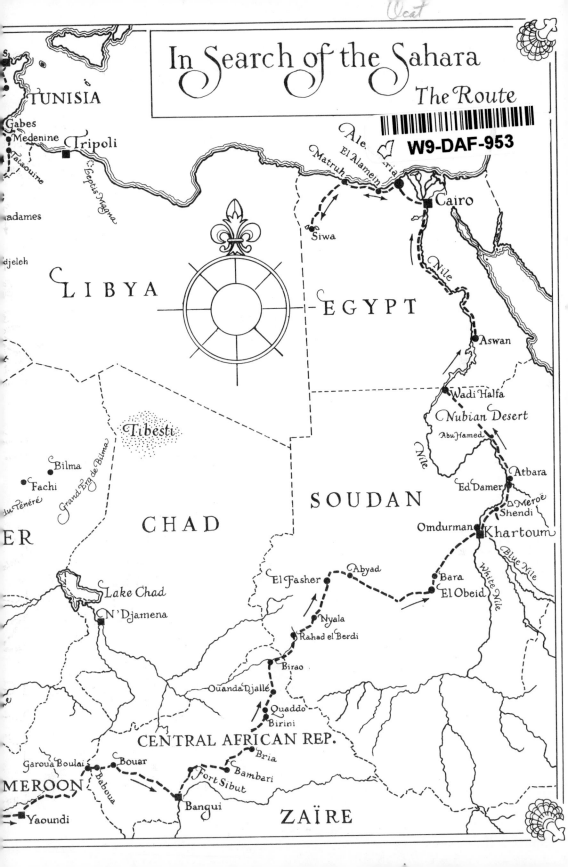

IN SEARCH OF THE OF THE SAHARA

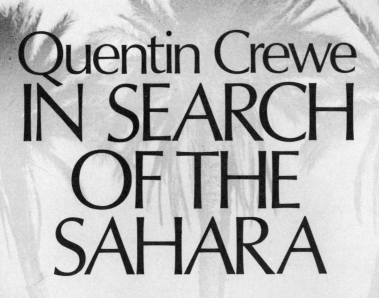

Quentin Crewe
IN SEARCH
OF THE
SAHARA

photographs by Tim Beddow

MACMILLAN PUBLISHING COMPANY
New York

Macmillan Publishing Company
866 Third Avenue, New York, N.Y. 10022
Collier Macmillan Canada, Inc.

The publishers wish to thank John Murray Ltd. for permission to use an extract from *Sahara* by Angus Buchanan, and Hamish Hamilton Ltd. for an extract from *The Blue Nile* by Alan Moorehead, © Alan Moorehead 1962.

Library of Congress Cataloging in Publication Data

Crewe, Quentin.
  In search of the Sahara.
  Bibliography: p.
  Includes index.
  1. Sahara—Description and travel. 2. Crewe, Quentin. I. Title.
DT333.C732 1984   916.4'8045   84-7873
ISBN 0-02-528890-3

Macmillan books are available at special discounts for bulk purchases for sales promotions, premiums, fund-raising, or educational use. Special editions or book excerpts can also be created to specification. For details, contact:
Special Sales Director
Macmillan Publishing Company
866 Third Avenue
New York, New York 10022

10 9 8 7 6 5 4 3 2 1

Printed in the United States of America

CONTENTS

To my companions

LIST OF COLOUR PLATES

I would like to thank the following people for their
help and encouragement of many different kinds:

Michael Barker, Nairobi; Julie Bates, Dakar; C. M. Beddow; John and Annette Bennett, Nyala; Colonel Dermot Blundell, Khartoum; Mr Copperman, Honorary British Consul, Bangui; Colin Crewe; Chris and Rosie Dodgson, formerly Honorary British Consul, Nouakchott; Toby Dodwell; Fathi Fadali, Cairo; Sharif Fadali, Cairo; Colonel David Fanshawe, Khartoum; Julian Freeman-Attwood; Dick Fyjis-Walker CMG CVO, British Ambassador in Khartoum; A. G. Gibbins, National Westminster Bank, Market Drayton; Claire Gordon-Brown, Dakar; Margaret Keir, Nairobi; Simon Kenyon, Nyala; Mustafa Khalil, Khartoum; Mick Mahoney, Bamako; William Squire CMG MVO, formerly British Ambassador in Senegal; HE The Sudanese Ambassador to the Central African Republic; HE The Sudanese Ambassador to the Court of St James; Jeremy Swift, Niamey; Jean Thouvenin; Samid Tidjani, Ain Madhi; Paul Weldon; Dr Gordon Yates; Francis Zobel, Dakar.

The London Library; Nicholas Kiwi Limited; Plow Products Limited, for WD 40; Puritabs; The Royal Geographical Society; Vogue.

FOREWORD

This is the account of a journey across the Sahara from Tunisia to Mauritania and then to Khartoum, Cairo, and Siwa. Quentin Crewe with never less than three companions travelled in two Unimogs, until one was blown up by a mine in Mauritania and the other written off in a crash. They then managed to get hold of two Land Rovers and continued the journey in these. Quentin Crewe, who organised the expedition, has written a memorable account of their journey through Tunisia, Algeria, Niger, Mali, Mauritania, Nigeria, Cameroon, the Central African Republic, Sudan and Egypt. He was anxious to travel in Libya and Chad but could not get permission to do so.

Quentin Crewe is extraordinarily observant and has a very good memory. In lucid, unaffected prose, often with restrained humour, he narrates the events and everyday happenings on this long and arduous journey. He describes the sights he saw, the people of all sorts, both European and native, whom he encountered, and recounts the stories he was told and the information he collected. His descriptions of the great dunes, the different coloured sands, the wastes of black rock, the beauty of the oases, the villages, the Niger river, the Atlantic seashore and many other scenes are vivid, his portrayal of people effective. With remark-able detachment he reports the harassment to which they were subjected by government officials, the frequent delays and the innumerable passes and permits they were required to obtain, sometimes from an official hundreds of miles away. He learnt to mistrust the information they were given about their route, and promises of help which too often turned out to be merely polite insincerities.

Throughout the book he remains objective and avoids any inclination to write romantically about the desert, and the Twareg and other tribes who inhabit it. Yet he writes with sympathy and understanding about the societies he encountered, many of them faced with the inevitable death of their villages and towns from the increasing desiccation of the desert. He visited the oil fields in southern Algeria and is hopeful that the wealth resulting from these will benefit the population as a whole, by providing them with more and better schools, clinics and communications. He describes dispassionately the tourists, travelling in package tours and trans-African expeditions, that they encountered at Tamanrasset, Tassili, and later at Meroë on the Nile. So many of them appeared to pay no attention to their surroundings, to be concerned solely with the practicalities of travel. He didn't like them, but they are at present a feature of these places and as such he accepts them. He and his companions were happy, however, to enter Mauritania which even today remains virtually unspoilt.

Quentin Crewe includes fascinating descriptions of some characters from the past, such as de Foucauld, an arrogant, fat and unpleasant young rake and gourmet, who joined the Chasseurs d'Afrique, became an explorer, a monk and finally a hermit at Tamanrasset, where in 1916 he was murdered by the Twareg; or René Caillié, one of the greatest of Saharan explorers; or the Marquis de Morès, who was murdered by the Twareg after a desperate resistance. He describes bygone empires in Mali, the Twareg who once held sway over vast areas of the Sahara, and the tribal customs of remote people such as the Mozabites in the interior of Algeria – the book is full of such interesting information.

After the Unimog, in which Quentin Crewe was travelling, had been blown up, hurling him out of it on to the sand, his party was reduced to travelling across unfrequented desert in one car. Describing this part of the journey Quentin Crewe remarks facetiously that, if the car had broken down, his companions would have had difficulty pushing him to safety in his wheelchair. This is the only time he mentions that he is in any way handicapped. He is, in fact, completely crippled by muscular dystrophy, only able to move one hand with the help of the other. This journey, and it is only one of several which he has made since he was crippled, including a journey into the Empty Quarter of Saudi Arabia, was a notable achievement by his able-bodied companions – carried out by Quentin Crewe it was an outstanding feat. I am delighted he has written this book about it. Not only is it an engrossing narrative of travel but it is a characteristically unconscious tribute to the unbelievable courage and resolution of the author.

Wilfred Thesiger

THE COMPANIONS

THE PEOPLE who travelled with me on the long journeys I made through the Sahara were a haphazard group. I knew none of them, other than briefly, before we set out; nor did they know each other. Three of them came in answer to an advertisement. Two were suggested by friends in common. One joined half-way through the first journey in answer to a cry for help. One was a cousin of my wife's, who announced that she was coming on the second journey. Three stayed the whole course.

Tim Beddow, the photographer; with curly hair and a long, long face, he has the faint look of an amiable sheep. He travelled with a whoopee cushion, a water pistol and a frisbee. It was noticeable that we adopted, to some extent, his scatalogical, schoolboy humour – perhaps because it was so agreeable to see him laugh uncontrollably. At considerable inconvenience and with a fair measure of self-sacrifice, over a year we adapted our meals almost entirely to his deeply-convinced vegetarianism. The first time that he lunched with me, after the trip was over, was in a restaurant. Merrily he ordered lamb chops. 'Oh, I have given up all that,' he said. It was a good thing, I thought at that murderous moment, that his photographs were so beautiful and that I liked him so much.

Anthony Cazalet was the mechanic after Peter had left. When he joined us at Tamanrasset, I was aware of nothing but a wild volcanic laugh, emerging from an enormous mountain of a man. He came with a huge folding bed, which he had had specially made for £300. He is possibly the most extravagant, perhaps one of the most generous and certainly the laziest person I have ever met. He talks entirely in clichés and it was possible at any time to press a particular button, as it were, and juke-box-like he would trot out the requested phrase. It lent a comforting quality to the conversation. He is an unparalleled mechanical diagnostician, always knowing precisely what is wrong with the engine. Mending it is a less certain business, involving a steady stream of clichés, peppered with

I

oaths. One thousand miles from any reasonable garage he literally dropped a spanner in the works, the spinning fan driving it clean through the radiator, and the water trickled prettily into the sand. Anthony weighed sixteen stone at the beginning, twelve stone at the end. He still walks like a fat man.

Jocelyn de Moubray, whose role was principally pushing my wheelchair, was two people: the shy, blushing, earnest eighteen-year-old schoolboy who started the journey, and the almost easy-going young man who ended it. Both of him lost everything, forgot everything and was wholly unconcerned with everyday practicalities. Among other unsuspected skills he could name and provide the ancestry of every racehorse which has run anywhere in Britain since 1965. He liked to tilt back his chair in the evenings, read T. S. Eliot and smoke a nonchalant cigar. We called him the Pasha. The Arabs thought him wonderfully pretty and the Mozabites pinched his bottom. He had a cynically pessimistic view of human beings, of which his own spontaneous nature was the perfect contradiction. Much of what appears in this book I owe to his observation.

Rose Cecil was a traveller who set standards of endurance for all of us. She is mischievous, warm-hearted, formidable and totally certain that she is in the right. This last was a characteristic of unparalleled value when dealing with recalcitrant officials. Rose would advance with heavy tread and menacing mien and the battle was usually over before it had started. Alternatively she would beguile them, which, being the more usual approach for a girl, took longer. No-one complained less of the discomforts and the frequent setbacks. She drew beautiful sketches, which she could never leave alone, adding and adding until they were black, like knitting in ink.

Ernie Cook was the organiser. He is an ex-Royal Marine of considerable resource. He had joined the marines, so he said, because he enjoyed killing people. Further to indulge this little whim, he transferred to the Sultan of Oman's army. Like many such ferocious-sounding folk, he has a soppy centre and constantly took the side of anyone whom the others were reviling. He never, to my regret, met Rose. While she was in the right, Ernie was simply right. 'When I say something definite,' he observed once, 'it is so. If there is a doubt, I mention it. Turn right.' One evening when he was wrong he threw the maps at me. Without him, on the other hand, the expedition would never have got started.

Peter Macdonald was the mechanic for the first few months, a lean young man who smoked prodigiously, always finishing the matches so that we had none with which to light the stoves. He had a Walter Mitty quality, and gave an interview to a local newspaper before we left. He was quoted as saying that he was born in Malta and therefore spoke Arabic, and that he was a skilled mechanic: 'There can't be many of us about.' I did not see the article until later. Ah well, I liked him; and he had an amazing capacity for making instant friends with strangers.

JOCELYN

ERNIE

ROSE TIM ANTHONY
QUENTIN

3

OLIVIA

TIM

Olivia Wentworth-Rump, the sunbather, was the daughter of a gentle Air Commodore and a dragon of a mother. Olivia wavered between preposterous debbery and immense practicality. She was seriously devoted to the Royal Family. I think only Olivia could have asked a man selling ice-cream in the most solemn Mozabite village whether the water had been boiled and the milk pasteurised. She cooked beautifully; after she left we never ate so well again. She complained bitterly of the irrelevant and worked twice as hard as anyone; and she could tease Ernie – a singular merit.

PROLOGUE

'THE MOST PERFECT DESERT IN THE WORLD'

THERE IS a rivalry among challenging landscapes, each offering to different people a particular attraction. Great mountains have their adherents, apparently just by being there. To others they are better left where they are and admired from a distance, the discomfort and perils of scaling them far outweighing the pleasure of getting to the top. Jungles, or rain forests as the cognoscenti would have us call them, appeal to people who evidently do not mind being bitten all night by mosquitoes and all day by flies, who enjoy a perpetual gloom, a pervading damp and an extremely limited horizon.

An affection for deserts may seem as puzzling to lovers of such landscapes as their tastes seem to me, but I would contend that the lure of the desert is as powerful as the lure of the sea, the desert having the additional charm of being populated by fascinating people, extraordinary animals and wonderful plants. Any old fish, as it were, can live in the sea, but it takes a very special fox or gazelle or even scorpion to survive in the desert.

The Sahara out of all the world's deserts must surely be the most intriguing. It is not the most dangerous, although it is the largest, covering three and a half million square miles – roughly one sixteenth of the whole land mass of the earth. It is not even the sandiest, for this distinction is claimed by the 'Empty Quarter' of Saudi Arabia, which is the broadest continuous tract of sand in the world. Undoubtedly the Sahara is the most varied desert, stretching from the Atlantic Ocean to the Red Sea, containing within it mountains rising to eleven thousand feet, depressions lying below sea level, salt mines, prehistoric cave paintings, Roman ruins, Egyptian temples, remnants of forgotten cities, hundreds of remote oases and, above all, a mixture of contrasting tribes, many living almost as they have lived for a thousand years. The Sahara is, as Théodore Monod expressed it, '. . . the most beautiful, the most perfect desert in the world.'

The fascination which the Sahara has exerted over Europeans began as early as the sixth century BC when Herodotus made a journey up the Nile to Aswan, a journey which was to remain arduous until 1869 when Thomas Cook took his first tourists in steamers to the same destination.* Herodotus speculated at length about the peoples of the desert to the south and to the west, and his speculations were to serve, certainly for the eastern Sahara, as the only information Europe had about the region until at least the eighteenth century.

At the western end of the Sahara, Europe knew of Timbuctoo; but knew of it only by hearsay or from the writings of Leo Africanus, which were by no means reliable and were in any case not generally available in English until the late eighteenth century.

The Sahara, then, was a land of mystery, inhabited perhaps by men with tails, by troglodytes and by other strange peoples. Timbuctoo, beyond a peradventure, was a city roofed in gold and glittering with emeralds.

The mystery and the hints of romance became a part of our heritage, so that Stendhal would eventually write, 'It is in the half-light of the Bedouin Arab tent that one must seek the model of true love.' That flavour of mystery was and, to a certain extent, still is a part of the lure of the desert.

Of more real importance are the mysteries of nature and geography, prompting questions that one seldom asks elsewhere. There is an Arab saying to the effect that Allah created the desert by removing from it all superfluous human and animal life, so that He might have a garden where He could walk in peace.

It is that very lack of superfluities which makes the desert a place where one observes what there is to see more closely. At first the stranger to such vast spaces may see nothing. His eye, accustomed to an abundance of event, roves unchecked over wide vistas of sand or gravel or rock. It takes a few days to adjust to the extremes of scale – both to the seemingly unending space and to the minutiae which become of vital importance to the traveller.

When his eye steadies, the newcomer often finds that the austere majesty of desert scenery surpasses the more readily acceptable landscapes of temperate climates.

Here the essential nature of the earth is not clothed in the soothing colours of vegetation. Instead the whole land is stripped and one has the impression that one is witness to the creation of the Earth. Everything looks in one sense as if it has just happened. The tumble of basalt rocks, the steep volcanic mountains, the flat sheets of granite, the pinnacles of sandstone, all seem so confused that it must be yesterday's disturbance that put them there. In another sense, everything appears timeless in the fierce silence of the desert. Those same granite sheets are worn smooth by the millenia, the gravel looks groomed on the endless plains and the pinnacles are the last bastions of sandstone in the ageless battle with an

---

* Though according to Amelia B Edwards, writing in 1877, these steamers, which she rather despised, were often to be seen stuck on a sandbank.

eternal wind. Nothing has changed for centuries, unless it be the dunes.

The dunes, with their fine, sculptured shapes and their delicately-rippled surfaces, lend a separate dimension to the grand sweeps of rock-land fashioned by aeons of wind and long forgotten rushes of water. Albeit barren and severe, the dunes with plumes of sand blowing from their razor-edged crests have a mixed quality of purity and impermanence which lightens the landscape.

While the newcomer at first misses the bright colours of a well-watered countryside, the variety of largely muted colours never ceases to surprise the desert traveller. In the middle of the day, the sun bleaches all colour from the land and even burns the blue out of the sky, so that it hangs like a grey-flannel sheet over the world. But in the evening, when the sun slants over the desert, the colour creeps back into the rocks and the dunes, as they reassume their shapes after the flattening day. The permutations are infinite. Outside Moujeria, in Mauritania, three sets of dunes roll up to the escarpment above the village – the first brown, the next fawn and the last pure white – almost like confectionery. Between Djanet and Tamanrasset, pure white sand lies this time among jet black columns of sunburnt rock. Above Ghardaia the land is pink and red. In the Fadnoun plateau all is black, unrelieved by sand but sometimes tinged with umber.

Often the colours seem uncertain. In the evening they may be green and yellow, fading to a whitish silver as the sun sinks and the moonlight takes over. The contrast can be so great that it is hard to believe that this is the same place in which you camped the night before; and the inexperienced, deceived by the reversal of light, will happily set off in quite the wrong direction.

There is nothing superfluous in the vast spaces and similarly, at the other end of the scale, the paucity of incident makes those small indications of life which do exist of paramount interest.

The sand is almost like a newspaper, with the same ephemeral quality of being useless once its news is a few days or even one day old. Often what it has to say is wiped out within the hour. For pleasure one may pick out the tracks of various animals or birds. It is amusing in the morning to read that a fennec fox has sniffed around the camp, that a jerboa has stolen some biscuits, or that a scorpion has disappeared into one of your party's sleeping bag.

Often the small signs are a matter of enormous importance. If you see a jackal track or hear the chatter of a sandgrouse, you know that you are within ten or twenty miles of water. A nomad, on seeing a set of camel tracks, will perform tricks of deduction which rival Sherlock Holmes. From the droppings he can judge where the camels have grazed, different grasses producing different coloured turds. He may even recognise the footprint of a particular camel or of a man walking with the camel. Airily, he will say, 'I see Hamadeha Kaddour was here a couple of days ago, on his way to In Salah to see his family.'

There is even something to be learned from the feel of the sand or the taste of it, in a way that is inexplicable to foreigners. In Mauritania, when I was looking for a guide to lead us across a particularly difficult belt of unmapped and unrelieved sand dunes, someone suggested a blind cousin of his who, he said, was infallible. Indeed in Mauritania there is a tradition of blind guides. Perhaps in a landscape which is constantly shifting, where there are no landmarks and each mile looks precisely like the last, sight is of no real use. A blind man can tell the general direction as easily as any other person; he can tell the position of the sun from the heat of its rays and he can feel the prevailing wind blowing in his face. For people with no compasses, there has to be something more than just plain sight and it may be that a blind man can develop that sense more finely than others and add to it touch and taste, which to a sighted person may mean little. In the end we took a different route, so I never saw the blind guide at work.

The minute detail of the desert becomes both fascinating and vital, for in the Sahara death is never far away. The bleached bones of desert romances are one of the few realities of such works. Hardly a mile will pass on any caravan route without one's seeing the curled skeleton of a camel, the half-dried corpse of a cow, or a sheep's skull. In almost every part of the desert there are stories of people perishing from thirst even in recent years. Near Hassi Messaoud I was warned against taking a particular track. The year before, a family of German tourists had tried it and had not been seen since. Even the nomads themselves miscalculate, particularly if they happen to be in a vehicle which is inclined to distort their judgement. They are accustomed to judge distance not in kilometres, but in time based on the speed at which a camel walks. Outside Mhamid in southern Morocco, a sign reads, '52 days to Timbuctoo' – the length of time it would take to get there by camel. Not long ago a group of Twareg, travelling by lorry, died on the little frequented track from Djanet to Bilma. It is easy enough, if the wind is blowing so that one's footsteps are wiped out, to get lost within a few hundred yards of camp. One evening Ernie, proud of his sense of direction, roared off for a spin on the motorbicycle, swooping up and down the dunes. Soon it grew dark and we realised that he simply could not find his way back and we had to direct the headlights of the cars up into the sky to guide him to the camp. In steep rolling dunes visibility may be only fifty yards and it is easy to forget from which direction one came. It is for this reason that the Twareg warn their children against following the *Zunkusharat* or Curve-billed Desert Lark. It has a way of flying a yard or two and then stopping. Boys, thinking it must be easy to catch, run after it paying no attention to the way. They are lost.

The corollary to the awareness of danger is a new sense of the tenacity of life. Whether it is life in the form of a plant, an insect, a bird, an animal or man himself, the ability, and even more the determination, to survive is a source of sheer wonder.

The desert near Djanet, Algeria

The Sodom apple (Calotropis procera), for instance, has an amazing capacity for survival, its complicated root system gathering moisture from the driest terrain and the poisonous latex in its leaves and branches protecting it from grazing animals. Of course, nothing in nature is invulnerable, so there is one grasshopper which revels in the bitter taste of the Sodom. I remember driving for two hours across the Fadnoun plateau and seeing no vegetation of any sort. Then there was one Sodom apple bush alone in a blank, black land. Not quite alone, for sitting in the bush was a black and white wheatear. Why does one bush survive when all others have failed? Nature at times seems to favour inequality. Or is it that this one bush was making a new start in absurd, vegetable optimism?

Red velvet mites, which eat termites, appear in the desert after rain. They are quite content to lie underground for a year waiting for the next rainfall and the next meal. The patience of desert ticks is even greater. Lacking a host, they can survive for ten years without nourishment or water.

Those same sandgrouse whose presence indicates water have, in the case of the males, special water-absorbent breast feathers so that they can carry water back to the nest to cool the eggs. (Birds in the desert do not sit on their eggs to keep them warm. Pratincoles and terns shade them with their wings to keep them cool. Others sit beside them.)

The addax and to a lesser extent the gazelle can survive on little or no water for considerable periods. The addax seldom drinks at all. It is a rather lumbering antelope which would have disappeared entirely from the Sahara were it not for its ability to live without water. It has retreated to the waterless areas where no-one can pursue it, especially to the 'Empty Quarter' of Mauritania.

Man in this environment, having had insufficient time for evolutionary physical changes, lives a most precarious existence, one in which a twenty-minute rainfall can make the difference between living and dying.

But this environment has a strong attraction for the European. For the British, perhaps it is the challenge which plays the greater part in drawing them to the desert; that and the masculine camaraderie.

In the late eighteenth and early nineteenth centuries, some fifteen British explorers died in the Sahara. It was not just the charm of a place in the history books. Desert exploration offered something more fundamental than fame. Partly, it might be the strange sense of freedom which the nomadic way of life offers, or you might term it irresponsibility. Life in the desert is reduced to three essentials - water, the way and, lastly, food. Nothing else is of the least importance. It is this paring down which appeals to the British, coupled with the simplicity of friendship which inevitably springs up between men travelling together in circumstances where trust has to be complete.

For the French the almost mystical pull of desert life was of supreme importance. Long before P C Wren wrote *Beau Geste*, the French were writing soppy novels about the clean-living, decent Frenchman who turns against the Industrial Revolution in France and all that it represents. He goes to the Sahara there to forge a clean, decent life, together with the clean, decent desert dweller - the inheritor of the mantle of Rousseau's noble savage. Provincial French libraries are full of such tosh. Nevertheless there were, throughout the nineteenth and early twentieth centuries, Frenchmen inspired by the ideals travestied in such books - soldiers, priests and others - some of whom we shall meet later in these pages. The man who perhaps expresses best the essential spirit of the French in the Sahara is Antoine de St Exupéry in *Wind, Sand and Stars*.

In the far western Sahara, lying at night on a high plateau where St Exupéry has landed his plane, he experiences a mystical soaring of the spirit. It is something which all desert lovers have felt to a greater or lesser degree when there is borne in on them the usually unattainable sense of the magnitude of space, coupled with that consciousness of the creation of the world.

In the eastern Sahara, St Exupéry nearly dies of thirst and exposure when his plane fails and he trudges blindly across the sands, following his instinct. There is no better account of the torture of the sun and the mockery of the deluded mind.

Above all, St Exupéry has in abundance the sense of optimism which is a *sine qua non* of desert travel. For many people the desert is an oppressive place. Their eye never steadies. The world is blank and empty. The heat by day is an unendurable agony; the cold by night an unbearable contrast. The *cafard*, as the French called it, seizes them and they sink into a bleak depression, mingled with fear. In Saudi Arabia, I travelled once with a city Arab to whom this happened, driving him literally to madness and attempted suicide.

The desert lover must look at these trials of the sands, the heat, the cold, the flies, the austerity and the privations quite differently.

St Exupéry wrote less about the heat and more about the hours of perfect temperature. To him the early evening, when the savagery of the sun has changed to a lambent glow filling the landscape with colour, and the early morning when the first rays of the sunrise drive away the bitter chill of the night, were like seasons of the year. Each day brought two springs to be greeted with delight. The less comfortable times were easily endured in happy expectation of the two peaks of pleasure.

What shines through his account of his nearly dying in the desert is the sense of victory, of a duel with the sun and the sand in which man was triumphant.

In all people who travel through the desert for pleasure there must be a measure of this sentiment.

from Tunis

Mediterranean Sea

Chott el Rharsa

Tamerza

Gafsa

Chott el Fedjadj

Tozeur

Nefta

Chott Djerid

Kebili

Douz

Gabes

Matmata

Medenine

M'Rrazig Camp

Tataouine

TUNISIA

Remada

ALGERIA

LIBYA

Tiaret

Michiguig

Bordj el Khadra

Bordj Messouda

Ghadames

N
W — E
S

0   100 km
0   50 miles

Peter McClure 1983

1

ROMANS, NOMADS AND MURDERERS

JOCELYN AND I had been in Tunis for a matter of days when we met Mohammed Ali Metoui. He was a tall man in his thirties, with a large, round face but rather small eyes. He was carefully dressed in European clothes and had a military bearing. Indeed, he had just retired from the army, in which he had held the rank of captain, in order to go into business.

He liked the British and he liked writers and above all he liked the desert. He would take all our arrangements in hand. By seven o'clock the next evening he would have a plan. I asked if he and his wife would like to dine with us the next day and we could discuss the plan. In that case, he said, he would send an assistant to our hotel with the plan and the maps. When we had studied it, we could come on to meet him at the restaurant.

The next evening no assistant arrived. So we waited and were rather late for dinner. Mrs Metoui had not come; she was unwell. But his assistant had come instead. Mohammed Mansour was a delightful young man of about twenty-four. He had spent eighteen months in Northern Ireland, teaching French in Londonderry. His accent in English was distinctive, being French with overtones of Ulster, imposed on the vigorous Arabic timbre of his native language. As it happened, we were not to hear much of it that evening, for Mr Metoui was in fine fettle. He was able to demonstrate how well-known he was in the restaurant and he told us of his excellent connections, particularly in Southern Tunisia. He adumbrated the possibility of sending Mohammed Mansour with us. At the end of dinner he suggested that we come to tea in his house the next day, when he would have a plan and maps.

We arrived at Mr Metoui's house about half-an-hour late, but it did not matter because he was not at home. His wife, happily recovered, was expecting us. She had baked a cake. Mrs Metoui was Scottish – a well-spoken, rather dowdy, earnest woman, perhaps the daughter of a doctor. She had come to

Tunis as a secretary in the British Embassy and had married Metoui when he was a glamorous young officer.

Their house was comparatively new, in what he had said was a beautiful part of Tunis, though it seemed to me to be in an area largely consisting of rubble. They had lived in it for five months. Even so, the only lighting came from naked bulbs hanging from the ceiling. The furniture was sparse. There were a few prints of the 'Cries of London' order, but otherwise nothing decorative.

It may be, of course, that this was on account of their two sons, one aged eight, the other four. These two quite pretty children had elevated disobedience and tiresomeness to a level I have never seen surpassed. Perhaps they broke everything. More plausibly, I suspect that Mrs Metoui had surrendered to her surroundings and forgotten any aesthetic leanings she may once have had.

This lack of taste and apparent absence of any need for man-made visual beauty was to be a source of wonder to me all the time I travelled in North Africa. Eventually I found some sort of explanation for it, but it is one of the great barriers between Europeans and the sedentary Arabs. Nomads have little scope for the exercise of artistic interest, although the few things they carry with them are often of considerable simple elegance. Moreover, they live in surroundings which provide an ever-changing landscape of infinite beauty. The housed Arab seems almost determined to cut himself off from all visual pleasure.

Metoui eventually arrived an hour late. No maps, no plan. He decided to dictate the plan to his wife. She sat pencil at the ready. He settled himself down and, in sonorous tones, began to dictate in English. 'The best plan for first encountering the desert is to start, in my opinion, in the Gafsa area . . .' Every so often he had to break off to lure his four-year-old son upstairs. His control of the brats was even feebler than his wife's.

The plan promised introductions to three governors, two of whose names he had temporarily forgotten, and to three military commanders. He would also advise on desert passes – 'a technicality'. The army would show us the desert, provide a free guide and possibly a military car.

Dutifully Mrs Metoui took all this down in longhand and then typed it out in exactly the words he had used. Not once did she correct his grammatical mistakes, however ridiculous.

He had not, at that point, made up his mind as to whether he could let us have Mansour, although the latter had told Jocelyn that he longed to come.

The next day Metoui telephoned to say that Mansour could join us. Later he came round to meet the rest of our party consisting of Olivia, Tim, Ernie and Peter, who had arrived with the two Mercedes Unimogs, driven from England.

He wished us well, told us not to worry about the desert passes and said that he would almost certainly join us for a few days in the south. He gave me a letter setting out what we might expect of Mohammed Mansour and pointing out that I was responsible for Mohammed's expenses. 'As an army man,' he wrote, 'I always prefer discretion and wish that the terms of this letter will remain confidential.'

Almost nowhere in the whole sphere of their influence is one so aware of the ancient Romans as one is in North Africa. Despite the savagery of Islam in the destruction of their cities, their temples and their monuments, an astonishing amount still remains.*

Leptis Magna, which lies ninety miles to the east of Tripoli, is probably the most remarkable ruined Roman city in the world, but Tunisia is littered with wonderful remnants of Roman architecture. El Djem is arguably the most beautiful colosseum, standing in a sandy waste. Aqueducts, triumphal arches, temples, roads, even wells which are still in use – every few miles there is something, so that it seems, outside Tunis, almost that the Roman occupation, which ended at least 1600 years ago, has left a more enduring mark on the landscape than the French occupation, which finished fewer than thirty years ago.

The more remarkable thing is that so many of the traces are in places where today no-one would consider building anything, for they now lie in barren desert. The reasonable assumption would be that the climate has changed and that the desert is spreading. The fact that the camel made its first appearance in the Sahara at about this period might seem to confirm this view. The Romans themselves always used horses, although Julius Caesar captured some camels after the battle of Thapsus, which had originally belonged to King Juba of Numidia. While it is true that the Sahara is growing, it is in the south that this is happening. The changes in the north have been very slight in recent centuries.

The difference lies in the amazing efficiency of the Romans. While at first, after the Punic Wars, they did not do much about North Africa, the early years of the Christian era posed difficult problems for the Romans – problems not altogether unlike those of the present day.

There was in Italy a flight from the land to the cities. The people demanded a more diverting existence. It was the time of bread and circuses. About 200 years after the fall of Carthage, the Romans set about making North Africa the granary of southern Europe. The land near the coast was fertile enough in many places, but there was insufficient good land to produce what was needed.

The Romans marked off, with a fosse, some one and a half million square miles of the new continent and undertook what must be the greatest agricultural project ever attempted in history. Using the Third Augusta Legion as engineers, the Romans devised a system of irrigation, making use of the wadis to capture the water which would otherwise drain pointlessly into the sands. They built

---

* The Romans themselves were even more savage in their destruction of Phoenician cities. Nothing remains of the original city of Carthage.

retaining walls and tanks and dams and ditches and barrages and conduits and terraces and channels.*

A French air force Colonel, Jean Baradez, spent several years in the 1940s making an aerial survey of the Algerian section of desert enclosed by the Roman fosse. It revealed not only a line of fortifications far south in the desert but, more importantly, a whole patchwork of farmsteads and farming villages where today there is empty gravel plain or rock-strewn plateau.

The prosperity this farmland brought sustained great cities like Leptis Magna, Caesarea, Sabratha and Gigthis.

From the east came the Vandals under King Genseric, and later the Arabs. Gradually the whole system, which the Romans had so carefully built up over two or three centuries, fell into disuse. Colonel Baradez believed that tens of thousands of square miles of cultivated land reverted to desert.

Occasionally one may see a small strip of green where a little water seems to linger in a desiccated region. Perhaps a man may sow a few lines of grain in this inexplicably near-fertile patch. He will have no idea that this was once an irrigation ditch and that the land around, some ninety generations ago, bore a crop which would give him a livelihood of which he never even dreams.

It soon became apparent that we were following a regular tourist route. It was pleasant enough to wander through Gafsa, once the Roman town of Capsa, where small boys dive terrifyingly from an overhanging tree into the deep, dark Roman cistern. To climb the spectacular road from Chebika to Tamerza and gaze out over the Chott el Rharsa and, beyond Tozeur, the Chott Djerid, two of the curious salt lakes which stretch across the northern Sahara from Morocco to Libya. To wander through the oasis of Nefta and wash in a *seguia*, or conduit, carrying water to the date palms, flowing for an allotted time to each section of the palm grove. To visit the zoo in Tozeur and see the doves with extra feathers just above their feet to facilitate, so the keeper maintained, landing and taking off in soft sand; to wonder at the invisibility of the highly poisonous horned viper and to feel sorry for the lioness, so plainly groggy with drugs. And to be impressed by what a fine ceremonial arch can be made out of crates of soft drinks when the President is coming to town. But this was not the real purpose of our journey.

Finally, at Douz we seemed to be on the edge of the true Sahara. This oasis is the centre of the M'Razig tribe, formerly a purely nomadic group, but now one which divides its time between pasturing its herds and growing dates – particularly since the government has implemented some irrigation schemes in the oasis and introduced a better variety of date, the *deglet nour* – fingers of light.

---

*Much the same system was considered highly innovatory when used to water a small area of Kenyan desert by Ewart Grogan in the 1930s.

It is the way of governments, as we shall see, to try to settle nomads on the land.

The M'Razig came to Tunisia in the thirteenth century and now roam the desert between Douz and Ghadames in Libya. Together with the far smaller groups of Achara, Sabria, Ghreib and Ouled Yacoub they are the only camel-rearing tribes of Southern Tunisia.

As we lunched under some tall eucalyptus, a group of about a dozen women were loading a large pile of bundles into a small trailer. Tim and Jocelyn offered to help. The women were brightly dressed in vivid colours, unlike the women of Nefta and Tozeur. Their chins and foreheads were tattooed and from their ears hung huge earrings. They laughed a lot and were somehow reminiscent of Spanish Gypsies. They laughed even more when Tim and Jocelyn found out how heavy the bundles were.

They had spent the winter in Douz, where they had houses and palm trees, and now they were setting off with their children to rejoin the men, who had stayed through the coldest months with their flocks in the desert. The women

The M'Razig are semi-nomadic; they wander freely across borders, ignoring rules and regulations

had hired a tractor and the trailer for £20 a day to transport them and their luggage. They were very vague as to exactly where they were going, giving the particularly indeterminate half-wave half-point, with nearly invisible directional finger hints, from which any Arab can seemingly absorb the details of a complicated route. Anyhow, it appeared that they were going in roughly the same direction as ourselves and, indeed, long after we had camped and dark had fallen, they came past and told us that they would be travelling on for an hour or so.

The next day we travelled through beautiful desert; sometimes rolling sand, nearly covered with waving grass like a 'foamy sea', as A J Liebling called it; sometimes pinkish rocky terrain; sometimes just dunes. We were not yet accustomed to such space and we stopped constantly to get out and to stretch our eyes over the suddenly enlarged world. It is surprising how in so large a landscape anything different stands out. I remember that that day Peter dropped some keys from the truck. He drove back ten miles and found the keys with no difficulty. An animal, a bird, especially a man, all stand out at huge distances.

The M'Razig family pack up their belongings

They are perhaps the superfluous that Allah meant to leave out and are therefore conspicuous. In any case, in the desert, you could mistake a bush for a man, but never would you think a man, however still, was a bush.

The way was another matter. The tracks were good and we found the route easily with a sensible map, but would never have known, from that imprecise wave, that we had followed the tractor. They must have stopped only for the briefest sleep, determined no doubt to get their money's worth, for it was quite late in the afternoon that we found them, tirelessly bumping over the fearful corrugations of the road.

They told us that they were about to turn off into the scrubland through which we were now travelling, because their men would be somewhere nearby. It would help if we could search for them, because we could travel so much faster over the scrub.

We wandered into the blank country, taking the one man of the party with us. He looked for signs of grazing.

Within twenty minutes he had found them about five miles from the track. After two and a half months, the reunion was happy but not exaggerated – restrained perhaps by our presence.

The head man, Bey Ahmed Brig, invited us to stay beside their camp for a couple of weeks.

There were seven men in the group which consisted of three families. Between them they tended a flock of a hundred goats, nine camels and ten or twelve sheep.

They told us that they were leaving early in the morning in order to go to fetch their tents, which they had left some months ago at a place some fifty kilometres away. We offered to collect the tents in one of the trucks. The next day at dawn, Ernie and Mohammed drove off with two of the nomads.

The rest of us spent the morning trying to do something about the ancient tractor which had broken down. Mohammed Habdaji, its driver, assured us that it was an excellent machine which would last many years, *inshallah*, once this little problem was solved. The problems seemed endless, but the principal one was that the radiator leaked like a colander. There was no hope that the tractor could return to Douz in that state. We poured in quantities of radiator sealing liquid and told Mohammed Habdaji to wait an hour or two. After that time we found that the leaks had been reduced to a steady but comparatively slow drip. Taking plenty of water, of which we had a lot, Mohammed Habdaji set blithely off.

I wondered, as I was to wonder so often in the desert, what would have happened if we had not been there. Mohammed Habdaji was in no danger, but the logistics of getting his tractor back to Douz or of repairing the radiator would seem nearly insurmountable. Yet he must have known when he set off that the probability was that this would happen.

Considering the dangers, it is quite astonishing how improvident the people of the Sahara can be. Often one sees a man pour out the last drops from his water bottle in order to perform his ritual ablutions before prayer. You know that there is no chance of his replenishing his bottle within a radius of fifty miles. He, on the other hand, presumably thinks that Allah will provide and, if He doesn't, *malish, mektoub*. Never mind, it is written.

When Ernie and Mohammed came back, the news was not good. Near where they had collected the tents, there was an army post. The military wanted to know what we were doing so far south without desert passes. Ernie explained that we had seen no sign on the road and that no-one had warned us that we were entering a military zone. This made no difference. Some Americans, they were told, were held under arrest for three days, although they were carrying vital equipment to an oil rig some fifty miles further on.

Then a sergeant turned up. He had known Mohammed when he was doing his military service. So they were allowed to go free.

On the other hand, they had brought the tents which were where the M'Razig had left them, untouched. The nomads said that no-one in the desert would touch another person's property. If we left our trucks there, unlocked, a year later everything would be just as we had left it.

As soon as the tents were up, the three nomad families divided, each with its own fire for the men and another fire for the women. Our camp was about fifty yards from theirs. Small courtesies were observed. They sent over goat's cheese; we sent them tins of rice pudding. Their older men came over once to try our tea. They did not like it and just left it. I thought of all the fuss European travellers make, forcing down food and drinks which they find repulsive, lest they offend their hosts by refusing the hospitality. No such absurd inhibitions disturb the Arab.

Their manners, nevertheless, are impeccable and their hospitality unstinted. They ask all the time for presents or favours but are not in the least put out by a refusal. Against that they never ask what they regard as impertinent questions. They are deeply inquisitive but never nosey. They would not think of asking your age, what you do, what your marital status is. The first ten minutes of any conversation is taken up with endless enquiries about your health, the health of your family and then further investigation as to your well-being, but after that it is up to you to reveal what you want. At the same time, every single thing you do will be observed and chattered about. In a sense, privacy is very real. If you say nothing and are not seen doing something, then no-one will know of it.

The rules of Arab manners are easily transgressed unknowingly. On the first night we arrived and when we were sitting round the communal fire, Mo-

OPPOSITE, Bey Ahmed Brig

21

hammed made a joke about Olivia and marriage with one of the younger men. Speaking rapidly and in French, the tractor driver warned Mohammed never to speak of marriage to a son, even in jest, when his father was present.

The old man, Bey Ahmed, was forgiving of any solecisms and chattered happily by his fire in the evenings. Primarily he liked to talk of herds, telling me that a camel was worth £300, a sheep £40 and a goat £30. He loved to hear about the pasture in my country and wanted to know how you could have land with no sand and few stones. When I talked to him of milk yields his face clearly showed that he thought I was inventing it all to impress him.

Bey Ahmed loved the desert and hated change. 'When I was a young man it was much more exciting; the charm of the desert is destroyed by engines. The pace of a man and a camel walking is more suitable.'

Everything foreign disturbed the peace of the desert, the engines and most of all the war. How peculiar it was that two sets of foreigners should feel they had the right to conduct their wars in M'Razig pastures. Bey Ahmed bore them no particular ill-will. If anything he felt greater sympathy with the British. 'Many of them died in that wadi,' he said, pointing to the north, 'and they lost the war too.' I asked him what he did while this was going on. 'My family and I kept out of the way, *al hamdulillah.*'

Bel Gaçem, the old man's nephew, was about sixteen. He used to listen quietly while Bey Ahmed talked and, in the morning, he would come over to our camp and discuss with me the things which had interested him. We sorted out who had won the war – Bel Gaçem had assumed it was the French, despite his uncle's belief that it was the Germans. He was more trusting of my account of European agriculture, having studied at the school in Douz. Until now all the young men I had met, mostly from the larger oases nearer Gafsa, had said that their ambition was to go to Tunis, possibly even abroad, but Bel Gaçem was different. He was not affected by the unemployment, nor was he tempted by the city. 'I will always live in the desert. I want no other way of life.'

There is a tendency among Europeans to romanticise the nomads, which I was anxious to avoid. Nevertheless, Bel Gaçem had been well-educated. His French was excellent. He was intelligent. In spite of these things he preferred the nomadic way of living, choosing what he saw as freedom. I could not help thinking that, compared with the boys who wanted to go to Tunis, Bel Gaçem was right.

The incident at the military post meant that we could not stay any longer. We had to get authorisation. Moreover Mohammed was plainly very agitated about this and, quite separately, very uncomfortable with the nomads. I got the feeling that Mohammed found it unsettling to think that these people were his

---

OPPOSITE, This M'Razig family from the oasis at Douz had hired an ancient tractor and trailer to haul their possessions across the desert

22

TOP, The M'Razig divide their time between growing dates and pasturing their flocks

ABOVE, Tamellahet: the high, painted dome over the tomb of Sidi el Haj Ali, a powerful nineteenth-century Tidjani Caliph

countrymen. He had more in common with the people of Londonderry than he had with the M'Razig and this he found hard to accept, the more so because we all seemed at ease with them. How could we have more in common with them than he had? I noticed that when he translated things which Bey Ahmed said he would change the emphasis. Sometimes it seemed pointless. When Bey Ahmed said precisely that they had nine camels, (something that I could understand) Mohammed reported, 'He says they haven't got many camels.' And he would brush aside much of the old man's expressions of pride in his desert existence.

On our last morning, Bey Ahmed came to ask us to give him an enamel cup. As we were packing up, an old woman, huge and with majestic gait, strode by sweeping up our washing-up bowls and bearing them off to her tent. Bel Gaçem, declaring that she was mad, somehow retrieved them. She cursed him and threatened to tell his father that he spent his mornings talking to me instead of looking after the goats. At least the goats didn't disappear like our washing bowls, said Bel Gaçem. Everyone laughed and we drove off towards the Matmata mountains.

The village and people of Matmata are perfectly extraordinary. I remember the place equally for its strangeness and for the unpleasant evening we spent there.

The people of Matmata are Berbers in origin, though now Arabic speakers, sedentary farmers growing olives and citrus fruit and some cereals. These were the ones who, when the original families came out of hiding from the Turks in the mountains, decided to dig their homes in a fertile valley, as opposed to their cousins who built 'perched' villages on the hillsides and preserved their language.

Seen from the air, Matmata has a look of a moonscape. The land is a mass of craters. Unlike most troglodytes these people do not dig into a hillside. They dig a deep hole in a hill from the top. This hole, which may be twenty-five or more feet deep and thirty feet in diameter, forms the courtyard of the house. From the courtyard, rooms are dug out all round, often at different levels. In a large house, more rooms may lead off the ones nearest to the courtyard and there may even be more courtyards. Finally, an entrance tunnel is burrowed out to emerge at the side of the hill.

The houses are unexpectedly agreeable – cool, shady and practical. Modernity is, of course, not suited by such cave dwelling. About half the four thousand inhabitants now live in a new village, built above ground not long after independence from France.

There is an hotel, with most modern comforts, dug in the old style and it was here that we paused after the long, rocky drive from the M'Razig camp. After a while Tim, Jocelyn and I drove off to find a place to camp before dark, the others saying they would follow and meet us at an agreed point in an hour.

We found a beautiful place albeit beside a deep, deep hole – presumably the abandoned beginnings of a house although at least twice as deep as most houses

23

and much narrower. Perhaps it was going to be a grain store. Either way, it was of no importance, merely a hole to beware of in the dark.

The others did not come. After waiting two hours or more we drove back down the tortuous track to the hotel. We expected to find them exasperated by some mechanical problem. We found them drunk.

Eventually we got them back to the place we had chosen. Ernie and Mohammed reeled around the camp singing endlessly one line of a song, *Just Another Tequila Sunrise*. They would eat nothing and teetered constantly at the edge of the hole, even wrestling on the lip of it until Ernie was hanging half in half out, over the sixty foot drop and I was bleating like an old nanny.

At last they went to bed after Ernie had broken the windscreen on one of the trucks by driving into a tree. Mohammed was sick all over Peter's sleeping bag.

Mohammed managed to speak to Mrs Metoui on the telephone. She said Metoui was annoyed to hear from the Sahara Brigade commander that we had been in area PS4 without passes. We were to go to Medenine to get desert passes.

Just outside Medenine we were stopped by the police who maintained that our vehicle papers were not in order. The Customs would want to fine us. This was the first of countless situations of this sort we were to find ourselves in in every country of the Sahara. I had yet to learn that there was little point in worrying about such troubles. If we were in the right, we could probably talk ourselves out of the difficulty, given time. If we were genuinely in the wrong, it might take a lot longer and cost a few pounds.

On this occasion we were technically at fault, but the hundred pounds which the customs chief demanded seemed excessive. He was in fact extremely likeable. 'To me it is an error of innocence,' he said. 'I will therefore telephone to Tunis to see if you may be excused.' Naturally, such a call could not be made so late in the day as this. Moreover, by its very nature, it was not an affair which should be hurried. Of course not, I agreed. Very well then, we must not move our vehicles from his yard. They were, after all, the error. We could sleep in the hallway of his office. An hour or so later he allowed us to take one truck, provided we left our passports, so that we could camp somewhere more reasonable.

Meanwhile Jocelyn and Tim had gone to the Governor's offices in order to get desert passes. After some prevarication the official agreed to let us have them, tomorrow *bien entendu*. Mohammed, who joined them after they had got the passes without any mention of Metoui's name, chatted to the official and puzzlingly reported to me that the official had said that Metoui was asking far too much.

We camped just outside the town, shivering on the gravel plain, waiting for one of St Exupéry's springtimes. It came. The customs man released us, Tunis having agreed to his lenient approach. The desert passes were ready. We drove to the pleasant market town of Tataouine.

Here we rather expected to meet Metoui, but it didn't turn out like that. When we arrived a ceremony was in progress. It was the installation of the new Governor, so Metoui's introduction to the old one was not much use. The leading family to whom he was meant to have written on our behalf looked blank. They owned a petrol station which was not very impressive, but that might mean nothing, Arabs being given to diversification in a way that Europeans have only recently learned. It was at this point that Mohammed declared that he could go no further. How, he wanted to know, would he get back?

As he had really done very little for us, although we all liked him, we felt this was tiresome of him as we would certainly need him to introduce us to Colonel Amar, the Sahara Brigade Commander. I pointed out that I had asked Metoui how Mohammed would get back from Bordj Khadra, the southernmost point of Tunisia, where we planned to cross into Algeria. 'No problem,' Metoui had said. 'He will find his way back from anywhere.' In fact, as Jocelyn happily observed to Mohammed's annoyance, Metoui had added, 'He can walk.'

We managed to persuade Mohammed to come on another fifty miles to the garrison town of Remada, where Colonel Amar would be, promising to take him back to Tataouine on the motor-bicycle.

At Remada, Mohammed found a captain to sign our papers, allowing us to go on to Bordj Khadra. Colonel Amar was not around. He would telephone Metoui to ask about the Colonel. We sat in a cafe, with a lot of soldiers, watching a World Cup match on television. When he came back, Mohammed said he had told Metoui of our attitude and Metoui had said he was to return at once. Peter drove him back to Tataouine.

Half relieved, we set off southwards through beautiful desert. Gradually the dunes grew higher as we crossed the corner of the great oriental *erg*, or sand sea. A group of gazelle leapt across the track in front of us. For hours on end we saw no other person, this country being almost barren of grazing.

Every so often we were stopped by the military, which was not surprising as we were running parallel with the Libyan border, sometimes less than ten miles away, and parallel also, on the other side, with the Tunisia oil pipeline. At Tiaret the soldiers gave us tea and suggested that we might have difficulty at the border – not from the Tunisian authorities who wanted everyone to be happy, but from the Algerians.

We came upon Bordj Khadra quite suddenly. It was fiercely hot as the midday sun bleached the sky. We were not yet accustomed to this interval between springtimes. Then we saw trees, a few acres of reedy water, a fort, a mosque and lots of barbed wire.

A group of soldiers were kicking a ball around in a desultory way. They told us we would probably not get through the Algerian border. They turned people back as there was no customs post.

Could we please try? They would ask the Commandant. They came back to

25

tell us that a telegram had come from Remada. 'It says your mission ends here. You have a permit to travel from Remada to here and back – no permit to leave.' Could we telephone to Remada? Not allowed. Could we speak to the Commandant? He would merely say the same thing. I suggested that it might be courteous for him to tell us himself. They went again to the Commandant.

The answer came quickly. No. And would we eat our lunch outside the compound. We had asked if we might eat it under the shade of some trees – the only shade for a hundred miles or so.

We were condemned to the noonday sun and to a diversion of some 1250 miles. We would never know whether it was Metoui or Mohammed who had inspired Colonel Amar to this rather irritating behaviour or whether Amar was fed up with Metoui.

I have deliberately told this story with some of the pique which I felt at the time. Now I feel none. A year later it would never have happened that way. The fault in fact was mine, for not understanding the difference in the way an Arab looks at something, the balance between what he must say and what he actually wants to do.

Metoui, I think, was probably genuinely anxious to help us. He had no real reason to understand the kind of material for which I was searching. And had we been content with his route, no doubt we would have seen everything to great advantage with the help of his introductions.

His offer to send Mohammed with us, I later realised, was one of those offers which are not supposed to be taken up. I fear that I pushed him into having to honour a promise which was never meant as a promise, and that we took amiable bombast for serious intention. I am sure he had never had any thought of joining us in the south. It was merely an expression of enthusiasm.

There are no more determined people in the world than the Arabs at telling others what they want to hear. It takes time to learn to distinguish between those statements which should be taken at face value and those which should not. In a sense both are equally sincere, because the reality and the fantasy are both felt. The first they can provide, the second they would if they could and they wish that they could.

As we headed north, again marvelling at the beauty of the dunes, we could take some comfort that our brush with authority and the inconvenience it caused us compared very tamely with what befell the Marquis de Morès in 1896, not far from where we were.

Near Tiaret (where the soldiers whom we had met on the way south said, 'Didn't we warn you about those Algerians? We knew they wouldn't let you through.'), we took a bumpy track eastwards to the fort at Michiguig. Many of the French Saharan forts have fallen into disuse. They stand, looking from a distance absurdly like a film set, romantically battlemented; and you expect to see kepi'd officers and soldiers ride out on white camels from the huge gate, pennants fluttering from their lances. When you get close you see how bleak the soldiers' lives must have been, virtually prisoners in their tiny quarters, now used as lavatories by passers-by. The *Beau Geste* fancy quickly fades.

At Michiguig, however, the fort stands proudly on a hilltop, very much alive, with soldiers on its battlements watching the Libyan border a bare four hundred yards away. Below the fort, one can discern the remnants of a village, where presumably the soldiers found some diversion. A little to one side is a graveyard. There is always a graveyard, sometimes with the simple military inscriptions still legible, more often not. A little further still is a high mound topped by a classical obelisk. This is a memorial to the Marquis de Morès. The inscription at the base was removed to Paris four years ago, so the lieutenant said.

The Marquis de Morès et de Montemaggiore is one of those people who, although they belong nearly enough to the present age, are completely impossible for us really to understand. He was born in Paris in 1858, the son of the Duc de Vallombrosa. His father's family was Spanish in origin, though they settled in Sardinia in the fourteenth century and finally moved to France in his grandfather's time. His mother came from a ducal French family.

De Morès' upbringing was completely conventional, ending at Saint Cyr and the cavalry school at Saumur, where he shared a room with the Vicomte de Foucauld (see Chapter Four). The photographs of him at that time show an absurdly arrogant young man with rather hooded eyes, a square jaw and an elaborately waxed moustache. Ridiculously touchy about 'honour', he killed two young men in duels while still at the academies. He joined first the *cuirassiers* and then the *hussards*.

He fought a brief campaign in Algiers, but in 1882 he married Medora-Marie von Hoffman, the daughter of an immensely rich New York banker. De Morès left the army and went to America, rather to the chagrin of his wife, who had married him partly for his position in Parisian society.

His career in America was spectacular, although ultimately unsuccessful. He acquired vast areas of land in the Bad Lands of what is now North Dakota and founded a town there which he named Medora. His plans were much more grandiose than simple ranching. He built a huge abbatoir and meat-packing plant, he acquired refrigerated rolling stock and shipped dressed meat to the east.

It was a sound economic idea. Until then, live cattle were shipped to Chicago. On the way they lost weight. De Morès could pay the ranchers more for their cattle because there was no loss of weight. At the other end he could sell the meat more cheaply because his transport costs did not include any waste material. This should have made everyone happier. But the big beef barons of Chicago saw de Morès only as a threat. They set out to break him; and they succeeded.

There is a question, nevertheless, whether it was as simple as that. De Morès also made himself exceedingly unpopular. He seems to have had no tact of any kind, but to have relied on winning men's admiration in order to get them to follow him. Those that did not fall under his spell often hated him, so that his schemes were always bitterly opposed, frequently by unscrupulous means. There were some eighteen attempts on his life while he was in America. In defending himself against one of these he killed a man. This was a common enough occurrence in the wild west, but his enemies used it to try to get rid of him. He was put on trial three times for this supposed murder. Each time he was acquitted.

De Morès' energy was astonishing. Apart from ranching and the meat packing, he shipped frozen salmon to the east, tried to run a stagecoach line, manufactured 'butterine' (a kind of animal margarine), ran a market garden, a pottery and a brickworks. He also had a share in a newspaper and a bank. By way of diversion he hunted, once deliberately taking on a large grizzly bear with only a hunting knife. Needless to say, he killed the bear with one blow.

When all his enterprises succumbed, as a result of his losing the beef war, de Morès returned to France in 1887.

Soon he was off to India on a tiger hunting expedition. On the ship home, he met some French officers who had been fighting in Tonkin, which later became Vietnam. When they described their supply problems, de Morès' entrepreneurial interest was aroused. He decided to build a railway which would help the army, but would also open up trade with China by pushing the line on into Yunnan. The British were already trying to do the same thing from Burma.

From the start this project was opposed by Jean Constans a former resident-general of French Indo-China. Constans was now in the naval department and was soon to be Minister of the Interior – a very powerful post in France. Despite this de Morès went to Indo-China where his scheme was received with such enthusiasm that, without waiting for authorisation or any hint of a concession, he started to build a dock at Tien Yen which was to be the port-terminus of his railway line.

It is true that the new Resident-General, Monsieur Richaud, was very encouraging, so it may not have seemed so rash an undertaking. From Richaud, de Morès learned about the dubious as well as inefficient administration which Constans had run. Constans meanwhile guessed what was happening. De Morès was summoned back to Paris. Richaud filed a report on his predecessor's misdeeds. He was instantly relieved of his post and ordered home. Richaud left for France, taking with him all the documentation about Constans. A few days out of port, Richaud was found dead in his cabin. His cabin boy was also dead. They were buried at sea. Death was attributed to cholera, though neither Richaud nor the boy had shown any sign of illness beforehand. No one else on

The Marquis de Morès et de Montemaggiore
(Courtesy of the estate of Donald Dresden.)

board got cholera. When the ship arrived at Marseilles, Richaud's papers were taken away by a government official.

De Morès never lacked courage. He launched a savage attack on Constans in the press. He campaigned, during the 1889 elections, in Toulouse where Constans was standing and was nearly stabbed by the minister's supporters.

Unfortunately, this drive for justice and probity in public affairs coincided with, or perhaps prompted, the development of all the most unattractive traits in the Marquis' character. He became what he thought was a socialist and an extreme patriot, but what we can recognise all too easily as an archetypal fascist.

He became a supporter of General Boulanger, a disaffected general who, with a measure of lunatic romanticism, saw himself riding his black charger up the steps of the Elysée to claim the leadership of France. Boulanger, who had a very large following, was threatened with arrest by Constans. He fled and in 1891, under sentence of deportation, committed suicide in Brussels on the grave of his mistress, the Vicomtesse de Bonnemain.

De Morès had launched himself into the realms of fringe politics, in particular adopting an attitude of rabid anti-semitism. He came to believe that the Jews were responsible for all of his misfortunes and those of France. He insulted as many Jewish people as he could, fighting duels with Camille Dreyfus and wounding him, and with Captain Mayer whom he killed. Full of honour, de Morès shook hands warmly with the Captain after piercing him with his sword. Mysteriously, Mayer responded most politely and died later in the day.

There is something about de Morès which makes one think of Sir Oswald Mosley. There were the same good looks and aristocratic background, the same entrepreneurial skill, something of the same political vision, the same misjudgement of men and the same decline into the politics of paranoia and megalomania. De Morès even dressed his bigoted working-class roughs in cowboy uniforms, just as forty years later Mosley was to dress his followers in black shirts.

Certainly de Morès had the same powers of persuasion. After Mayer's death, he was arresteed by Goron, the head of the Surete. Goron took de Mores to his office on the Quai des Orfèvres. There de Morès preached to Goron's underlings to such effect that Goron recorded: 'In two hours the sorcerer had them in his pocket. Another day and they would have been repeating everything he said.' He had, according to Goron, an irresistible fascination.

Perhaps above all, de Morès was a man of action. He could indulge in violent polemicism, and had even been put in prison for stirring up discontent, but his nature was physical rather than intellectual. The Sahara was the perfect place to demonstrate his deepest beliefs and his physical prowess. It was in some degree another wild west, but it had so much more to appeal to de Mores' misguided imagination.

Here in the desert France was expanding, reaching across the sands to the riches of central Africa. De Morès could further the interests of France. Then there was the British threat to claim more of Africa. De Morès could frustrate them. Here too were people oppressed by Jews. De Morès could help them. And in the desert were the fine, upstanding Twareg, men of noble stature and the very antithesis of corruption in Paris. De Morès would join with them. De Morès would also, incidentally, make some money by persuading his Twareg friends to guide the trade caravans to French ports in Algeria and Tunisia rather than to Tripolitania and Morocco.

For nearly two years the Marquis ranted round Algeria, denouncing the Jews and the British. France was to ally itself to Islam and march together with the Arabs 'in the peaceful conquest of Africa'. At the end of that time his plan was clear. He would set out from Tunisia for Ghadames and Ghat where he would negotiate with the Twareg. Then he would head east to Khartoum, where he would befriend the Mahdi and help him to drive the British out of Egypt.

From this point onwards, the facts of the story are hard to disentangle. The strands of treachery and deceit are difficult to distinguish from those of folly and arrogance. Moreover the story is full of contradictions. There had been many attempts on the part of the French authorities to dissuade de Morès from undertaking the journey at all. General de La Roque, the commanding officer in Algeria, had told him that the French army would do nothing to help him. It was for this reason that he elected to start from Tunisia. Commandant Rebillet, the military attaché in Algiers, raised every possible objection. On the day that de Morès was sailing for Tunisia, two of his men were arrested, presumably to discomfort the Marquis. De Morès was so furious with Rebillet that he let the men free.

When de Morès reached Gabes, things appeared to have changed. The French governor received him well and helped him on his way. Then came a telegram from General de La Roque's son, warning de Morès not to try to cross the frontier to Tripolitania at Beresof as there was a French officer waiting there to arrest him.

De Mores set out for Kebili. There he was met with great civility by Lieutenant Leboeuf. Leboeuf had received mildly contradictory orders about de Morès. The Resident-General had telegraphed telling Leboeuf to bear in mind that de Morès' expedition was a private one, 'so that you are not to assist him in any way whatsoever. You must make sure that he goes south by way of the Beresof oasis.' Leboeuf's other instructions came in a personal letter from Colonel Cauchemetz, the officer commanding the whole district, asking him to help de Morès in every possible way.

At dinner that night with his officers in the fort, de Morès seems to have exerted all his charm. He also talked too much. He told them he had fifteen thousand francs with him. He revealed his plan of joining up with the Mahdi.

He also claimed that he had sent Lord Salisbury a letter telling him of his intentions. The same evening de Morès got a telegram from General de La Roque telling him that Twareg guides would be waiting to escort him at Beresof. Was this an oblique way of reinforcing his son's warning? Somehow, it does not seem likely. In that case it must have been a trap. Whatever the answer, it confirmed de Morès' suspicion, which he aired to Leboeuf, that political enemies were trying to get rid of him. He went south, avoiding Beresof.

So much for the French. Now it is time to look at the Arabs who went with the Marquis. In Tunis he had hired, for a large sum, El Haj Ali, who claimed to be the nephew of the Turkish governor of Ghat. At the same time he took on an interpreter called Abdel Hack. Who recommended El Haj Ali is not known, but he was to prove wholly treacherous, so it is possible that the same political enemies were in some way responsible for getting de Mores to engage him. Abdel Hack, on the other hand, was completely honest.

At Kebili the *Caid*, the local chief, was a man of doubtful character called Si Ahmed ben Hammadi. It had been thought that he was likely to be deprived of his position by the French. Coincidentally with the arrival of de Morès in Tunisia, Si Ahmed came back from an urgent journey to Tunis having been firmly endorsed in his chieftainship by the authorities, much to everyone's surprise.

Si Ahmed told Leboeuf that Morès needed a trustworthy guide. He produced Ibrahim el Acheya, a known rogue. One account says that Si Ahmed gave Ibrahim specific instructions that de Morès must be killed, as he was an enemy of the French government. He gave him a letter to a Targui called Bechaoui ben Chaffaou, at Michiguig. The letter, Si Ahmed said, explained that whoever killed de Morès would not suffer any consequences.

There appear to have been more than one promise of this kind being put about. Si Hamma el Aroussi, the Tidjani leader at Guemar, near El Oued, had written to El Kheir ben Abdel Kadr, a Chamba tribal leader, telling him to go to Beresof to kill a Frenchman, who was travelling with great riches and with no official escort. Si Hamma guaranteed that anyone arrested would receive a free pardon.

When de Mores set out from Kebili, Leboeuf had some of his doubts assuaged by finding five ex-*Méhariste* cameleers among his escort. Ibrahim soon sorted that out. After a few days he told de Morès that they had not enough provisions to feed the *Méharistes* and that, in any case, they would not be welcome in Twareg country. They were sent back. Curiously enough El Haj Ali and Ibrahim allowed or could not prevent de Morès from hiring another Chamba guide, Ali ben Messis, whom they met on the way.

After a very few days Ali ben Messis warned de Morès about his escort and the danger to his life. De Morès chose to ignore this warning as he had ignored all others. Even more evidence soon piled up.

On 3 June, Bechaoui ben Chaffaou turned up in the camp. He seemed to know something about de Morès, because almost his first words to the Marquis were an offer to help him fight the British in return for a good supply of arms and ammunition. Abdel Hack, the interpreter, heard Bechaoui tell El Haj Ali that he had come to deal with de Morès. And he heard El Haj Ali say that he had been appointed to guide de Morès to his fate. Ali ben Messis confirmed that Bechaoui was a blackguard with a reputation for treachery. De Morès still did nothing. It was almost as if he wished to be murdered and to join the long list of victims of the Twareg. The Twareg by now had virtually infiltrated his camp, some thirty of them having joined Bechaoui. On 7 June El Kheir, the disaffected Chamba chief, turned up. On that day, too, the Twareg persuaded de Morès to dismiss Ali ben Messis, threatening that they would kill him if he did not go. Now he was entirely alone, except for the youthful interpreter, Abdel Hack, and a few servants.

On the morning of 9 June they struck. Why they waited so long, why they did not kill him in his sleep, why they ever started riding on the day of the murder are all questions which can have no certain answer. It may be that the sheer presence of the man was such that even the supposedly fearless tribesmen had trouble in screwing their courage to the sticking point. The fight that de Morès put up might be said to justify their hesitation.

The caravan started at seven in the morning. At that time of year it would already be very hot by eight o'clock. De Morès had ordered the guides to head north nominally to get more supplies, but probably because he at last realised the danger he was in. The guides were heading south. He rode to the head of the column on his indifferent camel – his fine, fast, white one was said to have strayed. He turned the caravan north once more. Still they waited. De Mores discovered that Abdel Hack and his servants were unarmed. El Haj Ali had

RIGHT, The monument to the Marquis de Mores

33

given their carbines to the Twareg. There was nothing to do. It was now after eight o'clock, not far from a place known as El Ouatia.

The track narrowed between some thorn bushes. The men pressed close on each side. Then Bechaoui leapt, and grabbed at de Morès' gun. Another man snatched at his revolver. The men tangled with each other. De Morès fell. His camel fell too and smashed his carbine. A lance cut his head. At once he was on his feet. He had his revolver. He shot two men dead and hit a third. Bechaoui skulked in the bushes. De Morès climbed a little knoll. The combined gangs of Twareg and Chamba formed a circle round the knoll. De Morès' cowboy hat was gone. He stood alone but they did not dare to approach. They cut Abel Hack's throat and stabbed de Morès' Arab servant. They quarrelled, the Twareg and the Chamba, each telling the other to attack. If one moved forward de Morès shot him. Still he stood, barehead in the sun, the blood streaking his face, holding forty men at bay.

At ten o'clock El Haj Ali came forward crawling, a white cloth tied to his lance. He offered safe conduct, if de Morès would promise to get them a pardon. De Morès laughed. When El Haj Ali made to go, the Marquis grabbed him, kicked him in the stomach and held him as a hostage.

The others moved closer. He shot three more. They started to run round and round the knoll, firing at random. De Morès whirled like the centre of a wheel, always picking off the closest man. El Haj Ali crawled away, de Morès shot him. Round and round. At last El Kheir came up behind him – shot him in the back. Another Chamba shot him in the jaw. Even then, he shot one more Targui.

Bechaoui ran up the hill, finished off El Haj Ali who was whimpering for water. El Kheir drove his dagger so deep into de Morès' back that the point came out by his navel.

It was the heroic fight that one would have expected from such a man and one that the tribesmen were not to forget for a long time. The French government, on the other hand, were eager to forget about it as soon as possible.

Edward VII said, 'If he had been English, I would have made him a viceroy.' The French did not even attempt to find his assassins. Three of them were eventually brought in, two years later, by an innocent chief – who was himself put in jail for his trouble on some ludicrous charge. One of the three died in jail. The other two, one of whom was El Kheir, were convicted in 1902. El Kheir was sentenced to death, but the widowed Marquise asked that his sentence be commuted. It was, to life with hard labour.

Bechaoui and the others were not even pursued. One of the Marquise's agents, Jules Delahaye, a newspaperman and a former *deputé*, spent six months in Africa investigating the case. He concluded that the murder was committed at the direct instigation of the military attaché, Rebillet, and that some omissive blame attached to the Resident-General of Tunis, Monsieur Millet.

It certainly looks as if the government planned the Marquis' death. But, in that case, why were such determined efforts made to stop his undertaking the journey which led to it? Could Constans really have corrupted so many officials, particularly soldiers who were inclined to like de Mores? It all seems improbable. Some reason then why de Mores must be prevented from making the journey? Rebillet's trading interests, which certainly existed for he had dealings with caravans from Ghat, were surely not enough to prompt murder.

There is one possibility which accords with the facts, but it is a shade wild for any real conviction. At the time of de Mores' journey, Captain Marchand was already on his way across Africa to establish a post on the Nile well south of Khartoum at Fashoda. The object of this incredible enterprise was to prevent the British from laying claim to the whole length of the Nile in a ploy to own half of Africa from north to south. This supposed ploy, of course, conflicted with French hopes of owning half of Africa from west to east.

The confrontation at Fashoda betwen Captain Marchand and General Kitchener was not to take place until 1898, two years after de Morès journey. When it did happen the French government backed down, abandoning poor Marchand, realising that a war with England was, in all sanity, unthinkable.

Could it be, then, that the government already knew that they would probably have to abandon Marchand? Did they fear that the enterprising de Morès might actually succeed in joining up with the Mahdi, which would (remembering the letter to Lord Salisbury) provoke the British beyond endurance, especially if the British thought he had official backing? So having failed to stop him with reason and small impediments, did they resort to killing him?

These were strange thoughts to entertain as I sat beside the obelisk at Michiguig, put up by French officers in 1911, looking out over the plain of El Ouatia. The border with Libya was only three or four hundred yards away, so I could not go across to look for the grand, granite cross put up at El Ouatia by the Orleans princess, the Duchess of Aosta, in 1928.

The Lieutenant at the fort at Michiguig knew little of the story and was surprised when I said I did not think de Morès was very likeable. He was more interested in convincing me that the murder had been committed by Libyans and not Tunisians.

Djebel Amour

House of Aurélie Picard

Chott Melrhir

Messaad

Ain-Madhi

Laghouat

Oulad-Nail

Djamaa

Sou

Oasis of Abou ben Ali

Guémar

El Oued

D a ï a s

M ' z a b

Touggourt

Tiabet

Temacine

Tamellahet

Ghardaia

Dunes of Dokhara

Metlili

The Pentapolis

Ghardaia

Beni Isguen

El Atteuf

Bou Nora

Melika

Ouargla

Sedrata

Hassi Messaoud

Grand Erg Occidental

Belhirane

ALGERIA

W   E

0   100 km

0   50 miles

Grand Erg Oriental

Peter McClure 1983

2

PURITANS AND THE ROMANCE OF A GENDARME'S DAUGHTER

THE SAND, when you come into Algeria near El Oued, is white. After the yellow sands of Tunisia, which look warm and friendly, these white dunes are somehow chilling, rather austerely chaste. When there is scrub on this white sand, or when gravel breaks through the surface, it looks rather dirty. But when the rippled dunes are unblemished they have a completely different beauty from the *erg* in Tunisia. The colours here are, in the evening, green and grey and silver; and, in the morning, instead of red and purple, the land looks washed with pink and blue.

These white dunes perhaps inspired the barrel-vaulting and the domes of the oasis, which prompted Isabelle Eberhardt, with typical exaggeration, to call El Oued 'the town with a thousand domes'.

Isabelle Eberhardt came at least twice to El Oued, the second time in 1900, when she was making rather desultory enquiries about the murder of the Marquis de Morès, for which research she was paid, rashly in advance, by the widowed Marquise.

At Behima, about eight miles outside El Oued, a member of the Tidjani sect slashed Isabelle with his sword, wounding her badly. This because she belonged to the rival brotherhood of Sidi Abd el Kader Djilani. She recovered in the French military hospital in the oasis and then was banned from the area by the commander.

Today the military look just as unreasonable. It was here that I first saw a group of a dozen soldiers, each with a large truncheon dangling from his waist, marching grimly through the town. Their appearance was made doubly sinister by the fact that their large military boots made no sound as they marched in the silent sand of the street. We were often to see similar groups, similarly armed and they always made me shiver; but it is fair to say that after Tunisia, where we were constantly stopped by military or police checks, we travelled through Algeria for weeks at a time without being stopped.

A few miles outside El Oued, when the houses are forgotten and the dunes roll higher and higher, is one of the most unexpected sights of the Sahara. On the left of the road is a no-entry sign at the beginning of a short avenue. The avenue leads to a large pair of gates in a long wall. Behind them is a palace. There is no other word for this extraordinary building, when it is compared with the simple mud houses which are the only dwellings for hundreds of miles.

The palace belongs to a businessman and hotelier called Mehra, who owns the Hotel Royale in Oran and the Hotel Chamonix in Paris. He was not there, but his wife sent their daughter, Nassouah, to show us round the gardens.

Nassouah was about twenty-four and exquisitely beautiful, with large, dark eyes and a perfect figure. She wore a dress with a lot of disco chat printed on it. She was a soignée, racée creature, again not to be compared with anything for hundreds of miles, unless it were the elegant gazelles which lived in a long enclosure at the far end of the gardens.

With immense self-possession she led us through the gardens which would not, in ordinary circumstances, have impressed one much, but here in this country of bare dunes they were perfectly amazing.

Mr Mehra, Nassouah told us, had built the house and created the garden in memory of his mother. All the flowers are imported, as was the specially treated soil. 'There are many gardeners here, but they are not used to flowers.' So someone flies out regularly from England to see how the plants are doing. He probably goes there more often than Mr Mehra, who only manages to visit the place three times a year.

We did not go into the main house where the family live, but gazed at its strange silver domes and then went round behind, where there was an acre of paving stones, rising by stages to another large building. In the middle was a swimming pool and beside it two large statues. One of a woman, the other of a man. The man was badly broken.

Nassouah took us into the building on the far side. It was a vast salon, eighty feet long and twenty-five feet wide. There were large pillars, the bases of which were fat palm trees. Between the pillars, were alcoves with gross armchairs and cushions covered in two different patterns.

This room was used for receptions to which seven hundred people would be invited. There were special extra servants quarters for the staff who were brought from Oran to serve on these occasions.

It seems that the seven hundred guests were not always very well behaved. The one beautiful thing about this room was the El Oued carpets. These carpets are wonderfully simple and restrained, their traditional patterns being knotted

Mr Mehra's house near El Oued

Aurélie Picard's house in the middle of the desert, reminiscent of a substantial Tuscan villa

only with black, dark brown and white wool. Nassouah said that originally the salon had had one single vast carpet. The guests destroyed it by stubbing out their cigarettes on it. It was the guests, too, who broke the statue by the swimming pool.

Everything about the place was extraordinary, but most of all the puzzle of so lavish and ostentatious a palace being built in a country which professes socialism. There is, of course, little Islamic objection to outward manifestations of success and it may well be that in Algeria the habit of Islam is more powerful than the affectation of socialism. Certainly the people of El Oued, where Mr Mehra was born, have no objection to his palace. They were impressed by his reaction to a tragedy during the building. Eight men died when the well they were digging collapsed. The next morning, I was told, he gave £2000 to the family of each man – 'even before there was any enquiry'.

The area in which El Oued lies is known as the Souf. The word is a Berber one meaning river, exactly the same as *oued* or *wadi*. The river in question is an underground stream or sea which here comes reasonably close to the surface, varying between roughly twenty and fifty feet below ground level. The palm trees of the oases in the Souf are watered quite differently from the other oases we had seen, where water from springs was spread about the palm groves by a system of irrigation channels. In the Souf, the practice is to dig deep into the sand until the surface of the earth is reached and then to plant the trees which send down their roots to the water. Date palms have the ability to push their roots down to a depth of one hundred feet or more.

By this system, the date grower is saved the considerable labour of daily irrigation and the need for vigilance in the matter of how many minutes of flow he is entitled to. (Actually, almost without exception, the man who allots the water and controls its flow is wholly incorruptible.) Life being what it is, these reliefs are more than offset by an eternal battle with the sand.

Round the lip of the depression which he has dug out and which may be hundreds of square yards in area, he will make a fence of palm leaves. Lower down in the saucer he will make a second fence. But the wind blows hard in the Souf, often savagely for days on end – rarely fewer than four days, often as many as nine. In these sandstorms which blot out the sun, a fence is meaningless. For days he will have to dig out the sand, which may have almost levelled his depression and covered even his fully-grown trees half way up their trunks.

Not far from El Oued, still within the Souf, I wanted to go to a little oasis called Ouibed, which from my map seemed to be well off any route. It proved to be so well off any route that we could not get to it in the vehicles. We struggled for an hour or so over soft dunes, following a faint track and learning, incidentally, more in that time about sand driving than we had learned in a month in Tunisia.

After no great distance we came to a straggly village called Abou ben Ali. An old man told us that the road to Ouibed was impassable. Even the lorry which came most days to Abou ben Ali was unable to get through after the recent winds. He said we were very welcome to stay there and he led us to a hollow which had plainly been a palm grove, but now only two trees grew in one corner. It was a perfect camp site and we happily unpacked all our gear while an audience of dozens of children gathered on the rim of our hollow and settled down to watch the entertainment.

The population of Abou ben Ali, who belong to the Ouled Sayrh tribe, is somewhat fewer than six hundred and it is increasing, although the life is hard and many of the young men want to go to the cities in the north of Algeria.

The village day starts at four in the morning when the men go to the mosque for prayers. After prayers, breakfast and then work until midday when the sun becomes too hot for the endless task of digging sand from the palm groves.

It is at midday that the villagers have their main meal, which may or may not have some lumps of mutton or goat in amongst the vegetables. It is better to have the main meal at midday because then you can eat the leftovers in the evening with a little cous-cous, for nobody likes to keep food overnight. By eight or nine most people are asleep.

The economy of the village depends largely on dates and melons and to a lesser extent on goats, sheep and camels, which are grazed in the valleys between the dunes where some scrub grows.

The dates of the Souf are regarded as being almost as good as those of Biskra. About one fifth of the half-million palm trees are *deglet nours* with tall, willowy trunks, most of the rest are *ghars*, a huge thick palm with fat, juicy fruit. At Abou ben Ali the dates are *deglet beida* or white fingers, rather dry dates of an inferior quality, but they come from a hardy palm which will thrive even on saline water.

The melons, for some reason which I never came to understand, are much less trouble. The old man, Ben Henna, who had greeted us and who was one of the two headmen of the village, thought melons were an excellent crop. 'All you have to do is prepare the seed bed, put a little fertilizer on and sow the seeds. After four or five days you clear any sand away from the plants and then sit back. You never have to visit them again until the harvest.'

When I asked why the melons didn't get covered by a sandstorm, which after all could cover a fair sized tree, Ben Henna just smiled and said, 'Ah yes, a sandstorm can cover a very big tree.'

Ben Henna was a great character and took an enormous interest in everything we did. He would spend a proportion of every day just sitting and watching. We used to ask him to eat with us, but he would never do that, although he

OPPOSITE, Ben Henna teaches us how to cook skinks

41

would eat any number of biscuits if we were so rash as to produce a packet while he was there.

In return for the biscuits, I daresay, he appeared one morning with a treat for us. Seven *poissons de sable*, otherwise skinks. He would teach us how to eat them. First, following the strict precepts of Moslem dietary laws, he cut their throats. I was glad of this as he would otherwise have tossed them on the fire alive. As it was, they wriggled in a disturbing way when he did put them on. After a few moments he took them out again, cut off their heads, gutted and cleaned them, sprinkled some salt on them and then toasted them on a skewer. They tasted a little like charred eel. I cannot say that any of us enjoyed them.

These skinks, when they are not eaten, serve as toys for the children. They tie a string to one of the skink's legs and they let it run along the ground for a bit and then snatch it into the air and whirl it around. It is one of the sad things of the desert that the children so seldom seem to play. The only toy one ever sees, apart from an occasional top or a hoop, is a small cart made out of stiff wire which they wheel around rather aimlessly. The children have no real childhood as we understand it; in many cases they are working, even if it is merely guarding the flocks, long before they are ten years old. They ape adult ways. It is a common sight to see a group of very young boys, sitting in a circle under the shade of a tree, just talking and discussing, in a way that no European children ever do.

There is a primary school in the village with one hundred and thirty pupils and five teachers. The number of children impresses on one that two thirds of the population of Algeria are under twenty. It is also a tribute to the progress made in Algeria since independence that there should be a school at all in this comparatively remote oasis. There is even another one at Ouibed, the temporarily inaccessible oasis beyond. When the children reach secondary school age they walk five miles every morning to Oumes Abed. From there a bus takes them another ten miles to Tiabet. In the evening they make the same journey in reverse. Usually the parents in the village take girls away from school when they are fourteen.

I did not think it polite to quiz Ben Henna too closely about various social aspects of village life, moreover he was not particularly forthcoming; not, I think, from any real reticence, but rather because most of the customs of the village he imagined to be universal standards of behaviour and therefore not of any particular interest. It is always an outsider living in a community who has most to tell.

Abd Karim is one of the five schoolteachers. 'You and I are equal. We are strangers in the village,' he said to me. He is about thirty and comes from El Oued. In consequence he looks upon the villagers with a certain measure of

OPPOSITE, Skinks also serve as toys for the children

superiority, while at the same time having a great respect for their industry and their sense of tradition.

Most of the villagers, according to Abd Karim, have two wives, if they can afford them. The girls get married when they are sixteen; the young men between eighteen and twenty-five. 'Only the students hold out longer than that, but they can get sex anywhere.'

The girls have no say in the question of their marriage. Their fathers arrange it and that is that. The bridegroom must pay the girl's father a bride-price of £1000, which is non-returnable whatever the circumstances. 'And, you know,' said Abd Karim, 'there is no variation in the bride-price for quality. Good or bad, pretty or ugly, clever or stupid, angry or happy, it always costs the same, £1000. Divorce, though, is quite easy, especially if the man doesn't like the woman.'

He went on to explain that all this is quite different in El Oued, not more than thirty miles away. In El Oued a girl can reject any man her father suggests. The question of love still does not seem of paramount importance. Abd Karim himself is married with three children under five. He got married when his father died, so that someone could look after his mother. The whole family stays in El Oued even during term time.

'There is no bride-price in El Oued. You must make your wife a really nice room and you have to invite everyone to the celebration, but it still works out a lot cheaper.'

Life in the village changes very slowly. The only doctor comes from Tiabet once every three months, but people can go to his clinic there. In an emergency he will come. A few days before we arrived the whole village had a *grippe*. The doctor came and dosed everyone – 'the women too,' said Ben Henna.

Against that there are four television sets in the village, so that life in the outside world is no longer a question of half-believed travellers' tales. By contrast, a lifetime of shifting the inexorable waves of sand is hardly appealing. It is no wonder that the young men want to leave.

Much of such speculation is, of course, relative. The sophistication of El Oued, apart from a phenomenon like Mr Mehra, is hardly great.

Abd Karim asked some of us for supper in the schoolhouse. We sat in the classroom into which the teachers had dragged their beds for us to sit on, round a low table. They fed us prodigious quantities of food and asked endless questions. Was London the principal city of Great Britain? I thought a schoolmaster might have known that.* Another question was about Liverpool. I was fairly well launched into a brief history of the port when Ernie, more perceptive than I, recognised that the question was really about football.

---

* Or was it a salutary rebuke to my national arrogance? On another occasion in Mali, someone asked where I was born. When I said London, he asked if that were in Czechoslovakia.

The teachers' views all had a second-hand air about them. The two great leaders in the world, they maintained, were Colonel Gaddafi and the Ayotollah Khomeini.

Could the Arabs ever rule the world, they asked? When I said, as I thought diplomatically, they might, having once been the leading civilised force, Ernie blew up. 'What nonsense,' he said. 'The Arabs always fight among themselves. They could never rule anything.' Surprisingly, the teachers all agreed with this somewhat sweeping analysis.

Ben Henna, who joined us after supper was silent on all political subjects. He sprang to life when the moon was discussed.

The camp site at Abou ben Ali

'Of course no man has ever landed on the moon,' he said. 'It stands to reason, when he got beyond the air, then gravity would pull him back.' A not unreasonable assumption, I thought. 'In any case, how would he get down again?' Ben Henna waved his arms in a swooping gesture. 'Swish. Boomp. Fiddlesticks.' And we all went laughing into the night.

The next day was our last. We spent the afternoon playing a football match against Abd Karim and his friends. All the children cheered and shrieked, particularly at Olivia who played in goal for our side, with much verve but little skill. A woman playing football was certainly the equivalent of Dr Johnson's woman preacher. Ernie cheated shamelessly, but the teachers were determined to win. They did, eight goals to one.

In the morning, Ben Henna came to watch our final packing-up. As each chair was put into the trucks, he moved to another one. When everything was in, he folded up the last chair and handed it to Tim. Then with a muttered Masalaama he went. Goodbyes in the desert are always to us strangely perfunctory. It is a much better arrangement.

It was some sort of national holiday and Abd Karim had his children out marching in honour of the day. He marched them past our hollow, just as we were leaving, and made them wave their flags.

The girl in the hotel where I was having a glass of apricot juice (anything more stimulating being forbidden), was about sixteen and very beautiful. She asked if she might borrow my pen. She came from Cherchell on the north coast, a small town now which was once the rich city of Caesarea, so called in honour of Augustus and ruled over by Juba II and his wife Selene, the moon daughter of Anthony and Cleopatra.

The young girl said she was the eldest of seven sisters. She was learning German, not because she wanted to but because there were three German teachers in her school and only one teacher of English and everyone wanted to learn English. At home with her family they spoke mostly French. Algerian boys rarely spoke French because they still hated the French. But girls spoke French, which was another reason why boys didn't speak it, because it was sissy. Didn't I hate the Mozabites? 'We all hate the Mozabites. We don't hate them as much as the Khybiles hate them. The Khybiles hate them three times as much as we do.' She made a measuring gesture with her hand, like someone describing the height of a child.

'Oh, but we hate them too; they are so hideous with their hooked noses and baggy trousers. They may be nice to foreigners like you but they are stiff and austere to Arabs. Hateful.' Her pretty face pouted at the thought of the Mozabites. I wondered why her family came here for a holiday, if they so disliked the Mozabites.

The hotel where I was having my apricot juice was in Ghardaia, the principal city of the five towns of the M'zab, the wadi from which the Mozabites get their name. As you may imagine from the intense prejudice they can arouse in an otherwise sweet and intelligent girl, the Mozabites are an unusual and separate people.

They are Berbers, speaking the Zenata dialect of Berber and they came to the M'zab nine hundred years ago, after a century or more of persecution.

Originally known as Ibadites – a right wing branch of the Kharijite sect, who broke away from the mainstream of Islam in protest against the decision of Ali, Mohammed's son-in-law, to approve an arbitration after the murder of Othman, rather than insisting on the death penalty – they maintained that anyone could be a *caliph*, even a black slave, if he were of sufficient moral probity, and that relationship to the Prophet was of no account.

Under the leadership of Abdul Rachman ibn Rostem, a Persian noble, the Ibadites founded a powerful kingdom in the seventh century at Tahert. Their territory stretched to the Djebel Nefoussa, now in Libya. The site of Tahert is today a small village called Tagdemt, near Tiaret.★ In 908 AD Tahert was sacked by the Shiite Fatimids, who held that all political power must reside with the descendants of Fatima, the Prophet's daughter.

The surviving Ibadites fled south into the Sahara, settling at Sedrata, near Ouargla, in 911. Here they created a civilised oasis with 400,000 palms and comfortable houses decorated with plaster work. But it was not to last. Barely a hundred years later, harrassed by rapacious nomads and hounded by religious enemies, the Ibadites set off again. The sand has covered nearly all traces of their settlement, but each year at the end of April their descendants, the Mozabites, make a pilgrimage to Sedrata, their erstwhile capital.

The Ibadites turned north-west and sought out the most inhospitable place imaginable that was at the same time compatible with survival. The Chebka, or net, is a rocky, reddish plateau with sparse vegetation, criss-crossed by a network of ravines and crevasses. In this forbidding place, the Ibadites found a wadi – the M'zab – which floods perhaps once a year. Here they dug wells, about 4000 in all, often to a depth of 180 feet and never less than thirty. They constructed a system of underground irrigation canals, or *foggaras*, some of which have survived nine hundred years.

The first glimpse of the towns of the M'zab is as astonishing as that of Venice or of the Grand Canyon. It is not so much the beauty of them, although they are beautiful, but the sheer surprise of their being there at all. We had travelled for many days through the sandy desert and then climbed to a rockier land. Nothing had happened for nearly two hundred miles since we had left the last oasis, and the previous one was a similar distance beyond that. There had been

---

★ The modern town of Tiaret was founded in 1843. The earlier town was razed to the ground two years earlier by General Bugeaud, the commander under whom Aurélie Picard's (see page 52) father served.

an occasional track leading off the road, probably to an oil drilling site. Sometimes, at night, a patch of sky would glow with flaring oil, like an artificial inadequate sunset. Gradually the land grew more barren even than it had been. There was no life to be seen, except for the occasional crested lark. The desolation had none of the grandeur of so much of the desert; it was raw emptiness. Then the hills grew steeper and, suddenly, on coming round a corner, we saw colour and patterns. Way below us, a long slash of green almost shocking in its vividness, while in the foreground a jumble of pastel-coloured cubes piled up one above the other to be crowned by a tall, tapering column of ochre.

It was Simone de Beauvoir who said that the towns of the M'zab were like splendidly constructed cubist pictures. And so they are. The rectangular, windowless houses are built on sharp hills, so that the houses form a rising pattern. They are washed in blue and yellow and white and terracotta. At the top of the hill is a mosque, with a roughly shaped minaret – a square narrowing as it rises to a top decorated only with stubby smooth pinnacles called *idudens*. The top of the minaret is as high as the plateau of the Chebka, so that it served also as a watch tower.

The towns are somewhat reminiscent of an Italian hill village, with narrow streets, just wide enough for a man on a donkey, climbing upwards, sometimes breaking into stairways. Several of the towns are still walled and Beni Isguen, the most sacred of them, has huge gates which until recently were closed every night.

Le Corbusier and Frank Lloyd Wright waxed somewhat pretentious about the architecture of the M'zab. Le Corbusier based his Ronchamp chapel on the mosque of Sidi Brahim in El Atteuf, the oldest of the five towns, founded in 1014. Whether or not they are perfect 'machines à habiter', the towns are quite different from anything else in the Sahara.

Their inhabitants are even more different. Although they are Berbers, they have curiously few Berber characteristics whether physical or temperamental. The people of the other Berber communities are tallish, dignified and handsome. The Mozabites are a thickset people with rather underdeveloped legs and necks. Their faces, too, are short and broad. Their noses are hooked and their lips thick. The men, at any rate, are remarkably plain.

Most Berbers are warlike. The Mozabites cannot bear fighting. Their treaty with France, which they made long before other tribes surrendered, specifically excluded any liability to conscription. They fought in neither of the world wars, when many Algerians fought with the Allies. According to RVC Bodley, though he is not always reliable, the most the Mozabites would do was to pay an Arab to fight in his place, an unthinkable arrangement for most Berbers.

Berbers, in general, are either agricultural, tending crops or raising cattle, or they are warriors like the Twareg, or they may even be fishermen as we shall see later. The Mozabites, on the other hand, are essentially urban.

The Mozabites are merchants. All over Algeria, and often further afield, even in France, they set up grocery shops and ironmongers shops. They work harder than other shopkeepers, they keep open longer, they are successful and they drive a hard bargain. It goes without saying that their success makes them profoundly unpopular.

Centuries of persecution and dislike have entrenched the Mozabites ever more firmly in their austere and rigid beliefs and confirmed them in their separateness. As their Puritanism has grown, even that spark which decorated the houses at Sedrata has gone. Their houses now are plain and their mosques are innocent of all embellishment. There is not even a pulpit – a reflection of the spirit of equality in their beliefs.

There are marked contradictions in their notions of equality when it comes to the role of women. In a religious context, women are equal with men. Girls are given an education so that they may understand their prayers. As all strict Moslem teaching is based in religion, their education is much the same as the boys' – at any rate for as long as they go to school.

In social terms, Mozabite women's lives are more circumscribed than those of almost all the other women of the desert. Until Algerian law forbade it, girls were often married before they reached the age of puberty, if that was what their fiancés demanded. There were some rather dubious safeguards for child brides, but they were devised by men. The marriages are, of course, arranged by the parents, although a recent relaxation of the code allows some girls to meet their future husbands once the betrothal arrangements are finalised.

Once married, women lead extremely cloistered lives. It is comparatively seldom that you see a woman in the streets. When you do, she is completely shrouded. Just one baleful eye may peer out from the enveloping black cloth; as often as not its owner will turn to the wall as a stranger passes. The women are watched over or spied upon by a powerful sisterhood, known as the washers of the dead – the *tiazzabin*. These rather formidable ladies were the counterpart of the assembly of scholarly men who traditionally governed each town. Apart from their functions with the deceased, they are in the business of issuing certificates of virginity and of chaperoning women whose husbands are away. On top of that, they have the power of excommunication, which bans a person not only from prayers but also from participating in any social life. The sins which can provoke the *tebria* are often trivial. A girl who wears too much jewellery or one who wears any when her husband is away; a girl who laughs too much even at home, or who wears foreign clothes, or who speaks to a foreigner – any such frivolity may at one time or another have been the cause of this sombre punishment. The washers of the dead meet once a year to review the list of sins and to discuss who may be the sinners.

The most important restriction of all is that no Mozabite woman may ever leave the M'zab.

49

In one sense, the restrictions are not all one-sided. The Mozabite men are accustomed to be away, often for two or three years at a time. While no-one would or could control what they may do abroad, they are forbidden to marry anyone who is not a Mozabite. If a man were to do so, he would never be allowed to bring his 'foreign' wife back to the M'zab. Both he and she would be banished. This rule ensures that, however confined the women's lives may be, they have a measure of control over their menfolk; for Mozabites are excessively home-loving and, if they want to live in the M'zab, they can only make a family life with a Mozabite woman.

Even more unexpected is the custom of *boumerkoude*, or 'the child which sleeps in the womb'. This may count in Islam as a heresy, but it is wonderfully convenient in social terms. While we might think a wife lacking in discretion if she gave birth to a child when her husband had been away for two years, a Mozabite husband will acknowledge any child born to his wife. If the period of gestation is hard to reconcile with the orthodox rules of gynaecology, the Mozabites believe that the child slept a while in the womb. This may allow others to think that the vigilance of the *tiazzabin* is exaggerated.

Unlike the girl from Cherchell, I found the Mozabites rather likeable. Despite the rigidity of their faith and their consequent tendency to disapproval, they are a hospitable people. Several of them, quite spontaneously, offered to let us camp in their gardens in the palm groves.

It was these palm groves in particular which struck a sympathetic chord. In no other Saharan oasis does anyone grow anything except for strictly practical purposes. Usually, under the palms, there are beds of onions, perhaps some leeks or some lettuce. Occasionally there may be a fruit tree, an apricot or an almond, although they are rare enough. In the M'zab, the palm groves are pleasure gardens. Mimosa, hibiscus, oleanders – there is colour where usually there is monotony. Huge fig trees spread out long branches. There is peach blossom, apricot and pomegranate. In among the palms, they build summer houses, cool in the shade of all their trees, and there spend the hottest months of the year.

Each of the five towns has its own character. Ghardaia is the largest, having two fifths of the total population of the pentapolis, which amounts in all to about 100,000. It is here that the tourists come, mostly to a big, modern hotel which looks down over the town and the palm groves and, in turn, spoils the sky-line from below. Outside the central, ancient heap of a town, there are banks and other establishments of modern commerce, but it is in the old town that one can feel something of what life in this cut-off world may have been like. The large arcaded market square, which is a lovely bustle of a place, with piles of glistening fruit and vegetables, is barely a hundred years old in its present form. Before that it was smaller and triangular. Twenty-four stones, dating from the fourteenth century, form a semi-circle on one side. On these the assembly men sat. Strangers were allowed no further into the town than this and, on another side, there is a platform, raised above the corrupting earth, for strangers to pray upon. No visitors were allowed in the mosque and, in any case, would not have wanted to go in, because the Mozabites were and still are, in many people's eyes, outrageous heretics, practising secret rites and holding sinister beliefs.

From the square, the narrow streets spread out, climbing the hill. In the lanes round the square, there are small shops and the workrooms of tradesmen – potters, brassworkers, jewellers, and endless cloth merchants. Soon these give way to quiet alleyways with the blank walls of houses lining them, but twisting and turning, here with steps, here with a covering arch, an intricate maze full of muted surprise. At the top is the mosque, its walls four feet thick at the bottom and soaring up to at least seventy feet.

While the name Ghardaia has its origins in a myth about a girl called Daia, who lived in a cave which can still be seen, the other towns have names with simpler associations. Melika, meaning the Queen, was the original holy city of the M'zab, until superseded by Beni Isguen. On the way to its cemetery there is the tomb of Sidi Aissa. He was a fourteenth-century sheik who followed the Malikite rite, the most usual in Algeria. He was converted by a dream to the ways of the Mozabites. It is a measure of their spiritual isolation that, in their delight at having a convert, they built a tomb of unmatched magnificence not only for him but for his wives and his children and his slaves.

Mozabite cemeteries are different from most Moslem graveyards. The tombs are more elaborate, often decorated with *idudens*, and they are surrounded by shards of broken pottery. There are niches for offerings and for oil lamps. It is the custom to put earthenware pots and jars on the tombs three days after the death – and then to smash them, supposedly in recognition of the ending of life.

Bou Noura means the one of light, and this town is so called because of its situation which is bathed in the rays of the sun, so that it seems to glow in the morning and the evening. El Atteuf, the bend, situated on a bend in the wadi, is the oldest of the towns, founded in 1014. It has two mosques, the result of quarrels within the town which was once divided in half by a kind of Berlin wall. It is the small Sidi Brahim mosque here which inspired Le Corbusier's chapel.

The last town is Beni Isguen, the city of piety. Here the original inhospitality of the Mozabites is tenuously maintained. The huge wooden gates may no longer be shut at night, but still no stranger may sleep within the town. While in Ghardaia no-one much notices the crowds of tourists, in Beni Isguen the people are thinly polite and wary. They do not like you to walk alone through the town, preferring you to take a guide who will stop you from taking photographs and will somehow not lead you to the mosque.

The fiercely private inhabitants manage to ignore outside influences, carrying on their bizarre customs oblivious of any other possibilities.

In the late afternoon they conduct their singular market, in which everything is sold by auction. A man will strut round the market square holding up whatever it may be that he has to sell. The buyers sit or stand all round the square making silent bids. It used to be that no bid was allowed to be more than one franc higher than the last bid. Round and round the seller would go until his price was reached. For an expensive item it might take hours for the bids to creep up in single steps. It could even take several days.

It appears that this rule has been relaxed. One man trotted briskly round holding up an ancient radio. He was calling out a price. Each time he came round, his baggy trousers flapping in the breeze, the price he called was lower. Then in the middle of the square an ordinary vocal auction broke out as bidders crowded round an old French wardrobe.

Whereas in the other towns a man who wants to sell his house will sit on the roof and take bids from the crowd below, in Beni Isguen he can only sell it in the market place.

The girl from Cherchell told me what a nice time she and I had had together. She hoped I would come to Cherchell. She swamped me with her eager, Mediterranean sentiment and she laughed at the little fire finches which darted out of the trees of the hotel garden and pecked at scraps under the table.

It was, I reflected, not surprising that she had nothing in common with the Mozabites. Hers was really a Latin culture, full of humour and very volatile.

The M'zab is a rather humourless place and in many ways its people are different from all other people, unless it be some strange group like the Amish in Pennsylvania. At the same time they share with all the people of the desert a total lack of sentimentality. The Sahara has stripped the Mozabites, as it has stripped nearly all its inhabitants, of every trace of self-indulgence, of superfluous emotion.

As we drove from Laghouat to Ain Madhi I tried to imagine what the landscape would have looked like to a provincial French girl of twenty-three who travelled this road in 1873. The Djebel Amour, a long range of purple hills, runs westward from the oasis, rising out of the flat desert. There are a few sudden patches of green, but the overall impression is of rough, flat land, stretching endlessly southward and shimmering in the heat. To our eyes, after weeks of travelling through the erg and the rocky wastes around Ghardaia, there was plenty of scrub, but to a girl who had lived all her life in northern France, it must have appeared unspeakably barren.

Aurélie Picard was the daughter of a gendarme. She was born in 1849 at Montigny-le-Roi. Her father had served in North Africa under Marshal Bugeaud, who was responsible for the brutal suppression of the revolt led by Abd-el Kader, the guerilla leader who tormented the French for fifteen years. The family had settled in Arc-en-Barrois, in the Haute-Marne.

The portraits of Sidi Ahmed Amar Tidjani and Aurélie Picard in the principal reception room at Courdane

Aurélie worked in the milliner's shop there. She must have stood out, even at eighteen, from the other shop girls. Madame Steenackers, the wife of the Director General of Posts, who had rented the château at Arc-en-Barrois, invited her to tea at the castle and then offered her a post as a companion housekeeper. This arrangement worked so well that, when the Germans advanced on Paris in 1870 and the government fled to Bordeaux, Madame Steenackers asked Aurélie to go with her and her husband. In Bordeaux they put up at the Grand Hotel. It was the first time that Aurélie had left the Haute-Marne. Also staying in the hotel was Sidi Ahmed Amar Tidjani and his brother Sidi el Bachir. Sidi Ahmed Amar was the chosen leader of the powerful Tidjani, a Moslem sect which was founded in the eighteenth century. Amar* was younger than his half brother Bachir and was actually the son of their father's concubine. Bachir, however, had been a sickly child and the fraternity had sought out Amar in order to appoint him the head of the sect when he was only fifteen. The Tidjani's relationship with France was uncertain, although Amar's father had withstood a seige at Ain Madhi in 1836, holding out against Abd-el Kader for eight months. At the same time the French did not wholly trust Amar who had set himself up as a kind of

---

* Although most writers refer to him as Ahmed, his descendants call him Amar. I have adopted their usage.

53

arbitrator between the French and the people of the desert. As they could not afford to have trouble in North Africa while the Germans were invading at home, they brought Amar and Bachir to France, ostensibly as guests, but in reality as hostages.

Aurélie and Amar fell in love. It is hard to say what drew Aurelie to this rather plump young man, with thick lips and very dark skin. (His mother came from southern slave stock.) To judge from his later photographs, he certainly cannot have been good-looking but, at the opera in Bordeaux in the Prefet's box, he must have struck her as a glamorous figure in his white robe and turban. For his part, Aurelie was an innocent dark-haired girl with, one imagines, a considerable presence. Amar first noticed her crossing the foyer of the hotel with four or five doves in her arms. This unlikely circumstance arose because of Monsieur Steenackers' role as Director General of Posts. The only means of communication with the besieged Parisians was by pigeon post and it was one of Aurélie's gentle duties to look after the pigeons. The doves supposedly reminded Amar of his home country.

Amar went to the Steenackers with an offer to buy Aurélie. Madame Steenackers behaved with characteristic French bourgeois ingenuity, protesting vigorously at the outrageous suggestion that a French girl might be for sale, but managing to convey that Aurélie might consider a respectable offer of marriage.

Aurélie's charms, coupled perhaps with the possible political advantages of having a French wife, were enough to make Amar overcome his hesitation about marrying a Christian, which was certainly an awkward step for a Moslem holy man to take. He proposed more conventionally. Monsieur Picard was sent for (by pigeon post) and a hard bargain was driven. The marriage was to be according to French law. Amar was to divorce any wives he already had and was never to marry additional wives.

Monsieur Picard went with Aurélie to Algiers where they discovered that mixed marriages were illegal under the colonial law. The Governor-General refused to make an exception even for the head of the Tidjani. Picard, however, fell in with Cardinal Lavigerie, the Archbishop of Algiers (and a great many other places besides). Lavigerie, despite his habit of sending his white fathers off to almost certain deaths, was genuinely without racial bias of any sort and was also ecumenical to the extent of believing that Islam and Christianity were not far apart in their creeds. He saw a marriage between Aurélie and Amar as a blow for racial equality and for the bridging of the gap between their two religions. Having made Amar swear an oath to repudiate his other wives and to eschew all concubines, he married them, at least according to God's law. After this, the least that the Mufti could do was to marry them according to the Islamic rite.

From Algiers the couple rode the two hundred and sixty miles over the Atlas mountains to Laghouat. After a few days there, they set off for Ain Madhi, the birthplace of the founder of the Tidjani sect and the home of his family. The distance is not great, a matter of forty-five miles, but even in winter the days are extremely hot. They might, it being October, have had to ford one river if it had been raining in the Djebel Amour. After that the track runs through very parched country. The only village they would see would be one with the gloomy name of Tadjemout, meaning 'crown of death'.

Ain Madhi itself at that time was a compact village with narrow steep streets, surrounded by a wall. Four massive gates barred the entrances. It is difficult to be sure that the present Tidjani house was the one that the family lived in at that time. (I was told categorically both that it was and that it was not.) It looks right and is the only house of any size in the old village. It presents a high blank wall to the outside, except for one pleasant loggia at some height, overlooking gardens and orange groves.

Aurélie's life was by no means easy. One of Amar's rejected wives tried to poison her, but she was up to that. She persuaded Amar to give her a position of some importance in a Tidjani *zaouia*, or monastic institution, at a considerable distance from Ain Madhi. Amar's finances were in a grievous mess, partly because the French had appointed a dishonest treasurer to look after his affairs while he was in Bordeaux. Aurélie had, in addition to her romantic side, a strong French sense of business. Amar, who became more and more indolent under Aurélie's care, handed over to her the running of his finances and those of the whole sect. Gradually she took it on herself to interfere in the sect's political affairs, although her influence with the French was not yet powerful enough to prevent another spell as a hostage, this time in Medea not far from Algiers where Aurélie had installed her family.

Bachir proved to be somewhat difficult, possibly from jealousy. Amar used to drink a lot of champagne which was said, as it was also said of the late Aga Khan's champagne, to turn to water in his mouth. No such divine intervention worked for Bachir, who one day became so drunk that he beat up one of his wives with such savagery that she came rushing to Amar and Aurélie streaming with blood. When Amar rebuked him, Bachir grabbed a shotgun and fired it drunkenly at his brother. Amar sent him to run the important *zaouia* at Tamellahet, near Touggourt.

After ten years Aurélie had been accepted. Her management of Tidjani affairs had brought prosperity and a lawsuit against the peculating treasurer had recovered positive riches. Aurélie decided to build a house. There was a spring called Courdane, near which she and Amar used to hunt game. Once they had slept there under a pistachio tree. This was the place that Aurélie chose for their house which she started to build in 1883.

Accounts of the building of this house tell of Italian architects and scores of labourers brought from Dakar. RVC Bodley, who claimed to have known Aurélie, wrote of camel loads of Italian marble, wrought iron work, stained glass windows and of fine furniture and superb carpets. The house took two years to build and Bodley compared it to Fontainebleau and wrote of a vast drawing-room and a high-ceilinged banqueting chamber. Another writer drew a comparison with Chenonceaux.

I had a faint hope that we might be able to find the foundations of this wonderful building and to see fully-grown some of the trees which I knew Aurelie had planted in the acres of gardens she was said to have made. I estimated roughly where I thought the house might have lain, under the Djebel Amour, five miles short of Ain Madhi. Then, about two miles away to the right of the road there were, indeed, trees which looked different, dark cypresses and pale green poplars. We turned off the road, bumping over rough clumps of sage and tussocks of grass growing thickly in the sand. When we got closer we were astonished to see a large stuccoed house. From half a mile away it looks a little like a sizeable villa in Tuscany. A long verandah on the first floor with twelve arches looks out over the desert. In front is a *parterre* with a colonnade to one side. At the corners of the house tall *sempervirens* stand like black candle-flames. As we got closer, we realised that the perfection is partly an illusion. The house is nearly derelict although most of the walls stand firm. The stucco is peeling, the iron balustrades are all crumbling with rust. The *parterre* is nearly completely overgrown and the colonnade is falling down. It can never have been comparable with a vast Loire château, but for the Sahara it was an amazing achievement.

There were some young men, most of them in western clothes, hanging about rather listlessly. They welcomed us with great friendliness and said that we could go into the house and wander about as we liked. We went in on the ground floor by a side door. We came into a room which stunned us all to silence. It seemed to be a breakfast room. Its furniture all belongs to the end of the last century. There is a portrait of Felix Faure, the French President in 1895, a pretty, painted cupboard, a round table and some chairs. Beyond the breakfast room, through an arch hung with brocade curtains, is a sitting-room. This has a large painted pillar in the middle of the room and the walls are painted with a red and green ivy pattern. There is a big gilt-framed looking-glass on one wall, a firescreen with a picture of a cat embroidered on it, some musical boxes, a bottle marked *Fleur Parfum* and a large volume of photographs entitled *Vues de Bordeaux 1870*. The curtains are of grand brocade and the carpets are beautiful. It is extraordinary enough to find, in the middle of the desert, a room furnished in the style of more than a hundred years ago, but what gives the place an almost eerie feeling is that everything is decaying. The chairs are broken, the brocades are hanging in strips, the paint is peeling and the plaster falling from the ceiling.

Upstairs is even more remarkable, for these were the grand rooms where Aurélie received visitors such as Colonel Flatters on his way to his death, the Vicomte de Foucauld (see page 86) when he was still in the army, even the Governor-General now that Aurélie was regarded as useful and respectable. It is hard to make out exactly which rooms would have been which in Aurélie's time.

There is a room arranged as a dining-room (which could not conceivably be described as a banqueting hall). Hanging on one wall is the head of a Barbary Stag. (This is Africa's only indigenous deer. It used to inhabit the whole Atlas range, but is now found only in Western Tunisia.) The rooms may, of course, have been rearranged, for it is fifty years since Aurélie died and her stepson lived in the house for many years. What appears to have been the sitting-room is the most amazing of all. The Arab tile floor is cracked, the ceiling and cornice are falling down but the furniture is in better condition than that of the other rooms.

The principal reception room upstairs at Courdane: in the chest of drawers were quantities of fashion magazines from nineteenth-century Paris

On one side stands an upright piano, made by Bord of Paris. On the piano is an ormolu clock and a pair of brass, church candlesticks for seven candles. Clocks must have been important to Aurélie. There is an elaborate brass one under a glass dome with figures in Arabic, a grandfather clock by Heardman of London and, most peculiar of all, a clock shaped like an enormous fob-watch also with an Arabic face, made by Ernst of Stockholm. Much of the furniture must have come from Egypt, being inlaid with mother-of-pearl. The walls are covered with a brown and gold paper and hung with guns and swords. There are coloured pictures of Aurelie and Amar. She is dressed in an embroidered dress with a train. She is carrying a fan and a black lace shawl. The effect, as was no doubt intended, is decidedly regal. Amar, on the other hand looks benignly pudgy and submissive, his rather weak face surrounded by a mass of white cloth.

Aurélie, unlike many women who were attracted by the romantic image of the desert, never took to wearing Arab dress. She was always in the latest Paris fashions. In a chest of drawers I found quantities of fashion magazines dating from 1873 well into the 1900s. It was her determination to remain French that

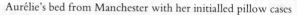

Aurélie's bed from Manchester with her initialled pillow cases

enhanced the respect in which she came to be held by both the Arabs and the French themselves. Had she done otherwise, the French would have accused her of going native and the Arabs would have relegated her to the inferior position in which their own women lived.

She certainly saw her own position as very superior. Her bedroom leads off the long arched balcony. The walls are green, patterned with a silver device suspiciously similar to a fleur-de-lys. Her bed has what the manufacturers describe as a 'woven wire mattress' and was made by Cresham and Crowen Engineers of Manchester. Over the bed is a crown. On the bed there are some pillows. The pillow cases are embroidered with the initials AT.

None of this is arranged or planned. There is no attempt to preserve anything in memory of Aurélie or her husband. It is just abandoned. On a shelf in an empty room, I found a collection of bottles: Eau de Tombouctou from H Olivier, Alger; Royal Windsor Hair Restorer (for tinting), Bière de la Loire (for washing hair, perhaps), lumbago medicine from Paris and many nameless beauty preparations.

When we had been around the house, the young men invited us to camp in the gardens and there we stayed for several days. The gardens are as decayed as the house. Originally they must have covered about thirty acres. It is possible to see how the gardens were set out, but there are few trees left. The poplars, which stand beside the stream created by the spring, are too young to have been planted by Aurélie. Many of the others must have died, but the cypresses remain and some gnarled apricot trees. There are no flowers, but where there must have been flower beds, beans and maize now grow.

In the garden on the south side of the house, amid what must have been a formal garden, there is a dome-shaped building enclosing a tree. This is Amar's tomb, built round the pistachio tree under which he and Aurélie slept while hunting, or so the young men said. His son Allel, by one of the repudiated wives, is buried next to him. Aurélie is buried just outside the tomb, among other members of the family. On her gravestone it says:

Ci Git
Mme Vve Aurélie Tidjani
Décédée le 28 Août 1933
a l'age de 84 ans
Mourrut Musulmane
devant plusieurs temoins
à Courdane

The young men turned out to be descendants of Allel, Amar's son by Zorah, the chief repudiated wife. The eldest is Abd el Samid, who is the head of the Courdane branch of the Tidjani family. Then there were Tahir, Samid's brother, Ahmed el Façi, whose father is the head of the family in Tamellahet, and Ali, a wild cousin. They were, in fact, all pretty wild. Ali had been in prison for brawling. Ahmed, despite being a gendarme, had been involved in three road accidents. In the most recent one he had broken a collar-bone. Then, he added, 'One of the family was killed in the accident ... a woman.' There was a newly-dug grave not far from Aurélie's. Beside it was a bottle of Eau de Cologne Riviera, which they used to sprinkle on the tombs.

Despite their wildness, or perhaps to some extent because of it, the young men were extremely hospitable and very entertaining. On the first evening they brought us delicious smelling sandalwood, gathered twenty miles away, to burn on our fire. They had an unexpected mixture of sophistication and innocence. They were all studying at the university in Laghouat, but it was clear that they believed the stories they told us about ghosts and evil spirits. The ghosts at Courdane took the form of exquisitely beautiful women, but only the senior members of the family could see them. When we told them that we were going to look at some caves in the Djebel Amour where there are rock-carvings, they warned us to be careful, because there is one group of caves which to enter is to come out mad. There are, Samid assured us, several lunatics in Ain Madhi as a consequence of ill-advised visits to these caves.

None of the family lives in the main part of the house, although it is open for visitors, not for Aurélie's sake, but because of Amar and his successors who lived there. The family now live in what must have been the servants' quarters. In Aurélie's time there were sixty-six house servants and a total of seven hundred people at Courdane, including servants and slaves for the house, the stables, the gardens and all of those concerned with the religious aspects of the Tidjani sect. Behind the house are the remains of what must have been almost a village. Even now there are people presumably descended from the slaves, to judge from their appearance. Samid was a trifle evasive on this point. At first he suggested that they are simply people 'who love the Tidjani'. Later he agreed that some were the children of slaves, who stayed on 'because they have no other place which is home and because they have a slave mentality'. It was a proposition that I was to hear advanced several times in different parts of the Sahara. Without any doubt one or two of them were treated exactly like the rest of the family. One in particular, another Ali, appeared to be very intimate with Samid.

Samid and the others have a great respect for Aurélie who they refer to as Lalla Yamina, although they like to play down the romantic side of her story. They prefer to believe that the marriage was primarily political on Amar's side. Amar's father had been involved in revolts against the French and his cousin was in prison at the time of the wedding, therefore the prime objective had been to soothe the French. At the same time they admired her skills and maintain that she was the only architect for the house.

After Amar's death in 1897, Bachir was chosen as the next head of the sect, in preference to Amar's son Allel because of Allel's liking for gambling and debauchery. Bachir was weak and had for years been jealous of Aurélie. It looked as if she might have to leave Courdane. Instead she married Bachir. It seems hard to imagine that she could really have been fond of this feeble creature who had once tried to murder her husband. One of Samid's uncles postulated the theory that she married him because she wanted children of hers to inherit Courdane. It is unlikely at the age of forty-eight that she entertained any very lively hope of having a first child. She had had none with Amar. More probably she just wanted to continue living there and also was apprehensive as to what would happen to the management of the sect under Bachir. In any event, she married him and continued through him to control the affairs of the Tidjani for another eleven years.

On our last night at Courdane, Samid killed a sheep and sent to Laghouat for bottles of wine, and we had a party in the gardens. We saw no ghosts of beautiful women, but as with our fingers we tore the meat off the whole sheep roasting over our open fire in the desolation of Aurélie's garden, I could not avoid the comparison with her parties with champagne and silver plates and the music from her Bord piano. Nevertheless, as I watched the sun rise in the morning, bringing a greenish glow to the Djebel Amour in the still sharp air, I wrote in my notebook: 'I would be sad to think that I would never return; Courdane is the sort of place which will grow even more attractive in retrospect.' And so it has.

The rest of Aurélie's story I heard later at Tamellahet, the Tidjani *zaouia* near Touggourt to which Bachir was sent after his drunken outburst of fury. Tamellahet is an attractive little village with a warren of arched passageways, lined with massive wooden doorways. The mosque dates from 1860. Beside it is the tomb of a powerful Tidjani caliph, Sidi el Haj Ali. The high dome has the most beautifully carved mud plaster ceiling, painted in many colours. From the ceiling hangs a Venetian glass chandelier, with one light bulb in it. On a bracket there is a clock called 'Veritable Westminster', which chimes faithfully every quarter of an hour.

The present leader of the Tidjani family in Tamellahet is Mohammed Hadi Tidjani. He is the father of the accident-prone Ahmed el Façi. He lives in a big house near the entrance to the warren of passages leading to the mosque. We sat in a large, cool room. The floor was covered with extremely fine carpets, but the rest of the room looked worn out. The tiles surrounding the fireplace were all chipped or cracked. I wondered how Aurélie, although no-one could claim that she had good taste, managed to overcome the Arabs' total indifference to their surroundings. There was a photograph of Mohammed Hadi's mother on top of the television, dressed in very western clothes. He himself was dressed in a pin-stripe suit with a thick, white, polo-neck sweater.

Mohammed Hadi had, at one time, been a communist. Now, he has come back, as he put it, 'To the fundamental beliefs. That is not just the best path, it is the only path.' He gave an unusually clear account of the founding of the Tidjani sect or brotherhood by Sidi Ahmed Tidjani. The Tidjani came, he said, from the east. They were descended from the Prophet, but the descendants of the Prophet were always squabbling politically so his ancestor sought peace in Ain Madhi. The founder was of the fifth generation to live there. The main dogmatic variation which led to the founding of the brotherhood was the question of whether Mohammed was more than just a prophet and whether it is permissible to pray to him as an intermediary to Allah. Most Moslems believe this to be specifically forbidden by the Koran.

The brotherhood was immensely powerful in Algeria, but now the group, 'is going through a quiet time. It is not so much that we are unpopular with the government; we have merely withdrawn a little. We are not, you understand, socialists.' The fact is that the Tidjani supported the French during the war of independence. 'Here we are guardians of the soul of the movement, but there are twenty thousand caliphs spread all over North Africa and the east. The biggest group of Tidjani is now in Senegal★ and there is a meeting there every year of representatives from many countries.'

Mohammed Hadi did not know Aurélie but said that she had had a great influence on the upbringing of his parents and grandparents. He showed me a photograph of what I thought was a little girl, dressed by Aurélie in the most preposterous clothes for an Arab child. My mistake caused Mohammed Hadi some offence as it was a picture of his grandfather.

He believed that Aurélie had married Bachir for purely political reasons. He maintained that the French would not believe that Amar was dead. He had died at Guemar, near El Oued where there was an important *zaouia*. It is true that there was a considerable fuss about Amar's body which Aurélie did not manage to have brought back for a year after his death. It seems highly unlikely that the French would not have known the truth, nor that they would have disbelieved Aurélie. Mohammed Hadi contends that they thought Amar had gone into hiding to plan a revolt. The only way to convince them was for Aurélie to marry Bachir – something which would have been unthinkable if Amar had been alive.

Mohammed Hadi said that after Bachir's death, Allel was chosen as the head of the sect. He and Aurélie agreed that they would never get on together, so she went to France. There she spent all her money and came back. Allel let her stay at Courdane as much as she liked, but for most of her last years she lived in Laghouat.

★ The President of Senegal is a Tidjani. Later, driving through Senegal I saw a village called Ainu Madhiu.

OPPOSITE, The Mozabite town of Ghardaia

ABOVE, Regal portraits of Aurélie and Amar hang in the *salon* upstairs

LEFT, The reception room on the ground floor of Aurélie Picard's house at Courdane.

The descendants of Aurélie's husband, Sidi Ahmed Amar Tidjani, who still live in the stables of the house. On the far right is Abd el Samid, leader of this branch of the Tidjani

When she was dying she asked to be taken to Courdane. Three days after she arrived, she died.

'Gradually over the years,' Mohammed Hadi insisted, 'she had embraced Islam. She died a Moslem. It is only evil people who said she did not.'

. . . devant plusieurs temoins a Courdane.

OPPOSITE, The escarpment above In Amenas, Algeria

3

LARES BY NIGHT, A LOST VALLEY AND A CRIME

T HE FLAMES from the oil wells, as they burn off the unwanted natural gas, can shoot up as high as eighty feet. On cold winter nights, travellers like to sleep on the warm sand near these ferocious torches, despite the hideous roar of the fire and the fact that it is expressly forbidden.

On 6 January 1956, the first oil burst out of a Saharan well at Edjeleh. All the old French desert hands wailed that this was the end of their beloved Sahara. The silence of the desert was destroyed for ever. The nomad would think only of how to buy a Chevrolet. The camel was as good as dead. RVC Bodley in *The Soundless Sahara* visualised a Chinese takeover, which would turn all Algerians into 'militant communists'. At the same time he devoted pages to complaints about the syntax and grammar of the agreement between France and Algeria for the development of the oil industry.

As with most such fears, the reality has turned out quite differently. The oil money has benefitted the whole population, providing roads, schools, communications, a measure of social service and much else besides. But Algeria is too vast a country, with a rapidly growing population, for even oil millions to transform the desert and the desert people or to make obsolete their customary way of life. Instead, there is the odd situation of the employees of the oil companies (or rather the concessionaires of Sonatrach, the nationalised oil industry) living an encapsulated existence, totally removed from anything to do with the desert.

There was little change in the appearance of the land as we went south from Ouargla. The dunes grew high again and, on the tarmac road, we seemed at times to be travelling in a liner of enormous tonnage, impervious to the swell of the ocean. The old desert hands were right about that. To exchange a camel for a motor vehicle is to lose much of the rhythm of desert life. The fine detail of the sands is gone and some of the immensity is lost as the vehicle shrinks the distances between wells or oases. Nevertheless when one is contending with the sand, or the rough rocks, or the bumpy gravel, there is an element of challenge. Some knowledge and some skill is called for; and the way is as easy to lose in trackless spaces whether you are mounted on a camel or driving in a car. But tarmac erases all connection with the desert. One might almost as well be travelling along the front at Frinton-on-Sea, unless a sandstorm should suddenly blot out the road and smother it, so that one is thrown back on the need for a compass.

At night, as we camped, we could recapture something of the real feel of the desert. I remember, near Ohanet, we startled half a dozen gazelle as we scrambled over some shale hillocks by our camp, and we found among the shale large, beautiful, black ammonites and, at no great distance, some petrified wood – evidence of long gone seas and forests. Again the flares glowed, now in all directions as we were in the centre of the oilfields.

So, after plunging down a dramatic escarpment known as the Moufflon's Leap, we came to In Amenas and the rules of security and also, as it happened, to mechanical trouble. At In Amenas they made us sleep in the police compound, which was filled with various groups of tourists. This was the only permitted site for camping for a radius of fifty kilometres. Here we met a French couple who gave us handfuls of exquisite dried apricots, and who were looking for other cars to travel with as, nominally, one is only allowed to travel south of In Amenas in a convoy of at least two cars. We could not help them, because the generator (or was it the regulator?) had broken on one of our trucks and it had to be mended. The French couple, on the other hand, helped us immensely by introducing us to Toto.

Toto is one of those small confident Frenchmen who assume command in any situation, while, at the same time, finding it droll that anyone should be agitated.

In Amenas is a dusty collection of buildings with no function other than as an operational base for the spread of oilfields. It has the sterile feeling of a place with no real connection with the surroundings, like an army camp, impermanent and ugly.

Toto has been coming here, for no-one can be said to belong here, for twenty-five years. He spends five weeks at a time working, and then flies home to France for two weeks. In France he has a wife and three sons. He has never brought his wife to In Amenas. She thinks it must be a glittering town, rotten with the corruption of the east, with night clubs and dancing girls and revelry. There was a half-way decent restaurant at one time but that has closed down.

Toto told us to take the truck, in the morning, up to the oil company's camp at the edge of town, where he works. The camp, fenced off from half a dozen similar establishments, consists of a short row of workshops and a cluster of cabins. The wind was blowing hard and the dust swirled in choking gusts. The

Europeans working there asked whether we would like showers and then some lunch. Such questions were almost bemusing after weeks in the desert.

After taking the generator to pieces, the mechanics decided it must be the regulator which was at fault. So we had showers and had lunch and sat in the air-conditioned cabin which they used as a communal living-room and bar.

Toto works for a French company which operates systems of testing to discover what lies at great depths beneath the surface of the earth. The principle was invented in the 1920s and has now been highly developed so that it requires radioactive materials to be used in the process. Huge complicated equipment mounted in enormous trucks, with computers and scanners and heaven knows what else, are needed for the task. The men who work all this have to have a high degree of varied scientific training.

There were about eight of them all told. In charge was Hans, a florid German with a rather mincing gait. There were two Englishmen – Martin, a somewhat academic looking man, with spectacles and a nervous generosity and David, stocky and extrovert, almost like a rugger player had it not been for his luminous blue eyes, made gentle by amazingly long eyelashes. There was an American, Mike, conventionally expansive, and only one Frenchman, Bernard, who had just been married. Another member of the team, a Peruvian, was away.

They worked on the same system as Toto, with five weeks on and two weeks off. Being a French company, their rota is based on the availability of women. In Algeria and Libya, where there is no chance of finding a woman to sleep with, the scientists have more frequent leaves. In Nigeria, where ladies are easily come by, the interval between home leaves is much longer. The pay is good, as well it might be because there is absolutely nothing for them to do when they are not working. Hans said they could earn four to six thousand dollars a month. More modestly, Martin said they got three hundred pounds a week. They have no expenses at In Amenas – food, wine and beer are all free.

Having decided it was not the regulator, they took the generator to pieces again. So we stayed the night, sitting drinking in the cabin living-room. By the end of the day we knew every one of their music tapes by heart, had grown weary of the pin-ups round the walls and were not able to encompass in our desert-filled eyes, the posters of green valleys. Fitfully, I read Patrick Leigh-Fermor, writing about baroque churches in Germany, and found it impossible to reconcile the two facets of our civilisation.

The atmosphere was brittle. Over the months the young men had built up a kind of teasing relationship, which presumably served as a wall of privacy. They carried their banter to lengths of ferocity which seemed dangerous to outsiders. Bernard had only arrived back that day and produced photographs of his new wife.

'*Pas mal,*' they said grudgingly, but with an uncomfortable measure of truth. She wasn't bad, but she wasn't that good either. Then, suddenly from one of them, 'Did she do this?' He sucked coarsely at the neck of a beer bottle.

In the morning, they thought that it must be the regulator. So we sat in the cabin. Outside, the sand whipped up more fiercely and we were glad not to be breathing it in. Those that were not working talked of their jobs. They had great contempt for the Algerians. They were hopelessly inefficient about the oilfields, not doing proper reservoir work, wasting oil so that it would run out long before it needed to.

The young scientists were much startled by my suggesting that the Algerians might prefer to run out sooner, rather than have to depend for skills on foreigners even more than they do already. They were good capitalist lads, imbued almost automatically with colonist notions. The Algerian operators, who worked much of their equipment, were lazy and dishonest, they said. Yet I could not but notice that the operators were cheerfully at work by seven in the morning, while the scientists slept until after eight.

Their contempt was based, possibly, on deeper considerations. They knew that their company gives guns as bribes to the authorities who hand out concessions. They knew also that the Algerian Government had not paid for their work in nine months.

It was probably the generator, Bernard said. Perhaps the Italians who were laying the new pipeline would be able to help. We climbed back up the Moufflon's Leap and found the large Italian camp. The board said: Italian Pipe Line, Parma. They were digging the trench while another Italian company, Saipem, actually laid the pipe. This was a very different establishment from Schlumberger. Here there were 150 Europeans working with vast numbers of huge caterpillared machines. There was a canteen, even a surgery.

The chief electrician, Guido, was a Sicilian. He worked on our generator all afternoon. He liked the money he earned. 'But,' he said in graphic Italian, 'I miss the fucking. I have to masturbate. I hadn't done that for years. Now, all the time.' A young Italian from Ancona, called Stefano, told me that he was engaged to a girl from Fano, but they wouldn't get married for two years or more. Until then he would work in Africa. There was an odd, sexually turgid atmosphere in the workshops. The Algerian mechanics working there were young and somehow flirtatious. In this isolation nothing would be surprising.

Guido thought it was probably the regulator. So we stayed the night. The doctor was an Indian. He was called Matthew, being a Christian from Kerala in the south. He had trained in Delhi, but had lived in Parma for fourteen years. He insisted that I sleep in his surgery. The Italians were rarely ill, he told me, but the Algerians often. 'They don't like work, you see.'

We ate that night in the canteen. First mountains of *rigatoni*, then steak with fresh vegetables. Everything was flown in from Italy. Cold, cold beer and strong espresso.

In the morning, Guido said we must have a new generator. The Algerian boys put everything together again. It struck me that the Italians were quite sharp with the Algerians, but Mohammed who was in charge of the Algerians seemed unconcerned and one youth said that they got on well with the Italians.

When we left, the canteen staff plied us with food, giving us quantities of meat and scores of oranges and grapefruit. For many days these rarities reminded us of the insulation we had experienced in the oil camps. In both camps they told us that they knew nothing of Algeria, nothing of the desert, nothing of the people who lived there. They were not even like an occupying army because they had no contact with anyone except the operators and the mechanics, who in any case were skilled people from the north and as unused to the desert as the Europeans.

The old desert hands need not have feared. The day after leaving In Amenas we were camped in the Erg Bourharet. Early, a man came by with two camels, one a fine white one which was twenty-one years old. He was a Targui, (Targui is the singular, Twareg the plural) called Zatab Mel. He worked for Fior-Texas, I think he said, as a watchman. Now he had two weeks holiday so he was going to Illizi, a distance of one hundred and sixty miles. He said it would take him three days, walking mostly beside his camels.

We travelled nearly a thousand miles before we managed to get a generator. It had to be flown from England.

It is south of Illizi that the desert changes so markedly. There have been some dunes rising hundreds of feet, some long miles of gravel plains, some rocky thousands of hilly acres. It has been beautiful and silent. The contrasts of the yellow-grey world of the noon day and the colour-washed mornings and evenings have been exciting. The sudden green bustle of the oases have lent surprise and variety to the journey. The life of the people has been hard but imaginable.

Then comes the Fadnoun plateau. Nothing has prepared one for this blank, black land. The road climbs up beyond Illizi, through lumpy tumbles of red and dark brown rock. A few acacias grow in the dips, but the tamarisks soon give up. I say road, but it is mostly a rock strewn track which shakes the trucks in interminable bumping and swaying. After hours, during which we were lucky to cover ten miles in each hour, we appeared to be on the top of the world. For countless miles the scorched black rock spewed in every direction. For long, long stretches there was no plant, no sign of any life. This, I thought, is what the world would be like after a nuclear disaster. One of our party – Tim, I think, who is always succumbing to the temptations of belief in UFOs, astrology, Nostrodamus and any such nonsense – was reading Vellikovsky. On the Fadnoun plateau it was easy to believe in the searing passage of a comet travelling too close to the earth. One could readily credit that once the world stood still and then spun the other way, that north became south and west, east.

Unquestionably manna was the only thing that might keep a man alive in this void. I searched his too-many pages for any reference to the Sahara – the one place where it is easy to see that the whole climate has changed from lush to arid and where it looks as if the change might as well have been abrupt and violent – but the silly man never mentioned it.

For two days or more we travelled through the new landscape. Sometimes the track plunged into precipitous valleys. At others one could see the track ahead winding for miles through mountains, so that it looked almost more like a road on a relief map than the reality. At one point there was a deep cleft and water lay hidden at the bottom. While the others scrambled between the high cliffs of the sun-free *guelta* (shaded rock pool), I sat motionless as two enormous black and yellow hornets climbed over my spectacles. We were momentarily back in the world of the living. That evening, miles later, we camped under a pile of black, burnt boulders and it was there that I saw the solitary Sodom apple and the wheatear perched in it. In the night, under the star-pricked sky, I thought that however many nuclear bombs are dropped, somewhere man will survive on earth.

The next day, we turned off the main track. While that had been bumpy, and at times quite difficult, this side road was greatly frightening. It wound this way and that through the roughest terrain, often finding that there was no way round and having to go straight through seemingly impossible obstacles. Much of the time I kept my eyes shut from terror. On our left, far, far below I imagined a momentary flash of green. Then we went round another immense column of rock and started a descent which it made no sense to undertake. The trucks slithered and ground over what looked more like a mountain-stream bed than a track. All at once, after two hours, it was over. We were down in a deep canyon and there were pink oleanders in bloom beside the way. Beyond, there were palm trees. For three days or more we had seen no more than a solitary plant. At once we were all laughing.

Iherir, as this place is called, has the lost quality of a Shangri-la and remains in my memory as the most perfect village in Algeria.

We went at once to the chief's house. He was a short, powerfully built man with a gentle face, which could harden up at a moment's notice, if he were not getting his way. When I asked his name he replied in French, '*Je suis le Chef de Barak du Tassili*'.

With infinite courtesy he took us to a large hut and said that lunch would be brought. The hut was circular and built of stones to a height of three or four feet, and mud-plastered on the inside. In the centre was a fat palm trunk, about eight feet high, balanced precariously on a not very flat stone. This supported the roof, thatched with palm leaves.

We sat with the *Chef* and another Targui who would reveal nothing about himself beyond the statement that he was a civilian. He owned, or at any rate drove, the Land Rover which was parked outside the *Chef*'s house. It was the only modern object we were to see in Iherir.

The *Chef* said that they had many tourists, but that the rules about photography were very strict. He was absolutely insistent that we should not take any pictures of people. He could arrange, if we really wanted it, a group photograph of the older men. It would cost £100, he said, quite unsmiling. He would provide a guide to take us up the canyon to the fort. That would be £7. This preposterous charge, I realised, was not to put one off as the price for a group photograph was intended to do. The £7 was to pay for lunch, thus allowing the laws of hospitality to be honoured with no embarrassment to us and no cost to him.

All that settled, the *Chef* relaxed. 'Why can't you walk?' he asked me. 'Is it because you eat too much and are too fat?' He thought this immensely funny. And from then on the conversation was all jokes and laughter. The cous-cous was excellent and the tea was delicious. At the end of the meal, I realised that the *Chef* had managed to tell us virtually nothing about his life or the life of the village.

The guide turned out to be the *Chef*'s twelve-year-old son Ibrahim, a boy of such astonishing beauty that even Ernie found himself questioning his own masculinity. Ibrahim was dressed in a light blue robe, with a white *cheche* round his head, giving him a dignity beyond his years, coupled with a girlish innocence.

We could drive only to the far end of the village, which comprised four little groups of houses, each group appearing to have a separate identity. The broad end of the valley, where we had lunched was plainly the more prosperous end. At the other end the valley narrowed until it became a canyon. A few hundred yards beyond the last, poorest huts, the high cliffs of the canyon enclosed a pool of clear water.

I stayed here, while the others walked with Ibrahim up the canyon to a red clay fort. Not much remains of it beyond some tumbledown walls, but it is one of the few relics of the Turks in the further desert. Ibrahim, despite his delicate appearance, walked faster than they could manage. Once away from his father's strict eye, he was delighted to be photographed.

I remembered my thought of the night before about man's ability to survive. Here is the place. Looking back along the wadi, there is the vivid green of the palms, the pink of the oleanders and the gentle sounds of pre-industrial living – a mortar thumping on a pestle, the bleating of goats which then echoes back from the wall of the canyon, the laughter of children.

The canyon wall is layered grey and red. Half-way up its four hundred feet, one thorn tree clings to a crack in the rock. A hawk, too high to identify, hovers over a swift which swoops lower down the cliff.

Shyly at first, the children gather round me. Hamoudi is the oldest, about the same age as Ibrahim, but much darker skinned. He too has a rather feminine

expression. His clothes are ragged. He speaks little else but Tamachek, for these people are Twareg, a group sufficient in number to be known as the Kel-Iherir. Hamoudi runs off and returns with an oleander flower, which he gives to me looking deeply into my eyes, though quite innocently. He is desperately anxious to please. He is an intelligent child and asks me to teach him the French names of the flowers and of the birds. He says he knows where to find prehistoric arrowheads and hunts in the distance under the high cliff, stopping every so often to wave to me to show that he hasn't forgotten. He comes back eventually with some chips of stone and some odd pebbles. I laugh at this dross and, at once, he throws it away and laughs too. Perhaps he is not so innocent in some ways.

When the others came back, Ibrahim greeted Hamoudi rather formally. The status of the two boys was established, the one the son of the chief, the other the descendant almost certainly of slaves.

The *Chef* had offered us the round hut for the night, but we preferred to sleep in the open near the *guelta*, a shaded rock pool – and were much bitten by mosquitoes.

Iherir, I like to think, is a place of survival. Up on the impossible plain above, there are caves full of prehistoric paintings. Once this was a fertile region. Now the Kel-Iherir emerge from their deep valley and must wander for scores of miles to find pasture for their animals. They have survived. The last crocodile in Algeria was caught in one of the pools of Iherir in 1924.

As we clawed our way back up the forbidding rubble of road it started to rain.

It was hard to leave Iherir and we would not have done so had not both Peter and the Unimog engines been sickly. Peter's health seemed to be connected to the condition of the trucks. When they ran well, he was well. When they had mechanical trouble he was ill. When one engine gave up entirely, Peter went virtually into a coma.

The question of how to take someone's temperature in the desert had never been suggested to me as a problem. When it is 110° in the shade, you can shake the thermometer down but it is back to over 100° before you can get it into the patient's mouth. One can only wait for night.

With our limping engines, we moved slowly from now on, for two months or so. Ernie's object was always to get to the next place. He was impatient of delay. Olivia liked sunbathing and was inclined to treat the Sahara as though it were Marbella beach; by now she began to notice the lack of cocktails and celebrities. Peter had the *cafard* and was the butt of everyone's dissatisfactions, being held

73

responsible for the failure of the engines, unfairly when their failure was really due to age. Tim withdrew into himself and dreamed, no doubt, of herbivorous Martians swooping down desert ley-lines in thought-powered space ships. Jocelyn, the most vulnerable, minded the tensions of others. It was a difficult time. Probably I was the happiest. It was my expedition – I could indulge my frustrations by abusing them all.

Human relationships are different in such circumstances as these. There is no privacy. The day is too busy to allow one to wander off much on one's own. We used to get up at about six, or shortly after sunrise. After that the flies would start fussing round one's eyes and ears, so that it was better to be up and moving about. When there are six people, it is extraordinary how long they take to get up, make breakfast – sometimes porridge; toast if we had been in a large oasis where they baked; cereal if we had any milk; semolina made with powdered milk as a last resort – wash up, pack up, load everything into the trucks. Two hours at least. When we were only four, it would take one hour. I never understood why.

Advisers had told me that the only way to run an expedition was on naval lines. Everyone must know his duty, be responsible for his particular task, suffer the consequences of any failure.

Somehow I could not arrange any of this. Every so often, when chaos mounted, I would announce rotas, declare rules, ordain timetables. No-one paid the least attention – largely, no doubt, because I was wholly unconvinced by such stuff, not wanting to live on naval lines. Anyhow, what consequences? I could hardly keel-haul malefactors. If anything went wrong, it went wrong not just for the one who might be responsible. It went wrong for all of us. That was punishment enough.

Each other's superficial characteristics we rapidly became aware of. When we were travelling we would stop for lunch at about noon. The books said that Unimogs did not like to travel much in the desert between eleven in the morning and four in the afternoon. Nor did they, but we used to put off stopping because of the heat – the breeze of travelling was hard to abandon. When we got out, the heat beat up at us from the sand, making us gasp. If there were such a thing, we would seek the thin shade of an acacia. If not we would rig up a huge red, silk parachute slung between the two vehicles. Under that we would sit motionless as lizards. There was usually a wind, but it offered no solace. Each gust felt as if someone had opened an oven door in one's face. We ate biscuits with disgusting 'spreads' or peanut butter. Sometimes we had chick peas or beans or lentils which had been cooked at breakfast time.

The middle of the day was not much use for photography because the flattening white sun, hanging in the flannel sky, beat the shapes out of the land and bleached the colours from the shimmering sand. Tim was conscientious and, even in the dead of day, he would stroll off with his easy, springing walk to photograph some unusual formation. It might happen that we stopped near some high dunes or by some steep piles of stones like giants' cairns. And Tim might climb one of these.

Abruptly, Ernie would jump up. 'Is that Tim up there? I can get higher than that.' And off he would run, ignoring the heat, until he stood on a higher level than Tim. So much of Ernie's life was spent in proving something, but it was a trait impossible for him to conceal – not something he wanted to reveal to us. In the first months, we learned little more about each other than we knew after the first week.

We usually left our stopping in the evening until too late. The standard joke of the problem of choosing a picnic site is multiplied a hundred-fold when it comes to selecting a camp site for the night. If you have two trucks and six people, all with opinions, it almost makes you long for naval discipline. Sometimes they would say to me, 'You are the leader why don't you lead? Just say, "We'll stop here".' The next night I would pronounce:

'We'll stop here.'

'What a bloody stupid place to stop,' they would say in unison. Then, splitting up, they would offer five new opinions as to where we should camp. And Ernie would curse what he called the Irish parliament.

By now it would be nearly dark and the next hour would hear plaintive questions as to the whereabouts of the torches, the top of the pressure cooker, the matches, the tent pegs, the salt. Ernie could always find everything he needed; Jocelyn nothing. Tim might well know where something was, but would be in too much of a private mist to notice that anyone had asked for it. Peter would do nothing, judging that looking after the engines was work enough, excusing him from cooking or washing up. Olivia got on with whatever needed to be done.

Olivia, Tim and Jocelyn did the cooking. In the evening we would eat spaghetti or rice, usually with tomatoes and onions. On some occasions we would open tins, but variety was made more difficult by Tim's refusing to eat meat.

We became conscious of the amount everyone ate. Special treats, like a tin of strawberries, would have to be shared out with meticulous care to see that no-one got more than anyone else. There were those among us who would cheat and those who would passionately resent others getting or taking a larger share. Ernie made a rule that anyone lingering in the back of the food truck was obliged to whistle, to prove he was not eating. Jocelyn's attitude to all this was the most sensible and sympathetic. If he was hungry, which was most of the time, he would eat whatever he came across with no thought of sharing. If someone else ate his share of something, he simply didn't care.

Our intercourse was almost entirely conducted at a trivial, day-to-day level. It was only very occasionally, as we sat round the fire at the end of the day, that the conversation took on a serious note and only once or twice did it take a personal turn. No-one ever talked about his family, except for one enlivening occasion when Olivia, to illustrate her mother's determined character, described the inept trimming of her pubic hair by some beauty salon and the scene which Mummy made in her support.

This keeping of our relationships on an unimportant level was our way of guarding privacy.

We used to go to bed early. As we went south and the year advanced, we forgot about tents and lay, as far apart as was reasonable, under the stars.

Whatever the circumstances, I was certainly not discontented, if only because our temperamental troubles coincided with our reaching the most beautiful part of the Sahara. The evening of the day we left Iherir brought us down from the Fadnoun plateau to a vast sandy plain, dotted with sudden outcrops of wildly-shaped rocks and edged with a line of low russet cliffs. Searching these for signs of rock-carvings, we came upon a place which no-one could dispute was a perfect camp site. Under a cliff lay a pool, sheltered always by an overhanging rock from the sun. Some amiable donkeys wandered in to drink. Sandgrouse chortled from above and Tim climbed up to see them and found another pool fifty feet above the first one. We camped beside the lower pool.

Each day after that, in the Tassili and in the Hoggar mountains, we found places to camp none of which was the same, but each of which had its particular magic. Some idiot has said that the Hoggar is Mahler's *Das Lied von der Erde*, while the Tassili is the twilight world of Wagner. The whole point of the beauty of the Sahara is that it is incomparable with anything conceived in European culture. This is no Norse or Alpine landscape, however doom-laden. It is unique, reminding even the most inveterate of comparers of nowhere else.

When we were about thirty miles from Djanet, one of the trucks overheated so that we had to stop for the night. The track here was going through high rock formations, so that it was confined to a width of about forty feet. We couldn't get off it and so slept on the road. We set out warning objects in both directions. In the night three Land Rovers raced past. They chose to go by on the narrowest side. There Ernie was sleeping. Apparently without waking, he rolled out of the way of the speeding cars.

In the cool of the morning the truck worked again. We dropped down about 1000 feet, running between the lower Tassili hills and the enormous Admer dunes. Djanet is a rather uninteresting oasis; what charms it may have had being ruined by successive military establishments and by tourists, for Djanet is the stopping place for people wanting to see the prehistoric frescoes of the Tassili. The oasis is long and narrow, lying in the gorge formed by the Oued Edjeriou. Sixty-four springs pour out an abundance of water.

At the time of the Turks, Djanet was subject to the Sultan of Ghat, a more

The Tassili plateau, site of the prehistoric cave painting

prosperous oasis on a main caravan route, one hundred and seventy miles away, now in Libya. The French built a fort, in 1911, to ward off the Senoussi from the east, who threatened the Hoggar. The Algerians keep a garrison there with a wary eye on Colonel Gaddafi and his expansive notions. Once again, with soundless tread, the soldiers marched past, their sinister truncheons dangling at their sides. They looked repressive rather than military, so that I wondered whether they were not there for keeping the Twareg in order, quite as much as keeping the Libyans out. Or the two aims might be connected.

Somewhat differently the tourists, by being there, change what they have come to see. The young Twareg men saunter by, their feet pointing outwards like ballet dancers', cool and arrogant; many of them enhance the mystery of their veiled faces by wearing dark glasses. They like particularly those which look like mirrors. They are peacock men, demeaned by being a tourist attraction. One I noticed had 'Y love you' tattooed on his arm beside a heart with initials.

An old man in the Post Office has come for his pension. He is a nomad; he has come too early in the month. A lively discussion takes place, everyone joining in. The pension book is passed round for everybody to examine. Opinion favours giving the old man his money now, for who knows where he may be on the due date. The officials are adamant. No money before the appointed, bureaucratic time.

Djanet is beset by officials and rules. It is almost as if the Algerians wished to discourage tourists. The only proper hotel is now shut. We had read how pleasant it was to sit on the terrace of this hotel, high up on the cliff, drinking cool beer. Now beer is forbidden. As camping is forbidden, all tourists are obliged to stay in a compound with stuffy palm-leaf huts.

It was not possible for me to go to see the rock carvings and paintings. They are accessible by car; I know someone who drove his Land Rover all over the plateau. Now this is not allowed, which may be no bad thing if the mess that the pedestrian tourists make is anything to go by. Indeed, the frescoes, despite their amazing number, need greater protection. Tourists have found that by throwing water over the paintings their colours are momentarily brought more alive. It can hardly improve them in other ways. One man offered to take me up on a camel. The unfriendly head of the tourist office vetoed that plan. It seemed more important that Tim should photograph the paintings than that I should see them. This, of course, was also forbidden – at least, he was obliged to leave his better equipment behind. Only snaps are permitted without special authorisation from Algiers. Tim and Jocelyn set off, with a profoundly irritating guide, for a three-day trip around the Tassili plateau.

The rock paintings and carvings of the Sahara are the most wholly astounding things in a place of perpetual surprises. The most barren part of the world is not where one expects to find its most vivid early examples of man's need for art. Much has been written about these prehistoric marvels, but often the interpretation of the drawings borders on the nonsensical.

James Wellard, in *The Great Sahara*, (a rather cross book) writes of a drawing which the Abbé Breuil confidently describes as a circumcision scene with eleven figures; two operators, one initiate, some singers to drown the shrieks of pain and some family members, looking the other way.

Wellard says it could be a castration of slaves, a fight, or the whole story of a man's life, ending with people bringing food to his tomb. With so many different possibilities, one's own interpretation is frequently the most satisfying.

Nevertheless, the paintings can tell us a lot about the history of the Sahara. The first paintings date from as early as 6000 BC, certainly before 4000 BC. They belong to what is known as the period of 'the round-headed men'. One can see why people with extra-terrestrial longings have suggested that many of the human figures look like spacemen. But then some of the figures have rather neat little horns and what look like grass skirts. Less prompting of fanciful

A Targui, Zatab Mel, sets out on a walk of a hundred and sixty miles, which he plans to complete in three days

OVERLEAF, Iherir, a Twareg oasis in a canyon in the northern Tassili

The Hoggar mountains rise to as high as 11,000 feet. They were once running with rivers and inhabited by tropical animals

speculation are the drawings of animals of this date. Elephant, hippopotamus, giraffe, crocodile, antelope – they all show that the Sahara at that time was lush, green and well-watered. The human inhabitants appear to have been negroid and their style of drawing owes nothing to any northern influence.

Gradually the Sahara became drier, perhaps more like southern Italy today. The second period, that of 'the cattle-herders', lasted roughly from 4000 BC to 1500 BC. The art of this time shows quite different influences. It is no longer so visionary, but tends towards a simpler realism. The way of life has changed from that of a purely hunting society to a pastoral existence. The people are still black, but more Ethiopian in feature. Henri Lhote, the person who has studied Saharan rock art more carefully than anyone else, believes that these people with their long-horned cattle are the ancestors of the Fulani and Bororo, who now live mostly in Nigeria, Niger, Mali and Senegal and whose origins seem obscure.

Next comes the period of 'chariots and horses'. From the east or the north-east there came white men with horses and chariots. Again no-one knows for certain who they were. The horse first came to Egypt somewhere around 1500 BC. All across the Sahara there are lapidary records of two-wheeled and four-wheeled chariots. Henri Lhote postulates a chariot route running from Tripoli, through the Tassili and the Hoggar all the way to Gao on the Niger. He has found chariot pictures at Hirafok, Tit, Tim Missao and Taoemekka (Arli), this last only six days' walk from Gao. From the flying gallop of the horses, which is Cretan in style, he concludes that these artists were Mediterranean people who, failing to seize Egypt, turned south-west across the Sahara. (The Cretans were fighting Rameses III in Libya in 1280 BC.) The pictures of this period show black and white people mixed together. The paintings are quite entertaining, though they are mostly rather disappointingly small. From photographs one imagines them larger.

The day of the horse lasted certainly a thousand years, for we find Herodotus talking in the fifth century BC about the Garamantes, who lived in southern Libya, fighting with two-wheeled chariots drawn by four horses. Their enemies were the Troglodytes who, according to Herodotus, squeaked like bats and ran at an astonishing speed. The Troglodytes, we may guess, were the ancestors of the Toubou who live in the Tibesti mountains and are known for their agility, perhaps maintained in order to avoid the slavers.

The last phase is known as the 'cameline', which started soon after the camel was introduced into Africa, when the progressively drier climate and the gradual erosion of the rocks into sand made it impossible for horses to survive. In terms of art, this period is uninteresting. The carvings seem childish and the zest has gone from the drawing. They are the first Saharan people, however, to use writing – making inscriptions in a Lybico-Berber script, which was the precursor of the writing that the modern Twareg use to scrawl messages of love on rocks that they hope their sweethearts will pass.

Tassili cave paintings: LEFT, a very early painting from the period of 'the round-headed men'; ABOVE, hunting still pre-dominates much later in the same period; BELOW, a late painting from the period of 'the cattle-herders'.

Whatever may be the final conclusions about the inspiration of these rock carvings and paintings; whether they be religious or secular; whether the sexual ones (which incidentally reveal a broad spectrum of amorous activity) are fertility symbols or saucy graffiti; whether they are decorative or magical; they are some of the most fascinating relics in the world. They will not last much longer for the caves in which they are contained are eroding. Many paintings which were inside are now outside, half the cave having fallen away, waiting to be erased by the wind. A few more centuries and they will nearly all be gone.

The only people I know of who continue with cave painting of any sort are the Dogon who are outside the scope of this book. They have lived in mountainous country near Mopti, in Mali, since the twelfth century, always resisting conversion to Islam. They number about a quarter of a million. Their beliefs are infinitely complicated involving a creation by a tiny particle called Amma, which produced two sets of twins, who went through diverse metamorphoses. The Dogon myth includes a Fall from Grace, an Ark story and much incest. They are obsessed with fertility and believe that white people are born secretly at night by the light of the moon. Most remarkable is their special celebration, Sigui, which takes place every sixty years. The timing of this festival coincides with the orbit of a companion star of Sirius, the Dog Star. This companion star is invisible to the naked eye and was not discovered by western astronomers until quite recently. The Dogon have no writing but a system of ideograms, which in some way accord with the nature of things, and a numerology associated with these symbols. On a cliff above the Dogon village of Songo is an enormous fresco made up of the signs and ideograms. Many of them represent animals which have long since died out in the region. The fresco is constantly retouched and renewed at the time of circumcision ceremonies. It is the best, but at the same time only one of many in the region.

While Tim and Jocelyn were on the plateau, I stayed with Ernie and Peter in the tourist compound called the Hôtel des Zéribas. The manager had a long face and slicked down hair which would otherwise have been curly. He was forever asking whether he could buy francs or dollars from me at the black market rate and pressing me to sell him whisky.

The Algerians long for foreign currency. In the depths of the desert a lorry driver will signal frantically. One imagines he is in distress, has run out of water or petrol. He will run across 'Tu as des francs ou des dollars? Je te donne double,' he will say in broken French.

Whisky is virtually currency. As I sat reading in the Zéribas an unctuous little fellow, who I thought was an electrician, came begging for a bottle of whisky. He offered twenty-five, then thirty then thirty-five pounds. Was an electrician

---

OPPOSITE, Hunters attack their quarry with bows and arrows

83

so well paid, I asked? It was not for him; it was for the two military commanders. The commander of the Illizi garrison was visiting the commander of the Djanet garrison. The hospitality must be of the best.

The Arabs are always asking for things; it is not exactly begging, more that they feel that the distribution of possessions should be better arranged. Foreigners have plainly got more than a fair share. It is only reasonable that there should be a redistribution.

'Give me that radio.'

'I am afraid I need it,' one says, feeling somehow foolish.

'You can get another one.'

'They cost a lot of money,' in useless justification.

'Exactly, that is why you must give it to me. I cannot afford to buy one.'

'No.'

He wanders off, quite undisturbed. If one gives it, it is the will of Allah. If one doesn't it is the same. It is written.

The children all ask, '*Donne-moi un stylo*'. Are pens in such short supply? Very probably. But one sweet apiece, I eventually found, was quite adequate. Later, in Niger and Mali, the approach from the children was even more direct. '*Donne-moi un cadeau.*' Once a grown man stood beside me in Mali, just repeating implacably, '*Cadeau, cadeau, cadeau . . .*' for a full minute.

Then there are the tourists – mostly Germans. Often they did not want to go onto the plateau. To be moving was all they needed, covering immense distances without making any contact with the people or the land. They would talk endlessly of routes, of how to adapt vehicles, of tyres. The logistics were all.

Heinz was Swiss, pigeon-chested and bow-legged. He had a straggly, half-hearted beard. He wore little green shorts. He made me think of an underbaked loaf, nothing about him being full-blooded. By trade he was a photo-litho-grapher and, he said, he liked to paint. 'But it is difficult to get money; you have to be lucky.' Perhaps he was no good.

He had come to the Sahara on the recommendation of an Englishman whom he had met in Indonesia. It was not the first time he had crossed a desert, having driven across the Gibson desert in Australia. For this trip he had sold his house in order to buy an orange Volkswagen 'camper', well fitted-out with a refrig-erator and other battery-consuming luxuries. He had painted in white, on the side of the car, maps of Africa and a hippopotamus, an ostrich, a kangaroo and a tiger.

Heinz had planned to travel with his girl friend. Three weeks before they were due to leave, they quarrelled irreparably. So he had cast around a bit and someone had suggested Gertrud. She was willing to come. Heinz pointed out that the Volkswagen had only one double bed, which they would have to share. That was perfectly all right with Gertrud. 'I am women's lib,' she said.

They set off from Switzerland in good spirits and crossed the Mediterranean to Algiers. Heinz did the driving and the cooking because he knew the car and the cooker. It was tiring. One day he asked Gertrud to take a turn at the wheel. 'I am not your chauffeur, you know. I am women's lib.' That night he asked if she would prepare the evening meal. 'I am not your cook, you know. I am women's lib.'

Gertrud would do nothing, not even put down the sand ladders when they were stuck. It would have been submissive. The extreme of anything, we are told, becomes its opposite. Gertrud, in her stout independence had become as useless as a fragile Edwardian lily. Heinz sent her back from Djanet by plane.

There is an aeroplane once or twice a week, from Algiers to Djanet. One of the pilots was a broad, plumpish, slightly effeminate man from Coventry, called Harry. He worked for British Air Ferries. The Algerians employed the British, Harry said, both here and in Libya, because the Algerians and the Libyans so often did not bother to turn up for work. The service to the oases was erratic enough without absenteeism.

After so long in Africa, Harry's particular brand of patient dissatisfaction struck me as comically British. The 'toilet facilities' were his primary concern. He minded them more than he minded the kitchen staff's slaughtering a sheep behind his hut, though he thought that 'uncouth'.

This was only the second time he had flown to Djanet and he did not like it. The approach was tricky and, because the cable from the power source to the beacon was so long, the signal from it was very feeble. You could only pick it up when you were within five miles. You couldn't speak on the radio until you were less than thirty miles away. If you missed Djanet there were thousands of miles of nothing to look forward to. Harry didn't much care for the look of the desert round here. Even on the ground, nothing would persuade him to go on the plateau. Last time he had been to Djanet a Swiss had been bitten by a horned viper up there. As if to confirm his forebodings, while we talked a woman was carried, gasping, past us, suffering from severe heat prostration. They soaked her in water and she revived, like those Japanese paper flowers dropped into tumblers.

Harry flew mostly in Libya. At least the desert there is largely flat sand. Though that didn't always help. Twenty years after the war was over, the Libyans found a Liberator which had made an emergency landing in the desert. Everything was intact. The crew decided to walk. Their footsteps were still in the sand. The one who went furthest had walked ninety miles before dying.

Although Libya was safer for flying, many people died in the desert there – careless oil workers usually, who took no precautions.

There was talk, Harry said, of the air service to Djanet being cancelled, probably because the Algerians couldn't pay British Air Ferries. 'Suits me,' said Harry. 'I would give up flying if I could afford to. It's the worst form of transport there is.'

When Tim and Jocelyn returned we wanted to leave. There is no bank in Djanet. The hotel will not accept anything but cash. We also needed petrol. In theory, the customs office will change travellers' cheques. The customs officer was unexpectedly civil. He had no money. It might come tomorrow, *inshallah*. I suggested that we give him some travellers' cheques now; when the money came he would pay the hotel and the garage. Impossible, quite out of the question. We sat and drank tea for a while, ruminating, the customs man and I, on the ways of the world. It was a hot morning. We tossed that about for a bit. All at once, he sent a boy to find out whether the hotel would agree to my suggestion. The manager was reportedly quite pleased with that arrangement. We agreed that what was true of the hotel must be true of the garage, *inshallah*. The garage man, reasonably enough, wanted a note from the customs man to say that he would be paid. I went back to the customs. Impossible. To write a note was beyond his authority; surely that was obvious, he said. I pointed out that without petrol I could not leave. 'That is your problem,' said the customs man. Then after a moment he added winningly, 'and our problem too.' We were sad together and the morning wore on. Then he had an idea. He would see if the hotel had some money. In half an hour he came back with wodges of money, far more than I needed. He gave me what I asked for and with it I solemnly paid both the hotel and the garage.

Problems with officials are frequently like this – at first, insurmountable; gradually, if you do not harry or hustle, they dissolve and both sides wonder why there ever was a difficulty. '*Voilà, pas de problème, alhamdulillah*'. The harry and the hustle had worn Olivia out by this time, and she flew back to England.

There was, throughout our whole journey, always something which forced us to retrace our steps. Time and again we would think we had left a place and then some misfortune would drag us back there. We became almost superstitious about it.

Peter had done a lot to improve the running of the engines, having been helped by a German who had travelled for years in an ancient Unimog. He modified the petrol supply, so that the fuel no longer vaporised before it reached the carburettor.

We travelled confidently back through the awesome fringes of the Tassili, past Zaoutalaz and out into the gravel plain which lies between the end of the Tassili and the foothills of the Hoggar mountains.

Jocelyn said, 'Nothing happens when I turn the wheel to the right. What do you think?'

I said I thought we should stop. The steering arm hung uselessly. A bolt had sheared off. We had no means of getting the end of the sheared bolt out of the solid plate into which it was screwed. We had no spare plate; it was not the sort of thing that normally breaks.

86

We remembered a derelict Unimog at Djanet. We had enquired about it, hoping to buy some oddments off it. At first we were told that it belonged to the Customs. The customs official said that on no account could they sell off parts of something which was government property. We should forget that idea and, in any case, he added with mystifying logic, they had sold the wreck to somebody else the week before. We traced the new owner, or rather his family. He had gone away for a month or two. They could not sell even the smallest part without his approval.

Certainly the part we now needed would be on that Unimog. There was no hope of negotiating a purchase. We decided to steal it. Ernie and Peter were to be the thieves. It was about one hundred and fifty miles back to Djanet, much of the way being over difficult sand. We unloaded everything from the healthy truck, so that they could travel more quickly. They left us enough water for a week and drove off.

We sat on the sandy, gravel plain. There was nothing to be seen in any direction, not a shrub, not even a boulder. The land rose a little to the east, so we could see no more than three hundred yards in that direction. To the west,

The Unimog breaks down outside Djanet

in the far distance, there were some hills. Jocelyn and I played picquet, but the cards blew away. We tried backgammon, but the wind blew harder and the board filled with sand.

The wind blows almost all the time in the Sahara. Sometimes it blows hard but the sand doesn't move. At other times the sand seems restless and the lightest breeze sends it scurrying about like smoke, making moiré patterns over the land. There must be a fixed speed at which wind can lift sand or, perhaps it depends on the contours. I could never tell when a storm was coming.

That morning the scurrying sand gradually rose higher and higher. So did the temperature. By midday, the world was just a yellowish fog, choking in the throat and grating on the teeth. A sandstorm invades like a rapist. Soon there is no part of you that is not gritty and dirty. The sand seeks a way deep into your ears, under the lids of your eyes, far up your nose. Clothes make no difference. All your body is assaulted. You breathe in hot, sand-laden air. Your hair is soon grizzled. Each line on your body is marked out with sand, like a pattern of iron filings held by a magnet. It is an insult and a degradation. There is no question of eating anything. When you pour water into a cup, it at once has a floating skin of sand. You try to breathe only through a *cheche*, or any cloth wound round your face. That makes you even hotter.

This time we were lucky. Towards the end of the afternoon, the wind dropped a little, the sand sank down and the air lost its yellow soupiness. Eventually we could even see the hills in the west, silhouetted by the setting sun. A pied crow came and pecked at the sand-ridden food we had had to throw away.

When I went to bed, I found that my pillow had been blown away. In the morning I searched downwind for a mile or two, but I couldn't find it. It must have made a strange sight – a white pillow bowling along, up and down the waves of the grey, rolling plain.

The next day Tim and Jocelyn tried to make pancakes, with some revolting 'mix', which we had brought with us. It would stick to the pan. The pied crow had a bountiful day.

Then, early in the morning, Ernie and Peter were back. We had expected to have to wait for four days, but everything had gone remarkably smoothly. With an unladen truck, they had made good time to Djanet, arriving early in the evening. They waited until well after dark and went to the Unimog. The part was there. The first clink of the hammer made such a noise that they realised that they would wake the whole neighbourhood if they continued. They decided to wait till morning and slept in the truck in a hidden place.

By good luck, the next day was some sort of holiday. The people of Djanet were all parading up the only street. No-one paid any attention to a couple of tourists working on an old truck. Ernie and Peter took only twenty minutes to get the piece off the derelict Unimog. It was never going to move again, but in case of miracles they left our old part, which, if someone could drill out the sheared bolt, was perfectly good.

They drove quickly away, getting back that evening somewhere near where they had left us. The track at this point was perhaps ten miles wide. They could not find us in the dark but had to wait till morning. We were on our way again by lunchtime.

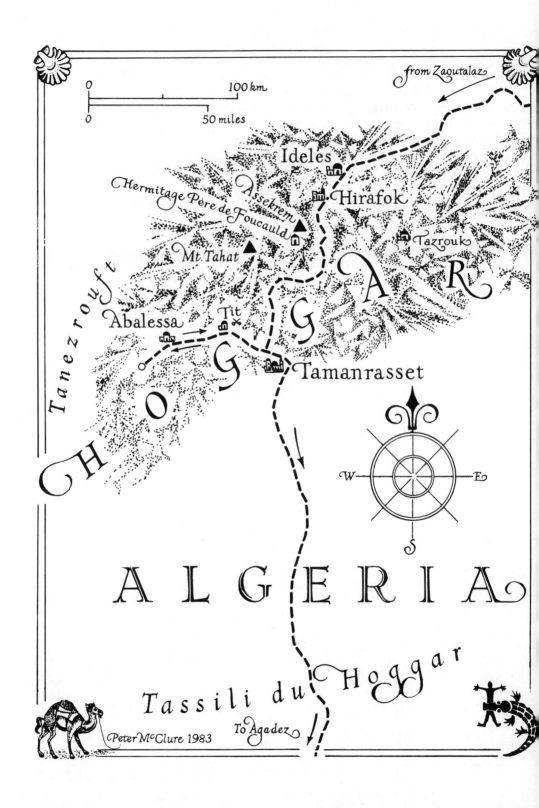

from Zaoutalaz

100 km

50 miles

Ideles

Hirafok

Hermitage Père de Foucauld

Assekrem

Tazrouk

Mt.Tahat

Tanezrouft

H O G G A R

Abalessa

Tit

Tamanrasset

W — E

S

A L G E R I A

Peter McClure 1983

Tassili du Hoggar

To Agadez

4

DESERT PRIESTS AND A MYTHICAL QUEEN

THE DESERT between Djanet and Tamanrasset is some of the most beautiful, almost wholly barren, land in the Sahara. Quite soon the gravel plain, on which we had sat while a crime was committed, rumpled up into the foothills of the Hoggar mountains. At first there were fairly low humps of mountain, quite different from the grotesque pinnacles and balanced boulders of the Tassili. These Hoggar mountains made pretty valleys and views. It still was not Mahler, but at a pinch, one could let the imagination clothe the lower slopes with trees, while the peaks, covered as they were with the whitest sand, did look like snowcaps. Yet it was the difference always, rather than any similarity, that was so wonderful. The distance and the silence. You cannot be further away or be quieter. Here we were further from Algiers than Algiers is from London. Of course, this was still the tourist route. Heinz, for instance, had gone ahead of us and was to cause us some alarm by not arriving in Tamanrasset for several days, having broken down. It was not until much later and much further west that we were to wander in deserts which saw no-one for months on end. It is true that we could have moved across hundreds of miles in Algeria where there were no tracks, but to struggle through untracked blankness serves no purpose for me. Remoteness is attractive provided that you have a destination or something, or better still someone, to find. Sheer emptiness for its own sake is pointless.

In among the early valleys, we came to an abandoned fort at Serouenout, another defence against the Senoussi. It looked romantic, commanding the whole valley. There was a yellow lorry parked inside the fort. The driver was a rather polished Arab, with a jaunty cap and dark glasses. While we were talking, a European woman emerged from one of the deserted barrack rooms. She was about forty, with dyed yellow hair arranged in a spiky, punk style. She wore a baggy, bright-blue track suit. In a stream of enthusiastic chatter, she informed us that she lived in Munich and had come with a party of half-a-dozen friends for a holiday. The friends wanted to take a six-day guided tour of the Tassili frescoes. She judged that it was more interesting to meet people, rather than stare at a lot of cave paintings, not, I was to mark, that she had anything against prehistoric art, or any art for that matter, but living people (and here she glanced at the lorry driver) were more stimulating than matchstick figures in a dusty cave, were they not? So she had elected to go to Tamanrasset on her own instead and this kind driver, who was taking she was not quite sure what from Djanet to Tamanrasset, had offered her a lift; was she not fortunate?

I lacked the courage to ask her whether she was sleeping with the lorry driver. I doubt that she would have been offended, but she might have offered more detail than I cared to hear. I wondered, though, what it meant to this dumpy, Bavarian chatterbox. Had the mirror-eyed driver, in his peaked cap, inherited the mantle of a desert sheik? Was his yellow lorry the equivalent of the pure white camel of all those romantic films and novels, in which the heroine is flung across the pommel and whirled away across the sands in a delicious ecstasy of terror? I do hope so. In any event, he told us of a diversion which led us past a landscape so exclusively black and white that, for a moment, I too could imagine myself in an ancient film.

The variety in the landscape here is astonishing to anyone who thinks that the desert is an endless flat space. In the course of a morning you drive up a narrow black and white valley, half-filled with hard rippling white sand; then you are climbing on a broad gravelly slope, which narrows abruptly to a rocky pass. Soon you go down again into an open space, sprinkled with bushes and traversed by sickeningly bumpy wadis. All at once you realise that the sand is now yellow and the hillocks are tinged with umber. The different sands take time to get used to in practical terms. There are subtle differences in texture, which can tell you whether your car will fly over the next patch or sink ponderously up to the hub caps. Recognising the quality takes long experience; but the aversion therapy of hours of digging and pushing which follows any mistake concentrates the mind somewhat.

It must have been a day for speculation of one sort or another. About eighty miles from the fort we were in a fairly open region. The way varied between soft sand and quite firm going scattered with small volcanic rocks, some of them a strong, dark blue in colour, so striking that they were almost worth keeping. But not quite. We came to a place where someone had arranged some more ordinary stones.

There was a large circle of them about thirty feet in diameter. Inside that were more stones forming the word 'Prioux'. It was almost big enough to be read from a small aircraft; but what aircraft? In any case, it did not seem like the name of a place. Anyhow, it was not a place. There was nothing to single out this spot from any other. There was no well, certainly. There was no cross road, nor anywhere for a cross road to go. We were still forty miles short of the next human habitation at Ideles. 'Prioux'? A person, then? I visualised a young lieutenant in the French army killed by the Senoussi while on patrol in 1916, perhaps, when Père de Foucauld died (see page 95). Surely, they would have carried his body back to the fort. It seemed too big for a grave, and unusually lacking in information – no date, no age, no cause of death. Just 'Prioux'. Perhaps he made an heroic stand here and was buried with full military pomp elsewhere. Then his name would be known to history. Or was he an aviator who crashed here? There was no sign of wreckage – and nothing disappears in this desert. So who or what was 'Prioux'?

We will never know, probably. It will remain one of the mysteries of the Sahara. It is quite unimportant, no doubt, but it is strange to think that in this unchanging part of the Hoggar, those stones may lie there for thousands of years. Age is meaningless in the Sahara. How long have they been there now? It is impossible to say. Equally impossible to say how long they will stay undisturbed. In a fanciful mood, one could imagine them there until the day when the alphabet they are written in is forgotten and people will puzzle over the slender evidence of six letters, which, as it happens, already today mean nothing.

Ideles lies in the valley of the Oued Tarouda. There is no more fertile patch in the whole of the Hoggar. There are nearly a hundred acres of lush gardens, with apricots, peaches and even grapes and figs. The vegetables are plump and full of taste. The birds flutter among the palm trees. It could never have hoped to equal Iherir for exotic charm, but it must have been a delightful place before . . . before what exactly? Really before a whole host of things, all of them important in the transformation of the Sahara. First, there is the climatic change, which has been going on ever since the days of the 'round-headed men'. Each decade, the desert becomes appreciably drier. The springs still flow at Ideles, but the deep, under-ground water is harder to bring up than it was formerly.

The social changes are even more significant. Originally Ideles was an oasis of the Twareg, worked by the vassals and serfs of the Kel-Ahaggar Twareg. Besides the farmers, there were metal workers and, of course, the slaves. The French, as part of their arrangement with the ever-rebellious Twareg, left their social affairs pretty much alone, turning a dimmed eye even to the continuing slavery. The people themselves were simple enough, believing in all manner of magic – especially the Tanaghouat, a huge snake which can bleat like a goat, luring victims whom it kills with a poisonous bite.

Independence brought a more interfering spirit. Slavery was positively disapproved and Ideles, in 1962, was a reception centre for slaves who fled from their masters.

It is also in the nature of independent governments to disapprove of nomadism. They feel that some disgrace attaches to this way of life. Once again, Ideles was chosen as being a good place to settle any wanderers. The authorities put up pretty houses of dark red mud and a large school; it was all a considerable building project for so distant a place. The men who used to work in the fields and gardens found employment in building a far more rewarding labour. Others went to work for the companies prospecting for oil, on road making projects, or even in offices in Tamanrasset. Much of the land is now neglected.

Newcomers disrupted the traditional patterns. There were mixed marriages of Twareg and Arabs and a complete abandonment of the class system.

All this makes for a rather unsettled atmosphere. There is little of the warmth which is usually accorded to visitors. The men, in their flowery, blue robes stared at us in some hostility. Only one agreed to be photographed. The new broad street of Ideles reminded me of a scene in a Western at the moment when the baddies walk slowly into the town and everyone keeps to his house.

When we walked through the poorer quarter of the village, where they still live in zeribas, straw or brush enclosures, two chatty little boys came up. An older boy said we must not speak to little boys. Why not? 'They can't talk properly.'

The women were different. The older ones were nearly all involved in some occasion, possibly a wedding. They wore superbly elegant, dark-blue cloaks and heavy silver tassels hung down their backs. The younger ones were much more forthcoming. They were dressed in dreadful Lurex gowns which they wore over long dresses. They were, like all Twareg women, unveiled. They threw stones at the little boys to drive them away and then they crowded round to flirt. Twareg girls are traditionally easy-going. Tim disappeared into the gardens for what we thought was rather a long time, ostensibly to photograph one of the girls. While the rest of us talked to the girls, the men glowered, but did nothing.

We did not linger at Ideles. A doctor there told us that the most beautiful road to Tamanrasset was a small one, branching to the left at Hirafok. It was, he said, a first rate track presenting no difficulty, except at one pass where there was a fearsome group of hairpin bends. This track would lead us past Assekrem, the hermitage of Père de Foucauld. The doctor, from Algiers, had been along the track only a fortnight before, so he could vouch for it.

In Hirafok, we saw a Targui putting the finishing touches to the loading of his beautiful, white camel. We asked whether this was the turning for Assekrem and Tamanrasset.

'Tamanrasset?' he said. 'I will come with you.'

In a twinkling, he had unloaded his baggage from the camel and transferred it to one of our trucks. I thought of Wilfred Thesiger and the distress he would have felt at this preference for mechanical transport. And what of all those sentimental writers, who in every volume assure us that time is of no importance in the desert, that no-one is ever in a hurry? There is always a character in those books, who asks with weary oriental wisdom, 'And what would you have done with the time you would have saved?'

The Targui, whose name I did not manage to understand, spoke very little Arabic and hardly any French. He managed to convey the fact that he had only once been in a car before. This was relevant. As the afternoon wore on, we wondered whether we would be able to reach Assekrem before dark. The Targui knew the way perfectly well and he could explain that it lay behind a particular mountain. But how long would it take? He had no idea. I knew it was a little less than fifty miles. I could not say how long it would take him on a camel. He could not say how long it would take in a car.

The answer was a very long time. The road, which the doctor had described as being so easy, proved brutish. Much of the track was loose rock. Every so often there would be a deep, narrow wadi with high, crumbly banks, which demanded the lowest possible gear. The only smooth part was the series of twelve hairpin bends, which we sailed up with no difficulty.

It was always like that. No information, from almost any source, was reliable. It was not that people told one what one wanted to hear, because, quite as often someone would say that a road was virtually impassable. In the event it would turn out to be extremely easy. Every aspect of travel was the subject of misin-

A volcanic mountain amidst a jumble of basalt rock in the Hoggar range

formation. We were promised water where there was none. We were assured that there would be no petrol where there was plenty. The bank in Timbuctoo, they said, was only open on Tuesdays. In fact, it opened every day, even Friday. This was permitted, that was forbidden. This customs post was open, that road was closed to travellers. On and on it went; and it was nearly always nonsense.

The desert, I would have thought, is the one place where information should always be trustworthy. For the wrong news could easily mean death. Contrariwise, I suppose, it works well. Once you have learned to mistrust everything you hear, you are never caught unawares. However many assurances we were given, we took exactly the precautions we would have taken without them.

It was late when we came to Assekrem, but it was still light enough for us to gaze out in wonder from the eyrie where Père de Foucauld built his hermitage, 9000 feet up in the mountains. Weird sugar-loaf peaks, sprouting like porcupine quills, vast indigo distances, an incomparable solitude.

The lives of saints are fraught with difficulty for the temporally minded, principally because the writers, on whom one must to some extent depend, generally select material which gives an impression of sanctimony rather than sanctity and eschew material which might reveal a more sympathetic humanity. These writers have, conversely, a very awkward time with the story of Père de Foucauld and consequently resort to considerable prevarication and outright suppression.

Charles Eugène de Foucauld was born in Strasbourg in 1858. His was an aristocratic, military family although his great-uncle had been the Prince Archbishop of Arles, who was savagely martyred during the French Revolution.

Both his father and his mother died when he was six. He and his sister, Marie, lived from then on with their maternal grandfather, Colonel de Morlet, who spoilt the young viscount absurdly.

When he was sixteen, he was sent to a Jesuit school in Paris, but he didn't last long. The priests discovered that he spent much of his time seducing shopgirls and more still eating. The Jesuits, ever oblique, asked the Colonel to remove his grandson on the basis of some invented illness.

De Foucauld was made to work with a tutor and, when he just passed the examination, his family sent him to the military academy at Saint Cyr. He was so fat that he looked grotesque in his uniform; but at night in the dormitory he would sit in bed eating spoonfuls of *foie gras*.

After Saint Cyr, he went to the cavalry school at Saumur, where he shared a room with the Marquis de Morès. By this time his grandfather was dead, and he had come of age and was rich. Freedom was a great spur to his turpitude.

At Saumur he was intolerable. He got from the doctor a spurious certificate to say that he should not be made to get up early; he disdained to collect his pay; he spent 70,000 francs in eleven months at Monsieur Budan's restaurant. It was almost surprising that he had the opportunity, because he was so frequently confined to barracks. Once this happened because he had simply disappeared for four days. He had been wandering round the countryside dressed as a beggar. He said he had wanted to know what it felt like to be hungry and despised.

On that occasion, he crept out of confinement in order to go to a party in Tours. Getting off the train his false beard slipped and the police arrested him, thinking he must be a thief or a spy.

The extraordinary thing is that he was not sacked. Despite his gross appearance (although by now he had taken to spending an inordinate amount on clothes), despite his arrogance, despite his apparent uselessness as a soldier, he survived the course. He must, one assumes, have had singular charm. The senior officers evidently quite enjoyed his outrageous behaviour and found his excuses witty and amusing. Plainly he was clever, with an exceptional ability to absorb and distil all manner of subjects. His tastes in literature were hardly military. He liked the classics and would read out to his companions extracts from Aristophanes. Nonetheless he passed out eighty-seventh, out of eighty-seven.

De Foucauld joined Les Quatrièmes Chasseurs d'Afrique. His regiment was ordered to Africa. Contrary to his usual principle of 'I rent by the day, not the week or the month', he had at this moment a permanent mistress, Mimi. He did not want to leave her. He bought her a ticket in the name of the Vicomtesse de Foucauld and sent her ahead to find a house for them both. For a while everyone was deceived and even the Colonel accepted Mimi, who must have had great style, as the Vicomtesse. This made the truth about Mimi doubly unpalatable to the Colonel when, inevitably, it emerged. The Colonel told de Foucauld to send her back to France. He refused and had to resign from the regiment.

For a while he set up with Mimi in Evian, but spent much of his time learning Arabic. It lasted only two or three months, until one day, as in some corny film, he read that Les Quatrièmes Chasseurs d'Afrique were off to put down an uprising. Abandoning Mimi, who packed her trunks with dignity, he applied to rejoin his regiment and, again for no reason that one can imagine, they accepted him. For about a year he really became a reasonable soldier, as always being popular with the men and his fellow officers. Then the restlessness, which beset him all his life, drove him to a new venture. He resigned his commission and became an explorer.

It was a peculiar interlude, because he decided to travel through Morocco, disguised as a Jew. The Jews were, of course, much despised. Against that, it was possibly not a bad disguise because Jews were hardly worth killing, while a Christian, if exposed, would surely be murdered. That he was well-disguised was proved by some of his former fellow officers, who passed him at the start of his journey lurking against a wall. 'Look at that Jew eating olives. He looks just like a monkey.' It was like *The Four Feathers* and almost as preposterous.

In the eleven months that he was in Morocco, he mapped nearly one thousand five hundred square miles, of which little had been explored before. In reality he had become a spy, while at the same time indulging his taste for self-abasement.

Back from Morocco de Foucauld fell in love. The girl was the daughter of a French geographer. He became engaged to her and then quite quickly broke it off. It is hard for anyone to present this episode in an attractive light, particularly as part of the reason for breaking it off were the snobbish objections of his family. His defenders, naturally, maintain that, if his love had been as true as he momentarily believed it to be, nothing would have deflected him.

This seems to have been a turning point in de Foucauld's life. He went back to Paris and gradually gave himself over to the Church. Everything he ever did, he overdid. After making his first confession for many years, he decided to dedicate his life to God and within a few months experienced a mystical sense of conversion. Therefore he made a journey to the Holy Land, which so impressed him that he decided to become a Trappist monk.

In 1890, de Foucauld became Brother Marie Albéric at a monastery in the Ardèche, planning never to see any of his family again. For the new de Foucauld, the austere regime was, he declared, not mortifying enough. He wanted greater poverty, more misery, less sleep and more work. They slept for six hours, if they were not keeping vigil. One might think that the other monks might have felt that Brother Marie Albéric's asking for more discomfort was belittling of their sacrifice, which they had every reason to regard as sufficient. This was not the case. They revered him, as René Bazin records in his book, *Charles de Foucauld*, 'as a second Francis of Assisi'.

After six months Brother Marie Albéric moved to Syria. Here everything was poor enough, but he went beyond the others working barefoot and eating less than enough to keep up his strength. Once again, they thought him wonderful.

Nevertheless the Trappists recognised that he was not cut out for obedience to their order. He might be a saint, but in his own not their fashion. He never took his final vows and was released from his lesser ones.

There followed three years in Nazareth and Jerusalem, where he worked for the Poor Clares as a servant, refusing the gardener's cottage, preferring to sleep in the tool-shed with a stone for a pillow. All he asked was to be allowed to adore the Sacred Host on the altar, which he did for hours on end.

Once more, the nuns decided he was a saint. They persuaded him that he should become a priest. So he forgot that he had never meant to leave the East and went back to Europe and was ordained. He also ignored or forgot that he was never going to see his family again. His sister came to his ordination. He was now forty-three.

De Foucauld's new plan was to go to North Africa and become a missionary, intending to found a Fraternity of the Little Brothers and Sisters of Jesus or the Brethren of the Sacred Heart of Jesus.

He went first to Beni Abbès, nearly six hundred miles south of Oran. The oasis lies at the edge of a wadi. Behind the village rise the dunes of the Great Occidental *Erg*. Today a main paved road passes near the oasis, running south towards Gao and Timbuctoo. There are petrol pumps, two hotels and an air of modernity. In de Foucauld's time, it must have seemed extremely remote. There was little there but palm trees. At the top of the cliff there was a garrison of French soldiers.

The soldiers helped de Foucauld build a small hermitage, the first of three that he was to have in the Sahara. He called it a Fraternity, for here he hoped to have followers who would share his austere way of life. He longed, at the same time, for solitude. In the end this contradiction did not matter, for the only candidate he ever found, Frère Michel, could not survive the rigorous existence and left after a few months to settle with the Carthusians, whose rule most people find strict but was a holiday for Michel.

It was no accident that de Foucauld chose a garrison town in which to build his first hermitage. There can be no doubt that, side by side with his perfectly genuine piety, there was a keen devotion to the army and to an ideal of French supremacy. While Englishmen believed that God had selected them to govern the world, de Foucauld was privy to His views about France. 'In choosing France as the cradle of the devotion of the Sacred Heart and for the apparitions of Lourdes, Our Lord has shown clearly that He keeps France in her rank of first-born.'

In 1903, Henri Lapperine, an old acquaintance at Saumur came to Beni Abbès. Lapperine was, as de Foucauld put it, to give 'the Sahara to France in spite of herself and unite our possessions in Algeria with our Sudanese colonies.'* He was at this time the commander responsible for all the remote oases.

Lapperine's ambition was to befriend the Twareg in the southern desert. The battle of Tit, in 1902, had so humbled the Twareg that they had retreated into hiding in the Hoggar and the Adrar n Iforas. De Foucauld called the battle of Tit, 'the greatest deed of arms in our time'. It was a phrase he was fond of. The battle of Taghit in July 1903, in which he had wanted to fight, he described as 'the finest feat of arms in Algeria for forty years'.

De Foucauld decided that he wanted to live among the Twareg and to study their language. After a number of rather unfortunate episodes, he had given up trying to baptise people or even to convert them. He had also stopped buying slaves in order to free them. His superior, Monseigneur Guérin, had pointed out that lapsed converts did more harm than good. From now on, de Foucauld would seek only to influence by example.

Lapperine recognised that this was, from his point of view, an extremely good approach. Moslems, even the rather unorthodox Twareg, are much

---

* The area south of Algeria was in those days called *Le Soudan*.

impressed by holiness; and this quality de Foucauld had to the full.

It is impossible to say how much Lapperine's needs affected de Foucauld's decisions. The coincidence of their aims was, at the least, fortunate. Together they set out to meet the Twareg.

After two journeys of reconnaissance, de Foucauld settled at Tamanrasset. As always, the accounts of his behaviour on the journeys made him sound unbearable. He would walk on the scorching sand barefoot. He would walk, when they wanted to get on. Lapperine finally made him ride. One officer brought him some water when he had had none for hours. He started to drink. Then: 'You are tempting me back to gluttony' and he poured the water away – something one would have thought inexcusable. But, as always, the soldiers loved him. And during the five months of his first journey, he managed to translate the gospels into Tamachek, the Twareg language.

His understanding of the Twareg seems to have been immediate. When he met Moussa ag Amastane, the *amenokal,* or chief, of the Kel-Ahaggar Twareg, he said of him, 'He is very good, he is most intelligent, very open, very pious, a Moslem seeking goodness in the way that a Moslem does, but at the same time ambitious, loving money, pleasure and honour as Mohammed, in his eyes the perfect teacher, loved them.'

Tamanrasset, when de Foucauld settled there in 1905, was merely an encampment for about twenty nomad families. He built a small hermitage which was the only permanent structure for hundreds of miles until Moussa ag Amastane, recognising this as a good site, built his own mud castle three miles away besides the huge rock Hadriane.

Of course, de Foucauld was never satisfied either with the degree of discomfort he could create for himself or with the measure of solitude he achieved. So he found sixty miles away a place immensely difficult to reach, one hour's walk from the nearest water. This was Assekrem. Here on a high ridge, surrounded by nearly perpendicular columns of rock, de Foucauld built his last hermitage. It is a tiny place, little more than a stone but perched on a rock. He wrote to his sister:

'During the day the thermometer never rises above twenty-five degrees; and with this chill for most of the time, there is a wind which reminds me of the great winds of Louye; I love so much to hear it whistling in the country, and God here treats me in a way that suits my tastes. Whenever I open the window or the door, I am lost in admiration at the sight of those mountain peaks which surround me and which I dominate; it is a marvellous view and a really fine solitude. How good it is to be in this great calm, surrounded by the beauties of nature, so tormented and so strange, and then to lift one's heart towards the Creator and Jesus the Saviour.'

OPPOSITE, Charles de Foucauld (BBC Hulton Picture Library)

Here and at Tamanrasset, de Foucauld pursued his devotions and came to know the Twareg, better than anyone else has ever done. Before his time they had murdered all Christians; and since his time their way of life has been steadily eroded. De Foucauld compiled a dictionary of Tamachek and wrote copiously about their customs and their traditions.

He became a close friend of Moussa ag Amastane who, perhaps in consequence, remained always loyal to France. Almost better he came to know Dassine oult Khemma, the most beautiful poetess of the Twareg. Moussa had been in love with Dassine for years, reciting endless poems about her 'But', as one of the poems ended, 'she never turns her head towards him, she pays him no attention'.

Dassine never found anyone she really loved, though there were plenty who loved her to the point of idiocy. One admirer was sitting next to her during a musical party. Some others arrived and put the points of their lances into the ground as a sign of peace. One of the lances went through the admirer's leg. He said nothing, in case any disturbance should cause him to lose his place next to Dassine. He sat impaled until the party ended.

Dassine helped de Foucauld with his dictionary and, in return, he taught the Twareg women to knit and gave them presents of needles and hair dye. They loved the needles, having hitherto only used thorns.

De Foucauld's spiritual directors must have been well pleased with him, for the Pope gave him special and rare permission to say mass without a helper.

Equally, the army was delighted with him. He provided information which they could have got in no other way. And, as he himself wrote, '. . . my presence here gives the officers a chance of coming into the heart of this country'.

There were so many sides to Charles de Foucauld. There was the hermit who longed to get lost in the depths of the desert; the monk who wanted to found an order; the soldier who wanted to fight and slaughter Arabs for the glory of France; the spy who liked disguise; the aristocrat who could find a parallel between the hierarchical Twareg and the feudal system of ancient France; the colonist who could have (according to Lapperine) 'very little esteem for the negroes settled there [Tamanrasset] who are all lazy and of the lowest type.' Finally there was a Christian who longed for martyrdom. Again and again he said that he would love to suffer the same fate as his great-uncle the Prince Archbishop of Arles. In the circumstances, this ambition was not hard of achievement.

In 1914, de Foucauld the soldier wanted to go to France, if not to fight, then as a stretcher bearer or chaplain. He was refused permission. As far as the military were concerned, de Foucauld the spy had far greater value.

By 1916, the Sahara was much unsettled. The subdued tribes, aware of what

OPPOSITE AND OVERLEAF, Twareg nomads

was happening in Europe, reverted to their efforts to drive the French out of the desert. The leaders in this movement were the Senoussi, a sect founded in Algeria but based in Tripolitania, as Libya was then called. First Ghat fell, then the fort at Djanet. By this time de Foucauld had become the centre of intelligence in the area. He wrote to Lapperine in France: 'I have transformed my hermitage into a fort. When I look up at my battlements, I cannot help thinking of the fortified convents and churches of the Middle Ages. How the ancient things return . . .'

The leader of the Senoussi, Si Mohammed Labed, chose another Twareg chief to attack the holy fort. This man was El Keraan, an enemy of Moussa ag Amastane, who still stood staunchly by the French. It is doubtful whether a straightforward attack would have succeeded. The walls of the fort were six feet thick. There were no windows on the outside. In the enclosed courtyard was a deep well. The priest had plenty of guns and ammunition. There was only one small, narrow door. De Foucauld could defend himself easily.

El Keraan had rifles but nothing with which to blast a way in. Besides, his orders were to capture de Foucauld as a hostage; they did not want to kill him. Yet they had to be quick. French soldiers patrolled the area almost daily.

The raiders found El Madani, who did some work for de Foucauld. Under the threat of torture, the former black slave agreed to help them.

The thirty men surrounded the fort hiding in the trench which ran around it. El Madani called to the priest, 'I have the mail from the army'. It was the day for the mail to come. The bolts slid back. The door opened just a crack. A hand came out. At once they grabbed. They pulled the priest out and threw him in the trench. They set Serma ag Thora to guard him. He lay quiet leaning against the wall, a gun to his head.

The men ransacked the fort scattering the priest's papers. They took his guns and ammunition. It was a good haul. Paul Embarek, the priest's servant, crouched by the wall watching.

Then two soldiers came. The priest made a move to warn them. Serma fired.

'The saint neither moved nor cried out. I did not think he was wounded. It was only after some minutes that I saw the blood flow and the body of the saint slip gently down. He was dead.' That is what Paul saw.

The Church had very little success in the desert. De Foucauld made no lasting converts except for one old woman to whom he gave the last rites. She perked up and survived until 1935, her faith fortified, it may be, by the two francs a week which de Foucauld had arranged for her to have for life.

In this restraint in trying to make converts he was following the principle laid down by Cardinal Lavigerie, a man of burning certainty, who became Archbishop of Algiers in 1868. Like so many others who came to the desert, for whatever purpose, he was an extreme character.

His faith or fierce conviction had come to him as a child. In Bayonne, when he was ten, he would grab little Jewish boys in the street and forcibly baptise them in a stream or a fountain. If they cried, he gave them a few sous. He believed even then in simple solutions.

At home he insisted on being addressed by his family, even his grandmother, as if he were already a priest and the servants were obliged to confess to him, kneeling.

In Algeria he did much useful work, founding orphanages and schools, relieving famine and teaching modern methods of agriculture – all things which an enlightened government might have done, but didn't.

Lavigerie also founded the Society of Missionaries of Our Lady of Africa, which became known as the White Fathers. The Archbishop, whose view was never narrow, saw them as a spiritual army who were to bring the message of Christ to hundreds of millions of people throughout the whole continent. The Pope approved of this ambitious plan and made him, in addition to his archiepiscopal role in Algiers, Missionary Prefect of the Sahara and the Sudan. This included being Bishop of Timbuctoo, whose improbable diocese covered the Congo and East Africa.

The furthest south that his missionaries had reached at this time was Metlili near Ghardaia, where they made no attempts at conversion and were not even supposed to discuss Christianity with the native inhabitants. They were to impress by example, praying in public and performing good works.

An unseen diocese is to a Bishop much like a vacuum to nature. In 1876, Lavigerie sent three missionaries to find their way to Timbuctoo. They were Fathers Paulmier, Menoret and Bouchand. Their guides were to be five Twareg who had been involved in the murder, the year before, of the explorer Duperé. It was the Archbishop who had suggested that these marauders, instead of being punished, should be brought to Algiers to be shown the delights of French civilisation – whereupon, one supposes, they would long for these great benefits to be brought to the Hoggar.

They were to set off from Metlili. Metlili is a village of the Chamba tribe, about thirty miles from the M'zab. The local sheik warned the Fathers of the probably treacherous intentions of the Twareg. They paid no attention. The Sheik even sent his son, El Haj Bou Bekher, and some tribesmen to escort them. They set off, chanting the *Te Deum*.

The end was, as so often with these desert stories, like a bad film. Riding ahead, Father Paulmier was discussing swords with his Targui companion. The Targui drew his to show it to him. The Father bent his head to look, the Targui chopped it off. Just behind was Father Bouchand; his companion shot him. Father Menoret was stabbed.

Cardinal Lavigerie (BBC Hulton Picture Library)

Bou Bekher prepared to fight. The Twareg told him that he was not involved; they only wanted to kill Christians. Bou Bekher relaxed and put down his weapons. Then they shot him. They justified this extra barbarity on the basis of a blood feud. A year before a Chamba had killed a Targui.

Lavigerie was shocked, but managed to thank God 'for this kindness He has done to my children'. He wrote to their parents: 'You can finally rest assured of the happy though painful certainty that you longed for and, at the same time, dreaded: your sons have suffered death for God's cause! Your hearts, illuminated by faith, have thrilled with joy, I know – even while you have wept . . .'

However enjoyable it may have been for the victims, the murder of these missionaries aggravated the French government. They advised Lavigerie to forget about Timbuctoo and to bring back any missionaries from the desert oases. Lavigerie did nothing of the sort, but he waited.

In 1881, the mission led by Colonel Flatters to the southern Sahara, with the ridiculous object of reconnoitering a route for a trans-Saharan railway, met with disaster. Ninety men died, tricked and killed by the Twareg.

Not even this deterred the Archbishop. He could not send any missionaries through the French-occupied oases in Algeria. So he established a mission in Tripoli, still under nominal Turkish rule. Once more three priests, Fathers Richard, Pouplard and Morat, set out from Ghadames to head for Timbuctoo. As always seemed to happen with desert explorers, they were given many warnings and their guides' behaviour would have alerted the most obtuse and unsuspicious traveller. The priests chose to ignore their well-wishers and their common sense. 'Give us shade when it is hot, protect us against cold and rain, give us a staff to help us down steep slopes . . .' they prayed in idiot simplicity. They got thirteen miles from Ghadames and were then murdered. Father Pouplard was killed by the same Targui who had killed Father Menoret five years before – Ida ag Guemmoum, who had been nursed by the White Fathers when wounded after the murder of Dupéré.

The Pasha of Tripoli caught three of the assassins. Lavigerie asked him to spare them, and thanked 'our Lord all the more for doing us the honour of giving our Society some more martyrs'. The White Fathers did not manage to reach Timbuctoo until 1895, three years after Lavigerie had died.

One cannot help but be amazed at the strength and certitude of these men's faith. Lavigerie and de Foucauld must have recognised the impossibility of converting Moslems to Christianity. Lavigerie in particular, who succeeded so readily in the rest of Africa – his White Fathers baptising black Christians by their thousands – should surely have understood the quality of another faith. As EF Gautier put it, 'There has perhaps never been a Moslem who allowed himself to become a Christian in good faith'.

While admiring these devout men one cannot resist liking Father Dupuis, who was so pious as a young recruit to the White Fathers that he did not dare move from his kneeling position when Cardinal Lavigerie was preaching, even though the Cardinal, to emphasise his points, absent mindedly thumped Dupuis continually on the head with his bible.

Dupuis was one of the first White Fathers to settle in Timbuctoo. Martyrdom was not for Dupuis. He was still alive in the 1920s, known by then as Père Yakouba. He lived with a black lady called Salama and had several children. Above his door, not far from René Caillié's house, he put up a plaque, in French.

'Yes, here it is. Entry two francs. Fifty centimes
extra to see the beast in freedom on the terrace."

My companions hated Tamanrasset, but I thought it had a certain vitality. The colour of the houses is a pinkish red and the mud walls are scratched with wavy grooves, like drag painting. The market is pretty and full of activity. The Twareg look majestic in their blue robes and their crisp, white *cheche* wound round and round their heads, sometimes twenty feet of material. The avenues of trees are a real source of nostalgia.

What my companions really disliked was the immense number of tourists. Tamanrasset is on one of the two main routes for crossing the Sahara from north to south or vice versa. There are lorries laden with Australians, quantities of Volkswagen 'campers', Land Rovers and Land Cruisers, quite a number of

Anthony cools off

109

ordinary cars, the occasional bicycle and some pedestrians with back packs. We had become quite snobbish about tourists, most of whose ambition seemed to be to get blindly from one place to another.

Where there are tourists, there are busy officials – often on the look-out for a chance to be bribed. The French have left all their ex-colonies with a passion for 'papers'. At each main, or even minor, town or post in the southern Sahara one has, on arrival, to present one's papers to the police and the car's papers to the customs and all one's papers to any buffoon in a uniform at any time he feels like seeing them. Jocelyn, of course, had usually put the papers somewhere peculiar – the food chest or the medical chest, anywhere really that no-one would normally keep papers. So we might not have them with us. 'There is no country in the world,' an official said to me as we held up all the traffic to discuss the matter, 'where it is not a serious offence not to have all your papers with you.' Foolishly, I said I knew of several. Only the prospect of his having to wheel me to the *gendarmerie* saved me from arrest. It was in Tamanrasset that Ernie was arrested for singing in the customs. He had gone to make the usual report and had been kept waiting, so sang to cheer himself up. When we realised he had been missing for a couple of hours, I went down to the customs office.

'Have you seen my friend Mr Cook?'

'*Bien sûr*, he is under arrest.'

'For what crime?'

'Singing in the customs.'

'Oh my word, that is serious. In my country we nearly always shoot people for that.'

Ernie was let out at once. Arabs like jokes. Provided one can manage to make them laugh almost any problem can be overcome.

Père de Foucauld's fort still stands, just off the main street. At some distance one can still see the crumbling remains of Moussa ag Amastane's large house, and nearby his and Dassine's tombs. There is nothing else.

We camped under a high mountain. Not far away, a beautiful spring bubbled up with mildly fizzy water. We filled all our tanks and cans with it. Almost at once the fizz went out of it and in a few days it took on a nasty taste which scraped the back of one's throat.

At the spring there was a house where there was, at weekends, a perpetual party – this for Algerian tourists. A youth with large, devoted eyes had come more than four hundred miles from In Salah for a short holiday. His father was half Targui. 'He loves to go out into the desert, like you. I would not dream of it, but then my family think me very sissy.'

OPPOSITE, A merchant in the market place at Tamanrasset
OVERLEAF, The Hoggar mountains viewed from Assekrem, where Père de Foucauld had his hermitage

Peter went home from Tamanrasset, travelling with Heinz, who at last turned up and was glad of a companion, having dismissed Gertrud. Anthony arrived with a generator. He could barely credit the heat, to which we had become reasonably accustomed. In despair he would fill his large, Australian hat with water and cram it onto his head, letting the water trickle gradually down over his huge bulk.

We passed through Tit, the site of the battle in 1902 at which the intransigence of the Twareg was finally broken. It looked a singularly awkward place in which to fight. It was hard to visualise the superior vantage point to which ben Messis (whom we last met trying to knock some sense into the Marquis de Morès) led Lieutenant Cottonest, so that he was able to defeat a force four times larger than his own.

The road dropped down from the Hoggar mountains, heading west towards the Tanezrouft – a great, lifeless stretch of flat, featureless desert, covering more than a hundred thousand square miles. Tanezrouft means 'the great thirst' and its huge expanse, with only very few, easily-missed wells, is feared even by the Iforas Twareg who cross it to sell their flocks in the east. It was first crossed by a European in 1912. He was a French officer called Maurice Cortier who, incidentally, employed a nearly blind nomad as his guide.

We stopped short of the Tanezrouft at Abalessa, which lies beside a broad, sandy wadi much of which is cultivated. Where the farmers do not work, Sodom apples grow in profusion, flowering and fruiting at the same time. The people of the oasis were cautious and uncommunicative. But when Ernie, unthinking, shook out his mattress, and a passing donkey shied and its rider fell off, the rider laughed more than he did.

Raised up on a knoll is a ruined stone fort, commanding a wide view over the surrounding country. This fort is quite unlike anything else for at least a thousand miles in any direction. It is not now very big, but one can still see eight distinct rooms, their walls four feet thick and about that high in several places. They are surrounded by a stone wall.

When this fort was discovered, in 1925, there were eleven rooms, so it may well have been larger still and quite impressive in its original form. In one of the rooms the floor has been dug out to make a tomb. This was covered over with six great slabs of stone, seven feet long and five inches thick, but only one foot wide.

The man who mounted the expedition of discovery was Count Byron de Prorok, a most unreliable romantic, who was also a prude. He maintained that a venerable old Targui storyteller revealed to him the secret of the whereabouts of the burial place of the greatest ancestress of the Twareg, Queen Tin Hinan.

OPPOSITE, The sand dunes with their fine, sculptured shapes and delicately-rippled surfaces have a mixed quality of purity and impermanence

This led him to Abalessa. I find it hard to believe. De Prorok had with him Maurice Reygasse, an extremely distinguished French archaeologist, but somehow de Prorok in his account of the expedition gives him scant credit. I feel sure Reygasse knew what he was looking for and did not rely on chance meetings with ancient bards.

Nonetheless, they did find Abalessa and they did find the tomb. In the grave was a queen, or at any rate a woman of great importance. She was white and the form of her skeleton was said to be that of a woman very like Egyptian women on pharaonic monuments – tall and thin, wide-shouldered, with a small pelvis and slender legs.

She had seven silver bracelets on her right arm and seven gold ones on her left arm. By her head was a necklace of a hundred silver beads. Lower down there was a pearl pendant. Among other objects there was a third century Roman lamp and some coins of the Emperor Constantine. (De Prorok seems to have imagined a crown set with emeralds.)

The villagers assured us that the French had looted the tomb. In fact, all that was found in it is now in the Bardo Museum in Algiers.

Who this queen was has never been established; nor have the builders of the fort been identified. The likelihood is that the two were quite separate.

We can comfortably dismiss the egregious de Prorok's fancy that Queen Tin Hinan was Antinea, the last and white Queen of Atlantis, although Paul Benoit's novel of that name was conjured out of the legend of Tin Hinan. The Twareg believe her to have been the ancestor of their nobles and that she came from Tafilalet in Morocco, an exiled princess.

The fort is another matter. Certainly no Saharan people, whether prehistoric or of our era, built in stone in this way. Many of the basalt blocks are properly fashioned by masons. It could be a Roman fort although definite evidence of the Romans venturing to settle so far south in the Sahara is negligible. Henri Lhote, the ingenious historian of the Sahara, found in Pliny a reference to an expedition made to the Fezzan in Libya by Cornelius Balbus, in 19 BC. Two places named in the triumphal roll of this expedition were Alasi and Balsa. Lhote guesses that these were Illizi and Abalessa. It is, when one thinks of it, no odder that the Romans should have reached here than that the French should have. Indeed, it may well have been slightly easier to cross the desert in their time.

The possibility then is that this was a Roman fort built at about the turn of the millenium, or soon after, to watch over the trade routes from Central Africa. Tin Hinan's date is impossible to fix, but most probably she merely occupied, and was ultimately buried in, this conveniently abandoned fort.

Abandoned again, presumably for good, it makes me wonder what people feel who live beside monuments or ruins of civilisations obviously superior to their own. Do the empty streets of Leptis Magna serve as a reproach to the ignorant Bedouin who pasture their flocks in the desert beside it? What of the peasants who live in the shadow of the pyramids of Chichen Itza or the temples of Angkor Wat?

The Twareg of Abalessa barely notice the fort, only using it for grumbling propaganda against the French. De Prorok said that they made only slight protests at his excavations. He was wary of them in case they should feel he was defiling their ancestress, and also because he had heard that Twareg hospitality often included offering any guests their wives for the night. 'At least, none of the members of our party faced any such uncomfortable experience,' wrote the priggish count.

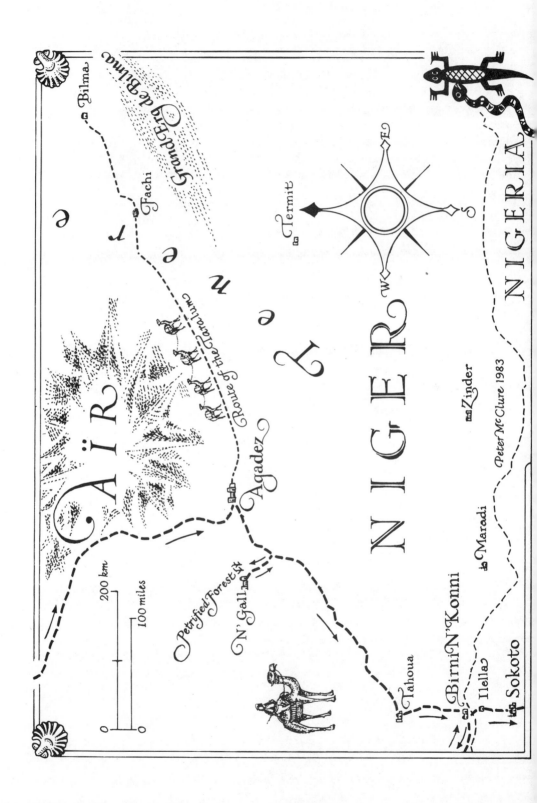

5

FORBIDDEN MOUNTAINS

THERE IS an excitement always in crossing a frontier. On the other side it will all be different. It is like starting a new game; another deal, and this time you will have all the high cards. The food will be better, the girls prettier, the drink cheaper.

It never works out quite like that, but you convince yourself that the land looks changed, that the people have a new cast of feature, that the architecture is fresh and interesting.

The excitement of arriving in Niger was muted by the fact that the frontier post was nothing but a hut or two set next to a clump of tamarisks. There was a well, but its water was so sulphurous as to be nasty even for washing. The post was also shut. We had reached it in good time, about eleven in the morning. It would re-open at three, they said. We played bridge under the tamarisks. The temperature was about 100°. Eventually the post opened at four-thirty and we just had time to push on and camp on an open gravel plain before dark.

In the desert, where the frontiers have been drawn by an arbitrary colonial pencil, it is even harder to sustain the illusion of change. The same sands, the same heat, the same wrecks by the wayside.

For some reason, it was in this stretch of desert between Tamanrasset and Arlit that we saw the pathetic end of so many hopeful journeys. Perhaps this was about the limit beyond which the average Volkswagen could no longer take the strain of grinding through the marshmallow sand, of thumping into the sudden ditches, of striking the hidden boulders. It was not just Volkswagens. Citroëns, Bedfords, Mercedes, buses, lorries, cars – they lay forsaken by their owners and then stripped by passers-by of every conceivable part which might be of any use. Just the shells remained – often with some originally jaunty, but now ironic, slogan on the side, 'Timbuctoo or bust', 'Africa here we come', 'Sahara Fizzer'.

These wrecks prompted so many forlorn thoughts. I imagined the amazement of the car worker in Clermont Ferrand or Coventry, if he could see the car that he sent off from the factory all bright and polished, lying now a skeleton so hot under the desert sun that to touch it would be to be badly burned. What, also, would this road look like in ten or twenty years? Nothing rots in the desert; the most that can happen is that driving sand polishes the metal, giving it a rusty gleam. Old guide books often say, 'bear left at the wrecked Deux-chevaux. . . .' There it still is ten years later. Each year more and more vehicles are just left sitting there. I once counted nine in a mile. Then, most of all, the wrecks are a reminder of the hazards. Here, in the season, often as many as ten cars a day may go by. But in the Tanezrouft, for example, no car may ever pass if you have wandered a little off your course. There was a day when we lost sight of all markers, all tracks, all signs of human life. We had made a simple mistake and had then become disoriented. Ernie's sense of direction, rather than the compass, brought us back to the track. You have only to miss an oasis or a well by a mile,

A game of bridge at Asamakka, Niger

following a slightly wrong bearing, and you head out virtually into infinity.

At Arlit, the first town we came to in Niger, our expectation of change was well satisfied. At once there were all the hallmarks of a free, as opposed to a socialist, economy. Above all, there was a bank. The shops were eager for custom, instead of being a scramble as in Tamanrasset, where customers fought to buy the few goods available. There were iced bottles of Coca-Cola and tonic water and even beer. There were also beggars and prostitutes. There were fewer regulations and those that there were, were enforced more openly.

It takes a little time to get used to the ways of a new country, in particular the different things which one can buy. In Algeria, for instance, the coffee was superb. We were never to get such good coffee again. Niger had better and cheaper drink than other countries. In Mali one could get jars of good mayonnaise which did not seem to exist anywhere else. Quite mysteriously, in the most remote oases of Mauritania we bought small tins of Tate and Lyle's Golden Syrup, which did not turn up even in the Sudan or Egypt where one might have expected to find a British product. The Sudan, wherever there was electricity, produced fruit juices whipped up with ice, which were delicious. In both the Sudan and Egypt there is an excellent pink drink called *karkadeh*. It is made from the flower of an hibiscus; not the common one, but one with a small, rather waxy flower. I never saw *karkadeh* anywhere else, though the plant would presumably grow in any Saharan country.

Arlit exists only because of its uranium mine. It is an unreal place, not just a camp like In Amenas or Hassi Messaoud but an imitation of a town, with even a place called a discothèque, which isn't one but has pop music blaring from it. There was nothing to keep us.

A tarmac road runs from Arlit to Agadez and, indeed, all the way to Niamey, the capital of Niger, six hundred and fifty miles beyond. Despite this road, Agadez is essentially a Saharan town, the capital of the Aïr region since it was founded in the fifteenth century, far removed in every way from the reasonably easy life on the banks of the Niger. The dust and the sand swirl about the uneven streets, which are lined with ochre-coloured mud houses. The Hotel de l'Aïr is the old Sultan's palace, supported inside by lofty, fat, round pillars almost reminiscent of Durham cathedral. The minaret of the mosque is a tall, tapering square tower, about ninety feet high. It is made of mud and the hundreds of poles which form its framework stick out two or three feet from its walls, giving it an engaging hedgehog appearance.

Somehow Agadez has preserved a very definite character despite the decline of the Twareg, the mining in the Aïr and the influx of tourists. But Agadez was probably always used to foreigners (but not Europeans) until well into the last century, when the slave trade was abolished. Many of the desert towns on the old slave route had Turkish, Arab and Egyptian agents living in them. They were there to keep an eye on the columns of slaves coming through, as they had come for many centuries. Agadez, also, is the first stopping place on the salt route from Bilma to Nigeria. Today it is the prefectural town for a large area.

Compared with Tamanrasset, which after all was really invented by the French, Agadez is delightful. The markets are not purely geared for tourists. The Twareg come from their gentler oases to sell, and from their mountain villages to buy. The Kanouri, once a warrior tribe, now mostly fishermen from the shores of Lake Chad, come across the Ténéré, because there is nowhere that they could find what Agadez can offer. The Hausas, with whom they now mix, call them Beriberi. The Fulani come to sell their long-horned cattle. The atmosphere is thoroughly cosmopolitan.

There was a persistent tout who took us to a silversmith. The others bought quantities of Agadez crosses and trinkets, which later turned out to have not a grain of silver in them. I sat in the street. At the end of it, the town ended. Beyond was only the desert and the sinking sun. A herd of goats, quite unattended, came trotting down the street. Then singly or in twos or threes, the goats would break away from the herd and, without hesitating, run swiftly into the houses on either side of the street. They were like suburban commuters coming home from the station, not needing to look to see which house to go into.

At the edge of the town there is a stadium. Part of the nationwide wrestling contest was in progress. The wrestlers were huge men with tassles stitched onto their shorts, giving them a faint look of Sumo wrestlers. The contests were far more fun than their Japanese equivalent. The immensely colourful crowd was bursting with enjoyment at each bout, their shrieks sounding across the town. The wrestlers were wonderfully sporting, prowling round each other like panthers, the losers laughing when they hit the ground. Tim started to photograph this happy scene. At once soldiers appeared. Only the Préfet could give permission for photography. The Préfet was sitting among the dignitaries. He, too, was enjoying himself, but he refused Tim's request.

We had with us at Agadez two people who had joined us in Tamanrasset in the hope of going with us into the Aïr mountains. Mechanical problems had delayed us. Now they had to fly back from Agadez without seeing the Aïr. So, two days before they left, we decided to make a brief excursion at least into the foothills. Just four of us went in one truck. As we left town we missed a police post and a policeman came roaring after us on a motor-bicycle. We managed to convince him that we had innocently not noticed the police post and that we were only going out for one night. We showed him the tickets for the aeroplane for the next day. He was young and uncertain, so he let us go but no doubt made a report.

We wandered through the foothills, past deserted villages and some inhabited ones. The people were shy but friendly. Three young boys agreed to be photographed and stood in a solemn row. Just at the moment of pressing the button, the eldest boy muttered urgently to the others and they all cast their eyes down to avoid the camera's theft of their spirit. The hills were beautiful. It was plain to see that the Aïr had, much more recently than the Hoggar or the Tassili, been green and full of life.

On our return, we saw our visitors off and prepared to go properly into the mountains. We had been told that the official guides were reluctant to let people talk to the mountain Twareg. Our persistent tout said he knew the right man to guide us. The man was Mohamed Tahir. He spoke good French and was plainly capable. He agreed to help us meet the Twareg, but he explained that we must be extremely discreet. In any case, we must engage him through the Tourist Office, saying that we had met him by chance.

We arranged this with the Tourist Office, who asked us to leave our passports with them overnight so that they could fill out the necessary papers. We were to collect them and Mohamed Tahir at seven in the morning.

I did not go to the Tourist Office in the morning, but waited for the others in the hotel. They came late, with strained faces. The Tourist Office had sent them to the Police. The Police said we were under arrest and were to be deported at once. They would send us under escort back to Algeria.

It was, I decided, an occasion for a show of dignity. Anthony, Jocelyn, Ernie and I put on suits and ties and went to the Police station. The temperature was 110°.

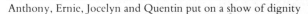

Anthony, Ernie, Jocelyn and Quentin put on a show of dignity

A tall, languid sergeant was in charge. He spoke with an indolent rudeness. I asked who had ordered our deportation. The Préfet. For what reason? The Préfet knew the reasons. Could I see the Préfet? No, if he wanted to see me, he wouldn't be deporting me. Could I see the Chief of Police? He would come.

We waited an hour and the day got warmer. I asked when the Chief would come. Are you ready to go? To go where? To Algeria, of course. I said I was not going to Algeria. I was going to Nigeria. You will enjoy Algeria. I have seen it already. Then you will see it a second time.

After another hour the Police Chief came. He told me he was a Brigadier. He wore a long *djellaba* by way of a uniform, with a small pill box hat. He looked smart, with a trim moustache and a civilised air. We shook hands. I said, pointing to a poster, that I was pleased to see that he was interested in the International Year of Disabled People, because I was a member of the British Committee. We exchanged a few more pleasantries.

Then he asked where I was going. Into the Aïr, I suggested? No, he said rather sharply. In that case, I would go on to Kano. '*Bien sûr, pourquoi pas?*' He said he would look into the problem and went away. After another hour he had not come back. The temperature was now 115°, so we took off our ties. At last the languid sergeant said we could go away to have lunch, as the Brigadier would not be back. We could find him at four in the afternoon.

At the hotel no tout spoke to us; everyone treated us with great caution. Mohamed Tahir had vanished. We were ostracised.

When we went back at four, the Brigadier was there. 'What have you decided?' he asked amiably, as if we were free to choose.

'I think we'll go to Kano,' I said.

'Of course, that will be perfectly all right. *Pas de problème,*' he said.

The languid sergeant shrugged his shoulders and prepared our papers. When we got back to the hotel all the touts were out again smiling and friendly.

We were never to know what had prompted this fierce reaction. It could have been Tim's attempts to photograph the wrestling, or our brief unauthorised excursion into the foothills, or our having told Mohamed Tahir of our wanting to talk to the Twareg.

There was at that time a serious alarm about the Twareg. Colonel Seyni Kountché is probably one of the more enlightened African leaders. He is aware of the dissatisfaction of the Twareg and, in order to appease them, he had included several Twareg in his government. One night the Twareg ministers all vanished. It was supposed that Colonel Gaddafi had bribed them away, possibly promising to support a Twareg uprising which would give them back their dignity and him possible control of the Aïr uranium.

It may have been none of these things, but merely the whim of the Préfet, who was known to be eccentric. He had, only a few weeks before, arrested an American agricultural adviser, asserting that he was a Libyan spy.

This was the first of many territories which were to be forbidden to us, but at least we were spared a two-thousand mile detour. I hardly know whether to attribute that reprieve to our suits, the International Year of the Disabled or merely the ordinary, good-natured common sense of the Brigadier.

The disappointment of not going to the Aïr, of not heading east to Fachi and Bilma and the forsaken oasis of Djado, was tempered by the thought that I could keep intact the impressions given by one of my favourite Saharan authors, Captain Angus Buchanan.

His book, *Sahara*, is a rough account of a journey that he made from Kano to Touggourt in 1922. His primary object was to collect specimens of birds for Lord Rothschild's museum and mammals for the Natural History Museum. Buchanan was not a writer in any professional sense. When in doubt, he reaches for a cliché, even using words like 'verily'. His camel is 'faithful, travel-wise, long tried'. His men, those that do not drop out 'through fear of the dangers of the journey, lack of heart for the endless hard work, physical weakness and incurable sickness' are 'loyal' and give 'of their strength to the uttermost'. He dedicates the book to 'Feri n'Gashi, only a camel, but steel-true and great of heart'.

Buchanan's world was full of such certainties. He had what he called a 'soft-hearted affection towards both man and beast ... Moreover, the whole caravan has come to embrace that free-and-easy, comprehending comradeship, that belongs to the wise when long on the great Open Road.'

The desert brings out thoughts which a fellow would never voice at home: 'I muse in my saddle over the strange gamble of it all, so similar, in plan, to the gamble of life, familiar to most of us who have intimately known the struggle for existence. But here the gamble is intensified, the material rude and raw, with vast wastes of barrenness immediate on all sides, and on the very threshold, ready to engulf and destroy the moment weakness is declared.'

Weakness, of course, is never declared. It is only in a chapter 'written' by Feri n'Gashi (a little arch perhaps, but informative) that we learn of Buchanan's being crushed in a camel stampede and his leg being seriously broken. He never refers to this again, although his wife in a description of his homecoming ('our wee girl Sheila ran to the gate ... and the faithful old Labrador, Niger, who was overjoyed at the sight of his long-lost master ...') says that this accident was nearly the end of the expedition.

I find the courage, the rectitude and the conviction absurdly appealing, because they are tempered by compassion, modesty and innocence. He is so touchingly pleased when his men, or his camel for that matter, show him affection or respect. More important now is that Buchanan was a wonderful observer and an astonishing naturalist. His breadth of knowledge is both a delight, and a reproach to one's own ignorance.

He lists one hundred and thirty different kinds of birds that he found in the

Sahara of which eleven were new sub-species. Out of forty-two mammals, ten were new species and ten new sub-species.

It is interesting to compare the number of animals and birds which he saw with those one could find today. All the time the variety of animals is declining. Heinrich Barth in 1850, in the Aïr, saw lion, giraffe, ostrich and monkeys. By 1909 Monsieur Jean, the French naturalist, reported that the ostrich and the giraffe had gone, though there were still lion and monkeys, presumably baboon. Buchanan found no lion and no tracks of lion. He believed that the last one was killed in 1918 at Baguezan. He did see baboon, warthog, porcupine, oryx, addax and arui.

I very much doubt if many of these still live in the Aïr. The probable exception is the arui, or moufflon, or wild Barbary sheep. The Aïr arui is a separate sub-species discovered by Buchanan. He said they were rare in the Aïr. but common compared with the Hoggar. Jeremy Swift managed to photograph five, running away, in the Tassili ten years ago, so they may still live in the heights of the Aïr.

This does not mean that all these animals have disappeared entirely from the Sahara. I have seen giraffe in Mali and baboon in Mauritania. There are certainly still addax in the far west.

The same decline applies to birds. Buchanan saw guinea-fowl but predicted their disappearance. They have surely gone and, I would expect, the barbets, the sunbirds, the Emerald cuckoos and the glossy starlings.

I had no chance to find out, but much more I minded not being able to follow the salt route to and from Bilma. Buchanan's description of the journey he made with the annual salt caravan is the most stirring part of his book.

The Taralum★ assembled at Tabello which was, even then, an abandoned village in the foothills of the Aïr, where I had made the little journey which may have led to our arrest. 'We had ridden in upon a camp of astounding proportions and unique picturesqueness. Before us stood *thousands of camels*, not a hundred or two which would have been amazing enough, but, literally, *thousands*; and the spectacle was one never to be forgotten.'

When the caravan set off on 25 October, Buchanan estimated that there were seven thousand camels and eleven hundred men. The train stretched at least six miles from front to back. On the first day they marched for fourteen hours, moving over rough stones and rocks of the *reg*, which reaches from the mountains to the sand sea of the Ténéré. When they reached the sand they camped.

'Like everyone else, I was tired, yet the sounds and scenes of that first camping of the Taralum were so astonishing that I almost forgot my fatigue.

'Camels being off-loaded are noisy at any time, but *tired* camels seem to believe in letting everyone within hearing know that they have a cause for complaint. The twenty to thirty of one's own line make noise enough. But

---

★ It is also called Azalai.

add to that the clamourings and complaints of *thousands*, and then try to imagine something of the astonishing uproar that resounded through the encampment ...

'The Bilma Desert is desert at its worst; an absolute sea of sand, destitute of the minutest object ...'★

For six days they kept up the same pace until they reached Fachi, which was the first place at which they could water the camels. The total distance to Bilma was three hundred miles. There the camels were loaded with cones of salt from the Bilma mines; each cone weighing thirty-five pounds and each camel carrying four or even six cones.

As soon as they were loaded, the caravan started back. The pressure was kept up. Each day they covered thirty-eight to forty miles, sometimes, in the heavy dunes between Bilma and Fachi, going for eighteen hours without a halt.

The job of guiding the Taralum belonged to one man, Efali, whose rule was absolute. 'He was famous as a traveller and as an old raider; but most famous of all as a guide in the desert.' This comparatively old, rather small man was responsible for the whole group.

The return journey laden with the salt was infinitely harder. Some camels had died on the outward journey, although the seven thousand 'were *the pick of the camels of the country*'. Buchanan was unable to estimate how many died on the way back, but on the third day before the end forty dropped out. In all, several hundred must have been lost.

'Men and animals weakened perceptibly ... nearly everyone limped ... suffering from numerous dry cracks that had opened cruelly in toes and soles of sandalled feet ...

'Even Efali, the fine old guide, had the appearance of a broken man in the end; limping, and stooping almost double, though, at the start, he had presented a trim, nimble figure remarkable for a man of his age.'

They got back to Tabello on 21 November, twenty-seven days after they set out.

The salt caravans continue today but there is no longer any need for the massed group to travel together. In 1922 the Sahara was by no means settled. It was only six years since the big Senoussi uprising. Caravans were liable to be attacked. The only way the salt bearers could be protected was by travelling to-gether, with a large escort of *Meharistes* sent from the north. At the moment it is quite safe, so the salt carriers can go in small groups. There is a steady stream throughout the autumn and winter, possibly involving almost as many camels in total as Buchanan saw together.

★ Buchanan would have been amazed to know that a few miles south of his route, at about this point, there is a positive graveyard of dinosaurs. One complete iguanontides skeleton in the Niamey museum was brought from there. Other bones lie on the dunes.

In recent years package tours to Bilma by aeroplane have been advertised. Buchanan spoke of a place a quarter of a mile south of Bilma which was the site of the original town of Bilma. The Arabs razed it to the ground two hundred and fifty years ago. '... all the inhabitants had gathered to the mosque on a festal occasion of Mohammedan worship, when they were swooped upon and trapped by their remorseless enemies; and a frightful massacre ensued, from which few escaped. The tragic remains of that awful day are still there for all to see, and I have looked with pity and awe on the ground that is thickly strewn with the sun-bleached bones of those who perished.' With less pity the *Guide Bleu* says that one may still see little boys playing football with a skull.

Except for the salt workings, Bilma does not sound very interesting. But Fachi is another matter. Buchanan found bones littered round that oasis too, because for centuries the people of Fachi were timorous and feeble. They were the victims of constant raids and attacks. Caravans stopping there, on their way from Libya to Nigeria, were regularly looted. One day there came a caravan led by a great Arab, full of wisdom and skill. He taught the people of Fachi how to build a village that could be defended against the fiercest attacks and raids.

Captain Angus Buchanan with Feri n'Gashi and guides
(Reproduced from *Sahara* by Captain Angus Buchanan, by kind permission of John Murray Limited)

The result was a village of shadows and mystery built entirely of salt, with narrow alleys, 'alleys that twist and turn in an amazing fashion, so that it is difficult to get an unobstructed view of more than a mere twenty or thirty feet of fairway.' The place was like a honeycomb, each section and each house in each section and each room in each house, easily sealed off by enormous doors made of palm planks. Any intruders would have to fight hand to hand with the defenders. 'At a moment's notice, the whole town can be barred and buttressed and placed under lock and key.'

Fifteen years before Buchanan went there, fifteen hundred men had attacked the town, of which the whole population was fewer than three hundred. They managed to destroy a few houses on the west, but the system worked and even that large a force could get no further. In the town there is a fort where Buchanan found 'a gigantic square-cut pit, with the bottom packed almost to overflowing, with giant earthen jars.' These jars, some of them eight feet high and seven feet in diameter (they even had steps up their sides) were used to store grain and dates. As there were several hundred of them and as there was a deep well in the centre of the fort, Fachi could have resisted a siege lasting many months.

So successful had the system of defence been that Buchanan suspected that the formerly timorous inhabitants had themselves become marauders. As well as the shadows hanging over the village – of attack, of hunger – there were, he thought, 'uncanny shadows in the threat of evil that lies behind barred doors and in the visages of cold-eyed men.'

Perhaps that impression is the most diverting to be left with. The poverty of Fachi must be as great, if not greater, today than it was sixty years ago. No caravans come from Libya. There can be no mystery left, no fear of raids, no hope of bounty.

After the Taralum and visits to n'Gall, Buchanan pushed on with his journey to Touggourt. He arrived there fourteen months after setting out from England.

'How altered from the start was my little band and its possessions! It had been composed of thirty-six camels and fifteen natives ... now all the camels had gone, except Feri n'Gashi ... Of the original natives only two remained: Ali, an Arab of Ghat, and Sakari, a Hausa of Kano. Lack of stamina, sickness, and failure in courage had claimed the rest at various stages of the journey. Only two had died as the result of the undertaking.'

When they reached Touggourt Buchanan planned to put Feri n'Gashi out to grass. He was entrusted to a Frenchman. Then this happened:

'Feri n'Gashi died, without the slightest sign of illness or pain, about one hour after our parting, marking one of the saddest experiences of my life and the passing of one of the noblest animals that ever lived.'

It was a very different sphere into which we now came. For so long we had

125

travelled in the central desert where, except for the oases, there was nothing but emptiness to be battled with and crossed. For centuries it had been like that, simply caravan routes across the wastes, relieved occasionally by the fortunate bubbling of water to the surface, a small settlement, an island refuge where one might rest for a night or two before pressing on to the further shore.

Now we were on the far side, nearing the various destinations of the caravan routes or the starting points of the slave routes.

In Niger's capital, Niamey, the spirit of commerce prevailed. In the hotel an Englishman was breakfasting. 'Findlay Cane-Roberts,' he said by way of introducing himself. He had that breezy, all-encompassing knowledge of commercial travellers. 'I shouldn't have the eggs, old boy. The yolks are about the same colour as the whites. Grey that is. I never have the eggs.' He was right, of course.

Cane-Roberts had been brought up in Nigeria and the Far East, but he did not speak Hausa or any African language. 'It doesn't do to speak too well, you know. They are suspicious of people who do, just as we would be if a black fellow spoke Welsh or Gaelic.' He was selling Tiger Balm, that panacea on which the Aw family in Singapore founded a large fortune.

I made some light-hearted remark about deceiving the public. 'Certainly not, old boy. I can tell you the natives are not at all gullible; they can detect a false menthol at once. They will only buy the genuine thing.'

Before being in Tiger Balm, Cane-Roberts had been in cigarettes and before that in medical supplies in South America.

I sounded him out on the politics of Niger. 'There are none, old boy. I should say commerce is the only thing. Everything around here is concerned with trade.'

Cane-Roberts was full of bizarre bits of information. 'You know, in Mali they like stale cigarettes. Anyone who's got a load of ten-year-old cigarettes they can't shift, they send them to Mali. It's just a question of knowing.

'The cigarette industry in Africa is the biggest one there is. You can't go wrong in cigarettes. A lot of them are smuggled. Take St Moritz. You see hoardings all over Nigeria advertising St Moritz. Ninety per cent of their total sales come from Nigeria. But not one packet is legally imported into the country.

'Pretty well everything is smuggled. Goods go round and round and it makes money. There is a cloth smuggler I know in Nigeria. He makes two million dollars a month, but he still lives in a mud hut. One way and another he has a family of twenty thousand people to support.'

Ernie left us at Niamey to return to England. He was nearly arrested again for taking a photograph of a sign outside the Presidential Palace, strategically placed so that the President cannot avoid seeing it every time he goes out. It reads: 'All Nigerians are under the same law'.

It was soon after this that Rose joined us, bringing with her a new spirit of energy. For a while now we were to travel in this new territory, the Sahel, which means shore in Arabic. It had started not far south of Agadez. At first the thorn trees looked more alive, then little patches of green appeared. Next a Baobab tree and larger stretches of green. At Tahouat there was a broad lawn in front of a municipal building. Its vivid grass looked almost vulgar, an affront to our yellowed eyes.

I disliked the Sahel, because it lacked the drama of the desert. It was flat and dreary. There were mosquitoes. And every camp-site became a torment because of the cram-cram (Cenchrus biflorus) burrs. These spiky seeds get into everything. They are almost impossible to get out of cloth and extremely uncomfortable in one's flesh. Many of the nomads carry tweezers so that they can get them out of their feet and hands.

The Sahel is depressing too, because here one can see how the Sahara is creeping southward and see also the appalling effect of the years of drought. Much of the region looks blasted, the trees dead and broken, as if fifty thousand elephant had trampled through the land.

The gloom is compounded by the evidence of mismanagement. In Niger there was excessive enthusiasm for the peanut in the years before the drought. Too many were planted. In 1970 the peanut represented sixty-five per cent of the country's total production. Other crops were forsaken. The peanuts took too much out of the soil and fertiliser programmes were quite inadequate. It was almost a conspiracy of folly. The peanut farmers cultivated land which had before been grazed by nomads. The nomads were driven north. At the same time, more wells were dug for the nomads so that they increased their herds. They increased them too, because, being denied the wealth which they used to gain from the caravans and with which they used to buy jewellery, their only symbol of riches was now the number of cows they owned. They increased them again, because the health of their cattle was improved by new medicines. In ten years the cattle population of Niger rose by more than one million. Huge herds were grazing less good land. Over-grazing in the north, over-using in the south reduced the Sahel to a wasteland. The long droughts completed the destruction. Coincidentally the price of peanuts dropped. The people and the cattle starved and died; and the Sahara crept forward.

In this bleak country there are two compensations. First, the birds. Now we were seeing all those that Buchanan had found in the Aïr. There were wydahs with their tails streaming behind them, like black tickertape in the wind. Hoopoes, plovers, hornbills and, above all, the superb Abyssinian roller with its unimaginably aquamarine wings, edged with dark blue and its long double tail. Once we saw a pair of huge lumbering bustards, but the ostriches eluded us.

The other pleasure was the Niger river. If one has never seen a grand African river their beauty comes as a wonderful surprise. Unlike a northern river, the

Niger lies on the land rather than cutting through it. At Niamey it lies at the edge of the city, a broad, still ribbon dotted with islands as green as lawns. When it is shallow, cattle graze on the rich pasture of the islands and sometimes farmers snatch a brief crop on the mud flats at the water's edge. The women set washing out in colourful patchwork on the flats and people wash themselves in the shallows. The men, as a rule, wash singly, sometimes covering their private parts with their hand, sometimes not. The little boys swim, but the little girls seldom do. The older girls and young women wash in groups, wearing nothing on top, but scrupulously careful to undress the rest of themselves under water.

We were to see the Niger at the extremes of the seasons. Before the rains, calm and flat as no European river is ever calm. Often, in the morning, the river is smoky with a haze blurring the shore line and, at sunset, it gleams like a metallic mirror. The *pirogues* move gently over the water, barely propelled by lazy, silhouetted figures who seem to be a part of the boat. Their reflections are as sharp as their reality. Now one could understand the hitherto strange choice of adjectives in the 'great grey-green greasy Limpopo', and wish that it were still left to say.

After the summer rains the mud flats were gone. The river was broader than ever and the cultivated islands were submerged. Now the river looked muscular and vast. Its surface was not rippled but it moved with the immense power of a huge python. Where two months before we had swum with idle strokes, we dared not put even a foot in the fierce current.

The river gives life to a strip of land never more than a mile wide. Beyond that the sun reasserts its authority and the earth is parched and lifeless.

It is hard to say precisely where the Sahara begins but as a rough guide the true desert seems to run close to latitude sixteen. When we regained this latitude the river was running astonishingly through sand dunes, often with no sign of vegetation on either bank. By that time we were in Mali.

OPPOSITE, Three boys on the banks of the Niger river

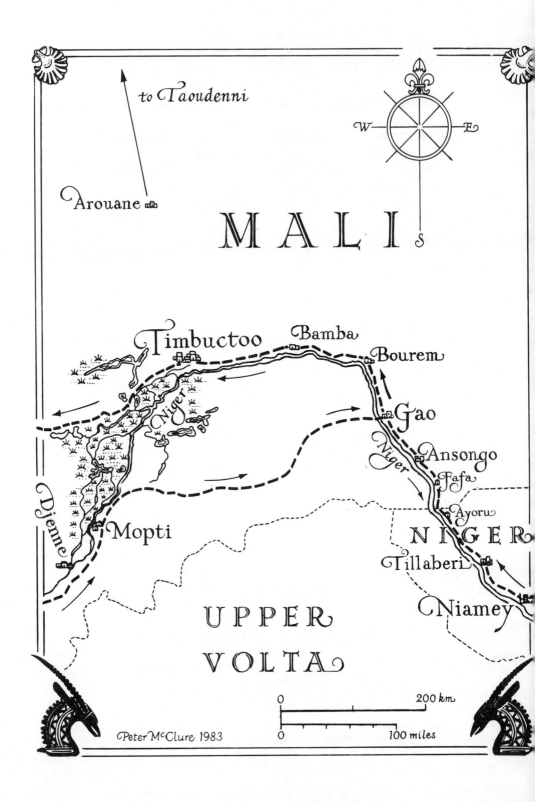

to Taoudenni

Arouane

MALI

Timbuctoo
Bamba
Bourem
Gao
Ansongo
Fafa
Ayoru
NIGER
Tillaberi
Niamey

Niger

Djenne

Mopti

UPPER
VOLTA

Peter McClure 1983

200 km

100 miles

6

THE ROAD TO TIMBUCTOO

EACH NEW country was more difficult than the last. At the Mali border the officials were slow and sloppy. Children crowded round us bleating, '*cadeau, cadeau, cadeau*'. Others brought nominally cool drinks for which they asked twice the normal price. The officials took away our passports and we waited for an hour. When at last it was done, the man brought the passports.

'Have you any medicine for me?' he asked.

'For what complaint?'

'*Maladie sexuelle*,' he whispered.

I hesitated to take the passports. He came from the Dogon country. His name was Boureima Guindo and I came to know him quite well as we passed that border post four times. I brought him some pills later, but whatever he had was obstinately resistant.

We were glad to plunge into the Niger at Fafa. The villagers told us it was dangerous to bathe there. The *capitaines* (Nile perch) were so big that they could kill a man. It was so hot that we did not care. There were indeed cheeky fish that gave one sharp nips, but the setting was pretty and the water gloriously cool. A flock of little waxbills fluttered in the bushes and rollers squawked in the palm trees. The children and young men gathered round to stare at us eating our lunch. We gave them empty bottles, which they prized highly.

Our next encounter with the officials of Mali was at Ansongo. Here the river widens out so that it looks almost like the sea and the village like a fishing port. Jocelyn raised his camera to take a photograph. An arm grabbed him, snatching away the camera. He was a little way away, so he shouted that he was to be put in jail and his camera broken, unless we paid a fine of forty pounds.

I went to the police station. It turned out that to take any photographs in Mali one must have a permit. Could we get a permit? They were issued in Gao sixty miles further on. You will pay? Or shall we keep the young man and break the camera? I suggested that this was rather drastic.

'What would you do in my position?' the policeman asked.

'I would recognise that some visitors had made an innocent mistake and that they had apologised profusely. I would explain the law to them and send them on their way with a caution.'

'What about the money?'

'Far too severe.'

'How much would you suggest?'

'Two pounds would be plenty.'

'Thirty.'

Eventually we settled for ten. The next time we came to Ansongo, he asked if we had got a permit all right.

'Oh yes, and they were so helpful and quite saw our point of view. In fact, they gave us the money back. Perhaps they will ask you for it.'

Of course they had done nothing of the sort, but it would do him no harm to wonder. At the same time I felt, as I felt so often in dealing with Saharan officials, a sense of cowardice. It was, I thought, feeble not to refuse to pay these bribes that were so frequently demanded. But the power of these corrupt officials is absolute. To fight them, you have not to care if you spend a week in jail or if your camera is broken. I lack that courage and I demean myself. It is a squalid sensation, relieved occasionally by laughter.

We were free to go to Gao and Jocelyn had his camera. Graham Greene once pointed out how quickly the most dismal place can become like home and how returning there can give one the safe feeling of a homecoming. Our first journey to Gao was a sad failure for dull reasons of mechanics. When we came again it was an unlooked-for pleasure.

Gao is, I suppose, a dismal place. The official buildings look battered and peeling. How long can it be since they were painted? One wonders how a place which is called 'underdeveloped' can also be in decay. There was once a cinema, but it has become a tumbledown market. The Hotel Atlantide is a sad relic of French colonial days. It is hideous inside, with blocks of pebble-dash on the walls of the main room and an inaccurate map painted on the plaster. Slow punkahs turn jerkily, if the electricity happens to come on. There are rooms supposedly equipped with showers, but no water comes. Instead an old man carries tubs to the rooms.

If you were to arrive in the heat of the day you might think that the town was as dead as it looks. Almost miraculously, on the stroke of four o'clock, St Exupéry's second spring arrives. The breeze is no longer the fanning from an oven door, but cooler than the air. The bead sellers return to their stalls under the arches opposite the Atlantide. Voices rise, children run, the acacias sway and motor bicycles fizz about, kicking up the sand in the streets.

The crowds, moving on silent feet, look like the patterns of a kaleidoscope with nearly all the pieces blue and green, with occasional yellow, but very rarely red. No two children are dressed alike. One will wear a tunic, another shorts. A girl will have a T-shirt on top of her skirt. A boy will wear a robe over trousers. Many have unmatching tops and bottoms of pyjamas. Only the stares are uniform.

When we arrived for the second time everyone remembered us and greeted us with elaborate, rhythmic welcomes. The traditional Arab greeting with its regular pattern of enquiry has been translated into French. *Ça va? Ça va bien? Ça va la famille? Ça va bien?* Even the dăh-dĕ-dāh, lăl-dĕ-lāl, dŭm-dĕ-doo rhythm is somehow carried over.

The young boys who wash travellers' clothes hailed us, the bead merchants welcomed us and even the head of the alarmingly named tourist organisation, SMERT, with whom we had parted on poor terms, was effusive. It is one of the greatest charms of the desert that a relationship once established is always thought worth renewing.

Gao is a town of about twenty thousand people, but at one time it had about seventy thousand inhabitants. It was the capital of the last of the three great Sahel empires – Ghana, Mali and Songhay. As early as the eighth century Gao was trading with Tahert in Algeria. The first royal dynasty of the Songhay, the Dia, was founded in the eleventh century, when the Berbers were drawn here by the gold, salt, and slave trades. Until the end of the fourteenth century, the Songhay kingdom was usually subject to the great Mali empire. By the fifteenth century the power of the Mali empire was dwindling. The Twareg seized Timbuctoo in 1433. Forty years later they lost it to Sonni Ali, the ruler of the Songhay.

Under a new dynasty, the Askiya, the Songhay empire was built up through-out the fifteenth and sixteenth centuries. It stretched over most, though not all, of the old Mali empire and reached, according to some authorities, as far as Kano. This is unlikely but certainly they made expeditions to Agadez. Leo Africanus, after a visit in 1512, said the kings of Mali paid tribute to the Songhay and were so reduced by them, 'that the king cannot even give food to his family'. In 1545, the Songhay raided the Mali capital (probably sited at Niani) and the Askiya's brother, Dawud, encouraged his soldiers to defecate in the king's palace. The degradation of Mali was complete, although it continued as a smaller kingdom for another two hundred years or so, well to the south of the Sahara.

The triumphant Songhay empire lasted an even shorter time than the Mali empire. In 1591 the Moroccans, armed with muskets, against which the Songhay could do nothing, seized Gao, Timbuctoo and Djenné.

The present town of Gao is on a new site, the Niger having changed course. The only building connected with the ancient empire is the tomb of the Askiyas, a mud structure with the usual hedgehog appearance, which dates from the sixteenth century. The original town lay to the north-east about five or six miles from the Gao of today. We went to visit the site, which we were told was of wonderful archaeological importance, with Bagna Touré, the head of SMERT in Gao.

On my first visit to Gao, I had found this man peculiarly irritating. He seemed fat and sleek in an area of great poverty. He always wanted to charge too much for anything he arranged. On our return, bolstered by the illusion of old acquaintance, he turned out to be quite the reverse of my first impression. There was no inconvenience to which he would not put himself in order to be helpful. On one occasion, without being asked, he travelled in the extreme discomfort of a communal taxi, to a place sixty miles away merely to see whether something we had lost there had turned up. He would not let us pay for anything.

Bagna Touré is a little over forty. He was brought up in Bamako the capital of modern Mali, by a German officer. How this came about he never explained. The officer, who is incidentally aged one hundred and seven, took him to Germany. He fell in love with a German girl and she with him. Her father forbade the marriage.

He is now married to a Malian and has three daughters and a son. Bagna also speaks darkly of an Italian woman, who comes to Gao for her holidays and who, he implies, is his mistress.

The archaeological site may be of great importance but it is hardly thrilling for the layman. The steles of Spanish marble which were said to have adorned the necropolis of Sané have gone to Bamako. On the other hand, the place is beautiful in the evening light. Standing in an open space which Bagna said was the site of a great mosque, one could look across to the glowing dune which marks the old course of the Niger. Young boys were herding the goats home at the end of the day. Elegant Twareg were riding their camels back to their camp after a day in Gao. It was the right setting to listen to Bagna's stories.

He pointed to a long stone with some writing on it. 'It was here that many Songhay killed themselves when they knew that they were defeated by the Moroccans. They entombed themselves, after engraving on a stone what they had seen in their lives, six of them together. From inside with a rope they let down the last stone – and they died.'

We stood for a while pondering this self-immuring pact. Then Bagna was off once again, explaining that he was of course of Moroccan descent, with the name of Touré. In consequence, the Moroccan state had a duty to look after him if need be, although there was the additional danger that he could be conscripted. The modern boundaries of invented nations, it struck me, mean nothing much even to servants of the state.

'You know,' said Bagna, 'the Emperor had magic powers which prevented the Moroccans from defeating the Songhay. For a long time the Moroccans could do nothing. Because they were a good people, the Songhay could not let the Moroccans die of thirst. So they made a truce with them, which allowed the Moroccans to pass along a passage to the Niger.

'Each day a beautiful Moroccan prince went down to the river. The Emperor's daughter saw him and she fell in love. The prince fell in love with her. They were not allowed to meet, so the princess sent her slave-girl as an intermediary. The prince and the slave-girl could not speak each other's language. They talked in sign language.'

Bagna, warming to his theme, made a series of dramatic and graphic hand-clasps.

'The princess revealed to the prince the secret of the Emperor's magic powers. The Moroccans attacked and defeated the Songhay.'

Needless to say the prince and princess got married. It was rather an odd marriage, because the beautiful prince was, as Bagna delicately expressed it, 'an incomplete man'. Luckily he had an adjutant of similar build and feature. Each night the prince would slip out of the marriage bed on some pretext and the

The Niger river at Gao

adjutant would take his place. This agreeable arrangement resulted in several children.

The story at this point, became rather confused. The marriage of the prince and princess did not settle the war. 'The daughters of their daughters married Songhay royalty, so after eighty years the war ended.'

It was hard to know quite how much of this stuff Bagna believed. A few days later I gave a friend of his, also called Touré, a lift to Bourem. Twenty-five miles from Gao, he said, 'This is where the Moroccans defeated the Songhay. The Songhay waited here with their bows and arrows to ambush the Moroccans. They did not know that they had guns. The Moroccans killed them all,' he said, ending with shrieks of laughter.

History is virtually meaningless to people of the desert, whether they are Arab, Berber or of black, slave descent. That is to say the very precise and accurate history which Europeans endeavour to achieve does not concern them. Story-telling, myth and legend, on the other hand, play a large part in the lives of people. It is not factual truth they seek, but rather the spirit or atmosphere of a time or a place.

We never went to Niani, the presumed capital of the Mali empire, but we did sleep in the remains of the supposed Ghana capital at Koumbi Saleh. The modern state of Ghana has no true connection with the ancient Sahelian empire. Some of the gold in which the early Ghanaians traded came from near the Akan forest on the border of the new Ghana and the Ivory Coast. The kola nut which was an important commodity of the Mali and Songhay empires came from the Akan forest itself. Those are the only links.

Koumbi Saleh lies within the borders of what is now Mauritania. The country is uninspiring, with huge permanent dunes covered with a fair amount of vegetation, and dotted with occasional villages of distressing poverty.

The clearest account we have of the appearance of the city of Ghana was written in 1067 by al-Bakri, who lived in Cordoba and actually never left Spain. He gathered information from travellers and other writers. He described a double city. One half was lived in by Moslems and boasted a dozen mosques, many wells with sweet water and vegetable gardens. The other half, six miles away, was the royal town; but the whole area between the two was built up.

Modern excavation and aerial photography at Koumbi Saleh reveal a town of about fifteen to twenty thousand people. The area discovered is plainly the Moslem half of the town; the royal section has not been positively identified.

For the layman, the place amounts to little more than large mounds of grey schist. An area known as the Great Avenue has been partly exposed by excavation. At the western end is a mosque, which experts say probably measured one

OPPOSITE, Fulani girl

hundred and fifty feet by seventy-five feet. I counted the bases of thirty-two pillars. The mosque and all the houses were built of small pieces of schist. The houses have small rooms, but in some cases, two storeys.

It was hard, even camping in the moonlight at the unexcavated end of the Great Avenue, to conjure up any picture of a town or to imagine any vigorous life in this grey place that reminded me more of a deserted quarry than anything else. Yet the kings and emperors of the ancient states did live in a certain style.

Ghana was first mentioned by al-Fazari writing in Baghdad at the end of the eighth century. The trade in gold had spread its fame that far. Although Ghana was briefly subjugated by the Almoravids, from the north, in 1076, it was free again by the beginning of the twelfth century. The conquest had the effect of converting the rulers to Islam. The fortunes of those empires went up and down. By the thirteenth century the town of Walata had become the most important town for the gold, salt and slave trades. At this time the kingdom of Soso was possibly the most powerful in the region, but the most interesting of the empires was on the verge of appearing.

The ruler of the Malinke had two sons, each by a different wife. Sundjata, the elder, was born a cripple. Dankaran-Tuma, the younger, was strong and handsome. When the king died, Dankaran-Tuma succeeded. By a bit of magic and the help of the chief blacksmith (leg irons of some sort, one wonders) Sundjata was suddenly able to walk. His step-mother tried to murder him. As the legends present it, Sundjata went into self-imposed exile in order to save the kingdom from strife. He took positions of valour and honour in neighbouring courts, rather as a knight in Europe might have done at the same period.

Then Dankaran-Tuma, repressed by the tyranny of Sumanguru the king of Soso, to whom the Malinke were subject, rose in rebellion. Sumanguru crushed him, ravaged his land and sacked his villages. Sundjata raised an army and, after a number of successful skirmishes, faced Sumanguru on the Niger at Kirina. Sundjata, as we might expect, defeated Sumanguru, but the battle was not without the help of a little magic. The trouble was that both leaders were magicians, so it was not an easy matter. By subterfuge, Sundjata acquired some of Sumanguru's wine, which he mixed into a poison. Quite why it had to be Sumanguru's wine is not clear as the Soso king was not to drink the poison. It was driven into him, not on the tip of an arrow because all kings were, as you might say, vaccinated against wounds of iron. The poison was put, sensibly, on the claw of a white cock. That was the end of Sumanguru. The Mali empire was born and was to last in one form or another until the sixteenth or seventeenth century.

The emperors of Mali brought kingship to its highest level. In the tenth century, al-Muhallabi had recorded that the people of Sahel worshipped their kings and that anyone who met the camels bringing the king's food to the palace was promptly executed. Everything to do with royal eating was taken seriously.

In eleventh-century Gao a drum was beaten when the king sat down to eat and no-one was allowed to move around until he had finished.

The kings of Ghana, according to al-Bakri, when dead were lain on a bed and put into a domed wooden structure. With them were put their arms and ornaments, and plenty of food and drink. For good measure, their servants were shut in with the body and the dome was covered with mats and then piled up with earth until it resembled a huge mound.

Court etiquette was strict. Anyone approaching the king, in Ghana or Mali, had to take off his outer robe, wrap himself in it, kneel, beat his breast and scatter dust or ashes on himself. There is a comical account of a Mali ambassador going to see the Moroccan Sultan. At every friendly remark of the Sultan's, the ambassador sprinkled dust on his head.

It was unthinkable to sneeze in the king's presence and, if the king sneezed,

Gao, soon after four o'clock when the town awakes from its afternoon slumber

everyone beat his breast in sympathy. The penalty for wearing sandals in the king's presence was death.

The laws of dress were strict. In Ghana, only the king was allowed to wear sewn clothes. Everyone else simply wrapped himself in lengths of cloth. Later, in Mali, the emperor wore European cloth as being the height of good tone. Moreover in Mali the equivalent of our honours system was related to trousers. Permission from the king to wear slightly wider trousers would be the same as the OBE. Considerably wider trousers might equate with a knighthood. Inordinately wide trousers would match a dukedom – but it goes without saying that the emperor wore the widest trousers of all.

Quite soon after the establishment of Islam in the west, royal pilgrims set out for Mecca. Two are known to have gone early in the eleventh century. A hundred years later chiefs from Ghana made the pilgrimage. The greatest of the pilgrims was Mansa Musa, emperor of Mali, who made the journey in 1324.

Mansa Musa, the most powerful of the Mali emperors, reigned for about twenty-five years. He was extremely devout and there is a suggestion that he undertook the pilgrimage partly in an agony of repentance over having accidentally killed his mother. In any event, he made the journey in the grandest style. His retinue of slaves, soldiers and officials numbered thousands; the lowest estimate being eight thousand, the highest sixty thousand. His wife, Inari Kunate, came too. She brought five hundred maids and slaves.

Having had to wait for a propitious day – a Saturday which fell on the twelfth day of the month – he travelled through the central desert, via Walata, Taghaza and Tuat in what must have been unbearable heat, for he arrived to camp beside the pyramids in July. By way of an introductory present to the Sultan of Egypt, Mansa Musa sent ahead fifty thousand gold dinars (about 500 lbs of gold). Nonetheless he, who was accustomed to people covering themselves in dust before him, was made to kiss the ground in front of the Mameluke ruler. He spent three weeks in Cairo and distributed golden largesse on such a scale that the value of gold dropped according to some accounts by as much as a quarter. (He was never seen eating.)

The result of this pilgrimage was the spreading of the fame of Mali and an enormous increase in the trans-Saharan trade. Stories of the gold trade had been circulating for many centuries. Herodotus had described the 'silent trade', the odd system by which traders from the north set their goods on a river bank and withdrew. Then the gold producers would come out of hiding, and put what they thought was an appropriate amount of gold beside the goods and retire again. The traders then would come forward to look. If they thought there was enough gold, they took it. If not they went back and waited for the gold sellers to add a bit more. This went on until the price was agreed, neither side ever speaking to or, in the case of the traders, seeing the other side.

Mansa Musa's pilgrimages increased the wonderful stories of gold and, until the new world was discovered, West Africa was a main source of gold for the civilised world. From this came all the myths and legends which, long after the mines were exhausted, were to draw European explorers to the supposedly mysterious and rich city of Timbuctoo.

European travellers, explorers and soldiers of the last century and the early part of this one were snobs, possibly romantic snobs, but still snobs. It was never the industrious, sedentary farmer that they admired among the people whose countries they visited or occupied. It was the warriors they loved. In South Africa they thought highly of the Zulu. In Kenya they found the Maasai heroic, despising most of the other tribes for having middle-class virtues. The Sahara provided perhaps the most attractive tribe of all.

The Twareg were warriors. They had a class system which was positively feudal. They were elegant and enigmatic. Their women were beautiful. One of their mottoes was, 'Shame enters the family that tills the soil'. With their poetry and their music, they were the perfect *noble* savages. That they were crooks and thugs did not seem to matter. Perhaps the Europeans attributed to them the same sort of glamour that, in fiction, they accorded to highwaymen.

In origin, the Twareg are Berber. Quite where they come from is unknown, but their own tradition suggests that they came from the Middle East. They are warlike, as are all Berber people apart from the Mozabites, but they made war, or rather fighting, into a way of life. For centuries they controlled the central desert and, therefore, the caravan routes of all trade between North Africa and West and Central Africa. On the face of it, their arrangements were perfectly simple. They either raided caravans passing through the desert, or they exacted protection money in return for escorting caravans to their destination.

The pattern of their lives was really more complicated than that. It was the white nobles or *Imochar** who did the fighting, the raiding and the extorting of protection money. Beneath them came the *Imrad* or vassals, also white. Each *Imrad* family was attached to a noble. The nobles used them almost as servants, although they were free men. They tended the herds, sought out pastures and supervised the logistics of nomadic life. If their noble wanted them, they were obliged to accompany him on raids or *razzia*. Then, of course, there were the slaves, *Iklan*, mostly black.

Running parallel, as it were, were two other classes in terms of the community rather than the ethnic tribe. First, the *haratin* or serfs, who tilled the oases in the areas controlled by the Twareg. They were dark skinned people from the Sahel or further south, nominally free, but wholly dependent on the nobles who, in

---

* *Imohagh* is the name by which they would prefer to be known. The word has an implication of freedom or independence. Twareg is a Chamba word with an Arabic root, meaning either 'abandoned' (by God) or 'people of the sand'.

return for their surplus produce, protected them from other raiders and marauders. Secondly, the *Inaden*, who were craftsmen – blacksmiths, silversmiths, woodworkers, saddle makers. They were mostly dark, though it has been suggested that their origin was Jewish.

These classifications varied slightly in the different regions. The Kel-Ahaggar were very xenophobic and kept rigidly to themselves. The Twareg in the south, particularly in Niger and Mali, mingled with the Hausa, the Fulani and the Songhay. Among them one found *Bella*, freed slaves, *Iraouellan*, descendants of captives from other Twareg groups, and *Ineslemen*, the holy men.

The customs of the Twareg were certainly intriguing. In the first place the traditional Moslem roles of men and women were, to a certain extent, reversed. While the Twareg were not matriarchal, inasmuch as the ruler or chief was a man, it was from its mother that a child took its status. If the mother were noble, the child was noble, no matter who the father was.* The maternal uncle was in some groups the most important figure in a boy's life. (Among the Iforas Twareg these rules did not apply.) The men went veiled while the women exposed their faces quite freely. It is because of this veil that the Twareg came to be called the 'blue men' (a term also used of Mauritanian nomads, who use the same dye). Usually the veil and enormously long head-dress was dark, dyed with indigo. The colour came out on those narrow parts of the face which they showed to the world. No-one has come up with a satisfactory explanation of the veil. The obvious one, that it was to keep out the sand, cannot be right. Otherwise the women would have worn them too. Furthermore they would have taken them off on occasions, whereas the men's determination never to uncover their mouths was almost obsessional. Even when eating or drinking, they somehow get the food or the glass to their mouths under the veil.

The freedom of women extended much further than simply not wearing a veil. At the *ahal* or court of love, at which boys serenaded girls and girls recited poetry to the boys, it was the girl who chose the boy she wanted. And, at the end of the evening, she took him away among the rocks to make love. It is hard to establish whether this really was so, or whether it was what the French wanted to believe about them.

All of this might well have been appealing to romantic natures, but the bloodshed and the treachery might equally have been expected to cancel the charms. Buchanan met one ancient raider whose biggest raid, with a band of one hundred, provided a haul of three hundred camels and seventy women and children. The men were presumably all killed. Most raids were smaller, involving about twenty men. Each man could manage three or four stolen camels.

The list of Europeans, mostly explorers, murdered by the Twareg is formid-

---

* Of course this is often the case with warrior tribes, as the father is liable to be killed. Among the people of Coorgh, which produces India's greatest generals, the same rules apply.

TOP, A girl on market day in Ayoru, Niger

ABOVE, The Niger river, still and slow in the dry season

A Targui nomad: the men traditionally never uncover their mouths, even managing to eat and drink under swathes of cotton

LEFT, A well near Agadez: the Fulani water their cattle in a vicious sandstorm

able. It starts in 1790 with an Englishman, Major Houghton, who died some-where near Timbuctoo. Then came Major Laing, the first European for many centuries to reach Timbuctoo, then John Davidson, the doctor son of a smart London tailor, butchered in 1834, three Frenchmen in 1873, the six White Fathers we have already met, and the ninety men of Colonel Flatters' expedition in 1885, which set out to seek a route for the fatuous notion of a trans-Saharan railway. There were plenty more.

In nearly every case the Twareg had undertaken to guide their victims and then turned on them when they were beyond reach of all help. Their behaviour was, in part, explicable by a perfectly reasonable desire to keep strangers out of their territory, particularly strangers who planned to occupy their land and interfere with their normal pursuits.

No tincture of any such honorable motive coloured the shabbiest of their murders. Alexandrine Tinne was an exceptional young woman with an unusual history. She was born in 1839 of an English merchant father and an aristocratic Dutch mother. Until she was seventeen, she lived in the Hague. She planned to marry a young English diplomatist, but at the last moment he revealed that he was already married.

Taking her mother and aunt (her father had died), she set off on a series of travels in order to get over her love affair. When finally she came to Egypt, she decided that Africa was where she wanted to live. A first expedition up the Nile to Nubia and the Sudan, with three large boats, was such a success that Alex-andrine planned a second one. With two German scientists, an Italian secretary and two Italian maids and, of course, the two Baronesses, she set off on a serious expedition to a virtually unexplored area, five hundred miles south of Khar-toum. The year was 1862, the same year that Speke and Grant were coming down the White Nile after discovering its source. The ladies also met Sir Stanley Baker at Gondokoro in 1863. Then disaster struck. Mother, aunt, the three Italians and one German scientist all died of fever.

This did not alter Alexandrine's resolve to stay in Africa. She had plans to build herself a house on an island in the Nile, but she was not popular with the authorities, largely because of her strident denunciations of the slave trade. Most of her servants were slaves she had liberated.

Alexandrine left Egypt and cruised up and down the North African coast in her steam yacht. At some point she became aware of the slave caravans which came from Bornu by Lake Chad, north through Bilma and up to Tripoli via Murzuk.* In 1868 Alexandrine decided to see for herself. As usual, she mounted a vast expedition amounting to fifty people and seventy camels.

---

* According to James Wellard, 'the last known (i.e. admitted) consignment of slaves to arrive in Murzuk was in 1929 after a two month march across the desert.'

OPPOSITE, The market place at Ayoru

She arrived quite safely at Murzuk which lies eight hundred miles south of Tripoli. There she met Dr Gustav Nachtigal, the first European to have visited the Tibesti mountains. It is probable that he deflected her from her original plan which was to go south, with Nachtigal to Bornu, and then head east hoping to reach Darfur and eventually the Nile at Khartoum. It had never been done. In any event, Alexandrine fell ill and stayed in Murzuk until the middle of 1869.

Then she set off, with a much reduced party, to head for Ghat with the idea of pressing on to Timbuctoo. Her guides and armed escort were Twareg from the Hoggar. The country through which they were to travel was controlled by rival Twareg. Alexandrine had made some arrangements with the rivals. It may be that the Hoggar Twareg thought that their rivals would attack and try to steal Alexandrine's luggage, which was reputed to consist largely of gold, and decided to anticipate them. Or it may be that they never had any intention of going anywhere. Either way, Alexandrine never reached Ghat.

When she was trying to settle a row among the cameleers, the Twareg escort attacked. Alexandrine raised her arm in a gesture of command. A Targui warrior severed it from her body and then hacked her neck. The Twareg left the beautiful twenty-nine-year old Alexandrine dead on the sand, surrounded by her murdered companions.

Apart from such acts of sheer barbarity, it could well be argued that the Twareg were right. The foreigners did threaten their livelihood and their whole way of life.

Today the Twareg are a sad people. Their social structure has had to be drastically adapted as a result of the supression of the slave trade, the disappearance of the great caravans and the policing of the desert. The only caravans which continue now are the salt caravans, from Bilma to Agadez and from Taoudenni to Timbuctoo. But even while the caravans still struggled across the desert, the French prevented raids and robbery.

Without loot there was nothing but tradition to bind the vassals to the nobles. When protection became unnecessary there was nothing to offer to the serfs. With the abolition of slavery there was nothing left at all. Everything militates against them. Their territories are far from the capitals of the modern states of the Sahara. They are, in every country, a minority. They have had less education than the people of sedentary tribes. Plans to settle them on the land, where there is any, conflict with their motto about tilling the soil. As if all this were not enough, nomads are, as we have seen, thought to be inferior. There is, I suspect, a measure of envy in the householder for the freedom of the nomad, but this merely serves to confirm his prejudice. Little is done for the Twareg in any of these countries and they are a disaffected group.

I had heard that there was a Twareg museum in Gao. 'It is somewhere in the *septième*,' people said airily, as if we were in Paris. The *septième* turned out to be a drab, dusty quarter. In a browny-grey street, with a large ditch running down one side, we found the grandly-named *Musée du Sahel*. It was in an ordinary looking house. There was no sign outside. In the courtyard there was a well and a tentative sort of tree. An old, blind woman lay on a bed in a loggia. For a while no-one paid much attention to us. It turned out that the key to the museum was missing. Eventually a laughing Targui found the key, but one of the double doors was stuck and my chair would not go through. No-one could do anything. In the end the door was found to be locked with a hidden bolt. Everyone laughed. Père de Foucauld said the Twareg like a lot of laughter. We went into a fairly small room. The Targui asked us to wait for the curator.

It was plain that the museum was not yet working. A thin layer of sand covered the floor of the room. All around there lay a jumble of objects. There were saddles, pots, some bed-posts. One very elaborately carved and decorated object, looking a bit like a short totem pole with a leather-fringed, cup-shaped top, was impossible to identify. The Targui told us it was for holding a milk bowl. After a short while, I realised that the total possessions of a family of Twareg would not fill half a small room.

We waited. The collection of objects looked more and more forlorn. A child of great beauty came and stared at us. Her skin was a wonderful, light-cocoa colour, her eyes black, but with whites gleaming in the darkened doorway. She wore a long robe and a brown headscarf. When we spoke to her she did not answer, but went away and drew water from the well, lifting the heavy bucket with surprising ease for a child of her size.

At last the curator, Eghless ag Foni, arrived. He was dressed in European clothes. His face was distinguished, yet curiously soft and feminine but with no hint of epicenity. We went through a long, formal greeting. He ordered tea, for the sake of hospitality, but it was plainly the wrong time to have called. I suggested that we come back later and he looked much relieved. We drank our tea quickly and left.

We came back in the early evening. The old, blind woman was asleep on the bed in the courtyard. Eghless took us around the rag-bag of exhibits. The ones in the room where we had waited he referred to as Collection A; in the next room was Collection B. The objects were identical.

The museum is sponsored by the Germans. The idea of two collections is that one should be in the museum and the other should be a travelling exhibition. So far nothing whatever has happened. There have been several dates appointed for the opening of the museum. Each date has come and gone. A new one was proposed now. When I went back to Gao some months after the next appointed date, it was still not open.

There was a further room which was more revealing than the first two. For here the quality of everything was inferior. The tents were no longer of hide but of indifferent cloth. The bowls and pots were cheap and nasty. Virtually nothing was decorated. These, Eghless explained, were the possessions of a

Twareg family since the great drought. More than half the herds died in the drought years. There were too few now to make tents from their skins.

A Twareg family can just about subsist if they own a herd of twenty goats. Nowadays twice that number, plus two camels, would be considered prosperity. 'But it is altogether impossible for the Twareg to follow the traditional nomadic patterns since the drought.'

Many of them go to Libya to work, for there they can earn money and buy camels. But they have to smuggle the camels and their earnings back to Mali, otherwise the Libyans or the Algerians would make them forfeit it all. Eghless' eyes brightened a little at the thought of the adventure this entailed, but he is a man of great responsibility, one of the few who can talk to the government and try to persuade them to do something for his people.

Eghless first went to a school for nomads in the Adrar n Iforas. He did so well that he moved rapidly from school to school, finishing his education in Bamako. Nevertheless he still thinks of himself as a nomad. As often as possible he escapes back to the desert and his family.

He invited us to go to visit his family. It was categorically forbidden. Kidal, the centre of the Iforas Twareg is in a military area, and when we applied to go there even Bagna Touré, who once opened the bank for me when it had been shut for the day, could do nothing to alter the official decision.

It was an infinite pity. The Twareg,

OPPOSITE, Twareg nomads

whom we had seen and met, were all, as it were, pasteurised. They might look beautiful in their blue and white robes. They might strut like peacocks, flashing their mirrored dark glasses. But they had no role, unless it be that of a tourist attraction. In Algeria they were not even allowed to carry their traditional swords. In Niamey they were reduced to being souvenir sellers. Eghless, however, made me wonder whether they may still survive in the forbidden zone.

When I asked Eghless about the old class structure, he maintained that in the Adrar it still obtained. The vassals still have a respect for the aristocracy, even though they now have nothing to offer. In fact, he asserted, the aristocrats have something to offer.

'We still have *razzias* and wars between the people of the east Adrar and the people of the west Adrar. The warriors still provide protection.'

Perhaps part of the reason we were not allowed to go to the Iforas is that the Twareg are even now not wholly defeated.

After many days or weeks in the desert, seeing no-one, towns come as an intense shock. One has been fussing about conserving water, the torch batteries are all flat, there has been no fresh food for a long time, washing has been forbidden for lack of water. Life has been reduced to its essentials.

Then there is a town; and the abundance of everything is almost bemusing. The most uninteresting town makes one feel as if one were back in the centre of things. It takes a day or two before one remembers that the nearest real city is more than a thousand miles away.

Timbuctoo produced a rather different effect on me. Certainly I felt the boost that the first days of water, vegetables, light and above all ice give to the spirits. But the name Timbuctoo does something else. Each morning, when I woke up and looked across from our camp in the dunes to the three minarets and the roof lines of Timbuctoo, I could not but be amazed that this was where I was. However commonplace a visit to Timbuctoo has become, the magic of the word still stirs the imagination.

Nearly everyone who goes to Timbuctoo is disappointed. René Caillié who went there in 1828, the first European for many centuries to see the town and return alive, was sadly disillusioned. 'This capital of the Soudan, which had for so long been the goal of all my ambitions,' turned out, 'more like a jumble of badly built houses ... ruled over by a heavy silence.'

Today there are even rather erratic package tours. In the run-down hotel, where the wires of the air-conditioning units hang hopelessly out of the bottom of the machines, there are stunned tourists reeking of disappointment. They are stuck because the aeroplane has not come. It quite often does not come. Mrs Viane, a lady from Sacramento with a good figure and an unusual breadth of interest, tells me about her husband in aviation engineering, her two sons and her grand-daughter, and her two German Shepherds, Nemo, eleven and Brutus, two. The dogs guard the three-hundred-yard drive to their adobe house with its strong redwood posts. Mrs Viane thought one day in Timbuctoo was enough. The aeroplane did not come for four days.

The reward for package tourists is being able to say they have been there, but I rather liked Timbuctoo. I found it easier here to visualise a glorious past than I had in Gao. Ibn al-Mukhtar, writing a hundred years later, described the town in the sixteenth century: 'Then, Timbuctoo had no equal among the towns of the black people . . . for the solidity of its institutions, for political freedom, purity of custom, safety of people and property, clemency to the poor and to strangers, consideration for students and scientists and help given to the latter.'

The population, at the height of its importance under the Askiyas, is estimated at as many as one hundred thousand. Now, it is about seven thousand, but the town, unlike Gao, is on the same site. The three ancient mosques still stand – the Djinguereber mosque, built by Mansa Musa on his return from Mecca, the Sankoré mosque, built by a rich woman at about the same time, and the Sidi Yahia mosque, built about a hundred years later. While modern Gao is laid out on a grid pattern, Timbuctoo has narrow, crooked streets. Some of the houses have a form of external decoration, usually pilasters, which I found encouraging after months with a total absence of decoration. Timbuctoo has that agreeable quality of surprise around each corner, whether it be an elaborate doorway, a communal baking oven, or just a little open space.

Down one of these alleyways, amid a number of derelict houses, is the house built of mud bricks where René Caillié stayed in April and May 1828. We went in. After going through two bare rooms with uneven earth floors, we came to a small courtyard, cloistered on three sides. In the middle of the courtyard there was just rough ground, piled with blown sand. On the sand lay an old bottle, some odd bits of cardboard and a broken doll.

By one of the arches of the cloister, a young girl in a green and yellow dress was sitting in a chair, feeding a tiny baby with a bottle. She told us that the house had been rebuilt ten years ago. Before that it had been a two-storeyed house, but the ground floor was rebuilt to the original plan. I wondered how it could have become so decayed in so short a time. I asked how long such a house could last. 'A long time . . . if it doesn't fall down.' Behind the girl was a door to what I took to be the children's room. Carefully written on a piece of paper pinned over the door were the words, 'Palais d'Etienne'. It was the only decoration in the place.

The girl said, 'It was my grandfather who received Monsieur Caillié. They could both talk Arabic. Of course, my grandfather died a long time ago.' In Africa, the word grandfather is likely to embrace all ancestors. The girl told us that visitors came almost every day to see the house. But her family made no charge for letting people see it. Didn't she find it tiresome? 'No, It is our duty.'

The story of René Caillié is one of astounding determination and courage. He was born, the son of a baker, near La Rochelle. He was small and rather frail, but he had a wild ambition to travel. He had no real education and absolutely no money. At the age of sixteen he managed to get to Africa, where he got 'fever'. He came back to France, but he was never deflected from his ambition to reach Timbuctoo. Some ten years later he got to Senegal. After three attempts to reach the Niger he achieved his first objective by travelling with a party of Malinke who were going to Djenné.

For the Malinke, he invented a story that he was an Egyptian boy, captured by Napoleon and taken to France as a slave. When Napoleon fell, he had been released and now he was trying, by any means or route, to get back to his homeland.

This was the story he was to stick to throughout his journey. He must have told it well, for although he often felt himself suspected, he was never exposed as an infidel, which would have meant death. The jouney to Djenné was ghastly. He became thin and weak. His mouth was diseased and his teeth fell out. In Djenné he was befriended by a chief who helped him on his way to Timbuctoo and gave him an introduction to Sidi Abdallahi Chebir, the 'grandfather' of the girl in the house.

After two months, during which he recovered some of his strength, he set off with a large caravan of six hundred camels, heading north. Sidi Abdallahi gave him a servant and some clothes. At Arouane another eight hundred camels joined the caravan. Caillié described this huge assembly of animals and people: 'On one side were camels laden with ivory, gum and bales of goods of all sorts; on the other, camels carrying on their backs negroes, men and children, who were on their way to be sold at the Morocco market, and further, men prostrate on the ground invoking the prophet.'

It was with enormous excitement that he started on this especially dangerous route. He had reached Timbuctoo, now he hoped to 'be the first European who had set out from west Africa to cross this ocean of sand and succeed in the undertaking.'

He did succeed, but only after the most fearful further privations. Once they were well away from Timbuctoo his servant, Ali, began to torment him, perhaps having a suspicion that Caillié was an impostor. Ali kept him short of water and food and encouraged even the slaves to tease and bully him. When he fell from his camel and suffered from concussion, it was only the intervention of some of the more important members of the caravan that prevented Ali's leaving him by the wayside. Nevertheless, this frail Frenchman arrived after a month near the foot of the Atlas. Here the caravan had to wait to negotiate a passage through the territory of the Atlas Berbers.

They were camped among Ali's people and, with his usual ingenuity, Caillié soon won them round. He made potions for unmarried girls, telling them that in a month's time they would find excellent husbands. The potions were made

René Caillié crossing the Tankisso (Mary Evan Picture Library)

by writing magic words on pieces of wood. The girls had to wash the ink off the wood with water and then drink the water. Luckily the caravan moved on after two weeks.

His progress was very slow. Having started from Timbuctoo at the end of May, it was the end of September by the time that the French consul in Tangier managed to smuggle Caillié, disguised as a sailor, aboard a French ship bound for Toulon.

Most touchingly, Caillié had rejected the advice of the Vice-Consul's 'Jew domestic' to 'carry the fruits of my travels to England where this nation had offered a reward of twenty-five thousand pounds for the accomplishment of the journey to Timbukto.'

'Instead of listening to so contemptible a proposition, I replied that I was a Frenchman and added: "The recompense to be derived from the French Government would undoubtedly be less considerable; but I should not hesitate a moment to offer to my native country and my king the homage of my modest labours."'

Poor Caillié was too modest. The French Geographical Society gave him ten thousand francs and their gold medal. Charles X gave him the Legion of Honour. The government promised him the Residency at Bamako, but this never materialised. The small pension he was given was rescinded after two years, but the new king, Louis Philippe, had it reinstated and increased. Even so, it amounted to less than two hundred pounds a year. It was a big sacrifice he had made for France.

Caillié lived only another ten years after his Sahara crossing, but in that time he married and had four children. He became mayor of Beurlay. His is always thought to be a sad story. It is true that he might have been accorded greater recognition, but most of the men who had the same ambition died miserable deaths, often no-one knows where. Caillié, after all, achieved what he set out to do.

Today, it is once again impossible to make the journey that Caillié made unless, possibly, disguised as he was. Even then I think it unlikely. I applied to the Governor for permission to travel north on that route. I was not allowed to go even to Arouane. Beyond Arouane lies Taoudenni, the third major source of salt in the Sahara. But Taoudenni is also a penal settlement where murderers and political prisoners are sent to work in the salt mines. One Malian remarked wryly to me, 'You know, we are proud to say we have no death penalty in this country. We do not need it. We send people to Taoudenni and it is a strong man who can survive there for more than two years.'

No-one is allowed to go anywhere near Taoudenni, but the route is further complicated by the fact that it runs through Tindouf which is the centre of operations for the Polisario. It is just possible that an innocent nomad going north to sell his camels or his wife's jewels might find a way through, but not a foreigner.

The last person to make this jouney, which can only be done by camel, was Richard Trench in 1974. With much of the same innocence as René Caillié, knowing hardly any Arabic, never having ridden a camel, having no experience in the desert, wholly uninformed about the customs of the people, this young man arrived in Tindouf, by himself, in the hope of travelling southward over the route which Caillié's caravan followed northward. (The Polisario were not yet established in Tindouf.)

He had no business to survive. However, he fell in with a helpful trader who was heading for Timbuctoo. Trench's account of this journey is too recent for me to rehearse it here, but it is a remarkable account, almost as alarming as Caillié's story of his journey. Indeed, Trench also fell from his camel in the dark and was almost lost. The major difference is that no-one would have killed Trench, but the other hazards of the trip were precisely the same as they had been one hundred and forty-five years before.

Timbuctoo today, despite a certain amount of building and a garrison of troops, is little more than a village. I had been amused, while waiting the prescribed hour or so in the bank, by a little turkey-cock of a man, comparatively white, with straight, slightly greying hair. He darted nervously about greeting everyone and making ineffectual efforts to conceal from the other customers the enormous wodges of notes which he had come to deposit.

Jeremy Swift had recommended me to visit a merchant called ben Batina. Jeremy had taken ben Batina's stepson, Mahmoud, on several journeys and he thought that he might be a helpful interpreter and guide for me. A friendly youth in a red T-shirt had attached himself to us in the town and he knew at once where ben Batina lived. When we got there, ben Batina turned out to be the fussy little figure from the bank. He greeted us in the street, carrying the courtesies to preposterous lengths. '*Ça va? Ça va bien? Et la famille ça va? Ça va bien, alors? Et le voyage? Le voyage ça va? Ça va bien? Ça va?*' All the time his busy, bulging eyes were darting up and down the street lest he should miss anything or anyone. If someone came by ben Batina would run through his '*Ça va?*' routine with him, while at the same time managing to keep his conversation with us going at full spate.

I asked if we might come to visit him to discuss the possibility of Mahmoud's coming with us. '*Voilà la maison . . . er . . . c'est a dire, ce soir.*' About what time this evening, I asked. '*Ah oui, . . . enfin . . . ça va? Tu sais, je suis tellement programmé.*' It was a phrase I decided to hoard for future use. I suggested that we come the next day instead. He looked immensely relieved. Just as we were leaving, I asked him where one could buy gas cylinders for cookers. His urgent programme dissolved at once. He took us a few doors down the street and opened up a little shop using one of about fifty keys which he carried with him always. The shop was stocked mostly with bolts of cloth. Ben Batina burrowed about under the counters and eventually came up with some gas cylinders, for which he charged

us a quarter more than the usual price. He offered us some tired-looking packets of spaghetti and various other dusty foods, We managed to refuse them, but arranged to come the following day, by which time he would have news of Mahmoud.

Ben Batina's house is on a broad street, near the main market. On that side there are four corrugated iron shutters fastened with shiny padlocks. Presumably there is another shop behind them, or a storehouse. The entrance to the house is round the corner in an alleyway, just wide enough for him to park his car. The front door, the status symbol of Arab houses, is highly embellished with metal medallions, studs and bosses.

We went through the ritual of our health, how we had slept, the welfare of our family, how the day had passed. All this in the doorway. Ben Batina then led us through some small, dark empty rooms and up a steep stairway to a loggia with a large terrace beyond. The terrace is surrounded by a high wall, the top half of which is latticed. The floor of the terrace is made of brick and it trembled alarmingly when anyone walked across it. On the far side there is a raised part on which there was a carpet, a mattress and half-a-dozen chairs. We sat on the chairs, ben Batina on the carpet. The youth with the red T-shirt had wandered in with us. I had no idea whether ben Batina knew him or not but he made him welcome. When, after a little while the boy made as if to go, ben Batina pressed him to stay.

Nothing much happened for quite a time. Then a servant brought a large tin tray with sixteen packets of wafer biscuits on it. No-one did anything about them. Visits to Arab houses are so often like this. Despite all that one has learnt about always being given three cups of tea and that not to drink three cups is rude and to stay long after the third is worse, the pattern seldom follows the exact rules. The small talk went jerkily on.

Ben Batina was nervous. Every so often he would get up, clear his throat and spit deftly through the lattice work on to the street below. Then he would sit down again, his torn underclothes showing through the vents in his robe. He kept on saying that tea would come, but it didn't.

At last he raised the matter of Jeremy Swift's Land Rover, as Jeremy had told me he would. Ben Batina wanted to buy it. He had a blue Toyota pick-up. He could not resist telling us that he had bought it for three thousand pounds from an Algerian who had to make a quick sale. Still, he would prefer to buy the Land Rover. Was it still available? Certainly, I said.

He told the boy in the red T-shirt to open the biscuits. Ben Batina put a dozen biscuits on a plate and made the boy sit in front of me holding out the plate. A servant brought two large, orange, enamel jugs full of rich cows' milk which tasted mildly sour. Finally the tea came, hot mint tea in tiny glasses.

OPPOSITE, Ben Batina

I thought to enlist ben Batina's help in getting us permits from the authorities to take the direct route westwards, across the sands to Walata in Mauritania. This would have saved us a long diversion through the dreary Sahel. He advised strongly against taking this route, as it was dangerous and difficult. Moreover no-one might travel over it for many months at a time, so we could expect no assistance if we were to break down. The advice was probably good, but, in any event, he plainly had no intention of helping with the police or the Governor's office.

'I am a simple merchant, I have nothing to do with the authorities.' His simplicity is relative. He is, he said, a pure Moor. His father had been a caravanner with a large herd of camels. He had lived most of the time at Arouane and made his living by bringing salt from Taoudenni to Timbuctoo.

'My father died in 1976 on December the fourth at nine o'clock in the morning. It was very sudden. I had been chatting with him at eight o'clock. He was aged ninety. Yes, it was in December. The fourth. At nine in the morning. It was a good time, nine o'clock, as it was between prayers. He could not have borne to have missed a prayer. Nor for anyone else to have done his ablutions for him. He wanted to be no trouble to anyone.'

It was now the cool of the evening and prayer time. Quite unselfconsciously, ben Batina got up to say his prayers, spreading out a little mat beyond the edge of the carpet.

When he settled down again he told us that primarily he is a cloth merchant. (In the early empires Timbuctoo was famous for weavers, tailors and trade in cloth.) He also trades in salt, buying it when the camel trains bring it in from Taoudenni, transporting it on the Niger and selling it in Mopti. Besides these interests, he has a boutique in Gao. 'Gao is much busier than Timbuctoo. The people of Timbuctoo are so lazy that one is astonished that they survive. It seems a little active now, but when the river is dry, it is a dead place.' He dabbles as well in property, but it is very risky. Each stone costs ten pence and house prices are very low. So he buys sites, builds walls round them and waits until a buyer appears before building.

While we talked various women and children flitted to and fro under the five arches of the loggia.

'My wife,' said ben Batina, 'is half Fulani. Her mother was a Fulani. *Mais oui, nous avons trois filles, mais pas des enfants.*' Girls apparently do not count as children. 'I don't know why but she seems to have stopped having children. She hasn't had one lately,' he said vaguely.

He called to his wife to be introduced to us. She was a majestic figure, much darker than her husband, whose shape suggested that perhaps the lull in children was over. For the introductions she put a scarf over her elaborately arranged hair, which had a white thing somewhere inside it to give the hair height, like an egg-cup in a pie-dish.

Ben Batina repeatedly called our attention to her beauty, not asking if we agreed, but stating an obvious fact.

'And it is on her account, as she is a Fulani, that I have become a cattle raiser.' He pointed in one direction. 'My cows are over there, some way away.' He pointed in another direction. 'My sheep are over there. And then there are my goats, which are not so far away.'

Ignoring, for the moment, the Toyota and the gas cylinders, ben Batina's life is not so very different from that of his ancestors at the time of René Caillié, or even of the days of Mansa Musa. He trades in at least two of the same commodities – salt and cloth. The gold, it is true, has long since gone, but his father most certainly saw the slave trade. His herds are the same as those of the cave paintings. Timbuctoo may have lost its mystery, but then its mystery was, in great part, imaginary.

After that, we ran into ben Batina every day. There was never any news of Mahmoud. In the end, he no doubt got fed up with our asking. He said he had found us the perfect interpreter. 'He is my apprentice, clean, well-educated. I will bring him to the hotel at four.'

He came punctually, bringing the interpreter, Mohammed Edhar, and a couple of friends. We all sat on the ground in the dust outside the hotel where the cars were parked.

'We will talk of this matter,' said ben Batina who then started talking of quite other matters to his friends. Mohammed sat, beaming. He had a lean, changeable face with a pleasant smile which curled the edges of his eyes.

I asked ben Batina whether he was free for an unspecified period – say one month or two? 'Ah, oui. He is quite free.' I then asked about food. Perhaps Mohammed would find our food nasty. What would happen when we were travelling in the empty desert?

'Just a little rice. He is very simple. Not lazy and a good driver.'

What about . . .?

'The money,' said ben Batina sharply. 'That is a matter. Yes.'

He at once reverted to chatting to his friends about cattle breeding. I muttered something about forty pounds a month. Ben Batina ignored me. Then, during a pause, he said, 'It is too little, you know, for this one. More like sixty pounds.' He went back to his conversation. The wind blew the dust about and the Arabs gathered their clothes more closely around them. I said fifty.

For the first time, he actually consulted Mohammed, who made a non-committal reply and produced a piece of paper. This revealed that in his last job, something to do with the water board, he had been paid thirty-eight pounds.

We settled, of course, for sixty.

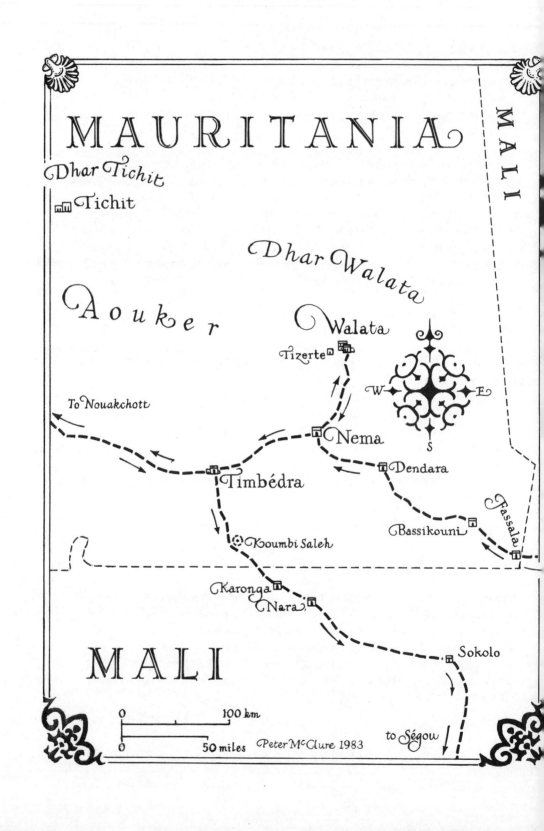

7

THE LAST WELLS
OF WALATA

WE CAME into Mauritania through Bassikouni on a little used route. At the customs post before the village, the chief was out for the day. If we really wanted to have our car documents stamped we would have to wait until the next day, because the chief had, as was proper, taken the rubber stamp with him. We left it at that.

Mohammed, the interpreter, had a sister in the village. He had not seen her for two years so he asked if he might go to visit her for ten minutes.

These villages on the fringe of the desert have a bleak appearance. The only reason for their existence is the haphazard chance that it is possible to dig a well there. The land round them has been eaten bare by the herds, so that it looks like a scab on a wound. The dust swirls up in pillars often as high as forty feet, mingling in the evening with the smoke of the cooking fires. An occasional fowl scrabbles at the earth. Round the well is a carpet of dried dung. A few pied crows squawk hideously from the roofs.

There are always lots of houses, like empty eye sockets, which have fallen down or been abandoned. Cattle with haunches like badly packed parcels revealing the shape of the contents, low miserably; and camels make a groaning sound like a giant rumbling stomach.

The poverty is extreme. That morning, still in Mali, a woman had thrust a whimpering baby through the window at Rose. She begged Rose to take it as she could not feed it.

Yet those people who survive still laugh and joke. Two youths asked us for a lift. We only had room on the roof, but the police said that they could not ride there. They had been waiting for a lift for ten days. They were running out of money. They offered to sell us a small black boy of about ten. 'A thousand pounds,' they said. Or we could have a charming whiter one. He was four or five thousand. At least I thought they were joking. Later on, I wondered.

At the first town, Fassala, the police were very welcoming. They were quite unused to foreigners. They wanted to kill a sheep for us. We could have a grand *mechoui* (whole lamb roasted on a spit) and stay perhaps for three or four days. We told them that we were already behindhand, so they gave us a mass of misinformation about Mauritania and sent us on our way.

The border certainly lived up to our expectations. After Timbuctoo and its tourists and the southward sweep through the Sahel we had taken in obedience to ben Batina's advice, Mauritania was as different as one could wish.

Here there have been no important trade routes for many centuries. Tourism has hardly been thought of. More than three quarters of the population are still nomadic.

Just before we arrived in Nema we stopped so that everyone could put on trousers rather than shorts. I always thought it offensive to wear shorts in devoutly Moslem regions. More than once, police had sent us away to put on trousers before they would stamp our documents. The road was running through hillier country than we had seen for a long time, but there was no sign of life, no indication that we were approaching the largest town in eastern Mauritania.

Nema lies in a hollow, at the edge of a low range of mountains stretching away to the north-east. It was known, at the time of the ancient empires, for its hot springs. Now it is a dusty garrison town. The only tap is three or four miles away at the airport. The airport is grand and new, with shiny checking-in scales and a lounge. One aeroplane a week comes, with few passengers. Heaven knows what folly of misused aid inspired the building of the airport.

The police in Nema were, at first, rather suspicious of us. It turned out that look-out soldiers in the hills had seen us stop to change our trousers. Quite what they found sinister in this I don't know, but the police chief put me through a persistent questioning. Gradually this took the form of a quiz about Mauritania. Finding that I knew the names of the principal towns and the whereabouts of the important mosques and ruins, he changed to people.

Did I think that people in the Sahel and the Sahara were all the same? When I said that I took it that the people of the Sahara were nomadic while the people I had seen in the Sahel were, broadly speaking, sedentary, he looked ferocious.

'The people of the north are white. The people of the south are black. If you are going to write a book, you must get your history right,' he said threateningly. Then he launched into a fiercely patriotic speech. The Mauritanians were independent. They were triumphant and great. They were infinitely superior to all the nations which surrounded them. They were a fine, free people.

The police chief was so moved by his own eloquence that he decided that my opinions must coincide with his. We were friends. He would like us to meet the Governor.

Our plan was to head north-east along the base of the mountain range to

Walata and then on to Tichit. The first part of the journey would not be too difficult. Beyond Walata there was no question of going without a guide. I decided to find one in Nema. We wandered round the town, asking here and there. Nema felt different from any other town we had been in. There was a measure of hostility in the way people looked at us. The older people were, for the most part, polite and helpful, but it was the children who allowed this feeling to grow. They were rude and disagreeable. Their jokes were coarse and offensive in a way that I had never seen before. I remembered the accounts of early explorers in the Sahara and it seemed that these were vestiges of the attitudes they had encountered. It began to dawn on me that Mauritania was almost a century behind the countries we had passed through. Do you get many tourists, I asked one man. 'Oh yes, we have a lot. Every year we have one, or even two.'

In a shop, the proprietor said that we should find a guide in Nema as the guides in Walata were no good. An old man, standing near, protested that this was nonsense. 'You can take a Walata guide out anywhere, blindfolded. Give him a few grains of sand and, without taking off his blindfold, he will tell you where you are.'

The Governor evidently did not want to see us, as the police chief never mentioned the idea again, so we set off for Walata.

Walata sits high up, looking over what must once have been a large river. There is not much left of the town now; just two or three tight clusters of inhabited houses. Behind them are the ruins of many hundred more houses and beyond them again the rocks at the lip of the valley – the ruins and the rocks blending together so that it is hard to tell where the one ends and the other begins.

To one side, on a higher hill, is a school and a modern building which serves as a dispensary. Rather above the main block of the village is the mosque. The sand creeps over the town, smothering many of the old houses and settling higher and higher round the mosque and even invading it. Three years ago, the army sent a hundred soldiers to sweep it out. After two years it was worse than before.

The view out over the valley is beautiful. Down below, to the right there are some new administration buildings, but it is the movement in the valley which attracts the eye. There are a number of wells along the bottom of the wadi and a very few trees, half engulfed by sand. At each well there are groups of camels being watered. In the supposed rainy season, there may be as many as three thousand camels coming in to drink every day. Even in what the inhabitants call the cold season, there are always three or four hundred.

Beyond the wells, the far side of the valley climbs steeply up two hundred feet. At the top there is a fort. The President was imprisoned there in colonial days. The military are very reluctant to let one anywhere near it. Perhaps it is still used as a prison.

The streets of Walata are steep, sandy and narrow. They are exciting, with sudden little views and odd corners. Every so often there is an elaborate doorway. The people move silently, like blue and white moths. Then, almost blasphemously, a man goes by with a transistor radio.

Very quickly we attracted a crowd of children, in particular one gnome of a child who looked about six years old, but his face was much older. He wore nothing but a short T-shirt. Whenever any of us smiled at him he would give a mad kind of salute, holding his hand by his head and then rapping it down in a violent gesture.

The atmosphere was far removed from that of Nema. Everyone wanted to help, especially when we said that we wanted to rent a house. After a while a rather earnest-looking man with spectacles appeared and said he had a house that we could have for twenty pounds a week.

The house was not far from the mosque. It was a new house and was not really finished. The entrance led through a short tunnel to a courtyard, which had two levels. The lower one had a large pile of wood for beams, a fair amount of rubble and a large oil drum. There was one small room at this level and Abdul Rachman, the bespectacled landlord, hoped we would not mind if an old lady spent part of the day there. The higher level formed a terrace onto which the two main rooms of the house opened. On the far side of these rooms was another rubbly, L-shaped courtyard. Round the corner was the lavatory – a tiny room with a none-too-deep hole in the floor. Happily it had not had time to become unpleasant.

The houses of Walata are built of stone, which is then covered with an ochre-coloured mud. A year later, another layer of mud is put on, this time mixed with cow dung which gives it a rich, dark red colour.

Every morning at about six o'clock, while we were in our house, a woman appeared with a fair supply of steaming dung which she deposited in the large oil drum in the front courtyard. She never said a word. The old woman came every morning at about seven and left at eleven. She never spoke either.

The insides of the houses are painted with a wash made with very pale dust. The result is a pleasant off-white. The rooms are high for coolness. The ceilings, which have exposed pole beams, are covered with matting between the beams; this gives an impression rather like a Japanese *tatami* floor. The rooms have plenty of windows, but they all open onto the courtyards of the houses. The walls are full of niches and pigeon holes for keeping things in. There is nothing else. Naturally, no water and no electricity.

In the grander houses there is, on the red walls of the courtyard, a decorated panel – usually circular. Sometimes there are more than one. They are quite unlike anything else that I saw anywhere in the Sahara. The patterns are traditional and they are executed now by only one old woman. She spent a day making a large medallion on a wall especially for us. She started by spreading a

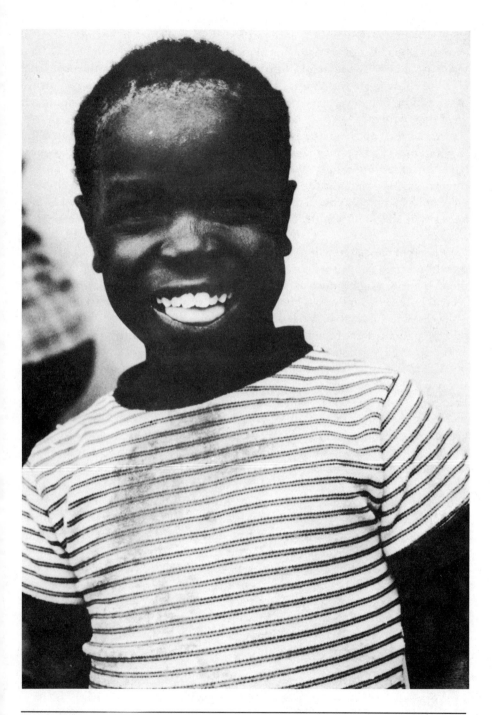

The gnome

circle of white clay over an area about four feet in diameter. Then she scraped away small patches of the white until the red wall was exposed and in this way made a pattern like lacework. Into some of the holes she put other coloured clays – yellow or brown. She worked quite automatically with the confidence of repetition. She never needed to step back to look at what she had done, but went doggedly on.

She had learned the patterns from her mother, but had no view as to what they meant – at least none that she could or would convey to me. Yet they must have had a meaning for her. When I asked her whether she ever wanted to vary the patterns, she thought for a while. Then she said, 'Yes, when my children were born I wanted to put them into the pictures, but I did not dare to.' It was not clear at all to me how the children could have been worked into so abstract a pattern.

Other people suggested to me that the patterns are to do with fertility. Newly-married couples who can afford them have their houses decorated with them, often paying as much as one hundred pounds for the work – a lot when a small house costs only two hundred pounds and a large one fifteen hundred. Still others said they have a religious significance and one elderly sage claimed that the patterns were brought from Iraq in the twelfth century.

We enjoyed our house. The view from the roof was beautiful and the peace of Walata was seductive. In the mornings and evenings hundreds of swifts swooped round and round overhead. The birds and the insects worked to a very exact timetable. At eleven in the morning, little russet, grey-headed sparrows would come pecking in what little shade they could find in the courtyard. Every evening between six and half past six a cloud of little bugs arrived to crawl over us. As the light faded, a great sweep of doves flew home to roost and always, just when it was too dim to make him out, some sort of owl made two passes over the courtyard. The moment it was dark the crawling bugs disappeared.

Soon we had a large acquaintance in the town, most of whom would call every day to see how we were getting on. Whenever anyone arrived, a horde of children, always including the saluting gnome, would rush in to stare at us and we had to drive them out with a great show of mock fury.

One of our first visitors was a superior young man called Maruani Bou. He had been born in Walata but, when his primary schooling was finished, he went to school and then college in Nouakchott, the capital. He had even been, *en stage*, to Tours. Now he works in the Treasury and comes home only once a year. In his view Walata is a dead hole, where everyone is in bed by eight or nine o'clock. 'There is only family life here and that, everyone knows, is insupportable.'

With his broad knowledge of the world, Maruani Bou is able to despise his

OPPOSITE, The artist works on a decorated panel

background and in pouring out his scorn he revealed several interesting things about Walata.

He said it was a mistake to suppose that everyone in Walata is poor. Despite the decaying appearance of the town, the leading families are still rich. The chief for instance, although he no longer has power, is well off. When his daughter had meningitis the chief chartered a plane to fly her from Nema to Nouakchott and she then flew on to Paris for treatment.

It is hard to imagine how anyone can be rich in this dying oasis where, within living memory, there were three hundred and sixty wells and now there are only six. Walata has no future and therefore its people either go away, like Maruani Bou, or they attempt to preserve the past. Many of the customs of Walata have completely died out elsewhere. No man, for example, would ever greet a woman in the street, with the exceptions of his mother or his wet nurse. The grandees still employ wet nurses.

The only thing which Maruani Bou thinks is satisfactory about Walata is that there is no crime. 'There is no need to lock anything up.' This theory I found hard to reconcile with the large number of padlocks which are to be seen everywhere and the huge bunches of keys which many of the women carry.

The Chief was away in the hospital at Nema, but his younger son, Nema ould Ba, used to come to see us every day. He is a gentle young man of twenty-three. He has a soft round face with permanently surprised-looking eyes. His complexion is very dark and his hair negroid. His handshake is a little damp.

Unlike Maruani Bou, Nema has little concept of the world outside Walata. His fifth or sixth 'grandfather' came to Walata from Tuat, in Algeria. He saw a pretty girl and married her. For many generations they talked of returning to Algeria but never did. He told us that his father's powers had been taken from him at the time of independence. He was rather vague about what those powers had been. The only one he could recall was the collecting of a tithe to pay for the upkeep of the communal wells. Now he pays for their upkeep out of his own pocket.

Nema is full of the legends of Walata. Among other stories, he told us of the first ancestor of the Walatans who, having dislodged the Bambaran inhabitants of the place, climbed up on the hill where the rocks now rise above the village. There he camped, where none dared sleep for fear of the panthers and jackals and wild boar. In the morning the people went up to see what they expected would be the remains of the saintly man and his followers. Instead, they found him sleeping safely, surrounded by the wild animals with their mouths pressed to the ground and wagging their tails – a sign of apology.

The myth quality of his stories is not confined to the misty past. He told me, one morning, of a bold contemporary of his elder brother who got bored in Walata and decided to make his fortune. He set off for Mali. Just after he crossed the border he met a large truck, full of Malians coming to Mauritania. He

Two sons of the chief of Walata; Nema ould Ba is on the right

stopped the lorry and told the passengers that they must pay for special passes which he would issue. He made so much money from the big lorry full of people that he was able to buy a ticket to fly from Bamako to Paris.

In Paris he met a merchant. He told the merchant that he had one hundred and twenty four-wheel-drive vehicles at the airport and that he would sell them to the merchant cheaply. The merchant paid up. The bold rascal skipped with the money to Germany.

There he lived well on the proceeds of the false sale and he became a friend of Chancellor Schmidt's son. After a year of friendship, he asked the Chancellor's son for a loan – a small cheque. He added so many noughts to the amount of the cheque that the cashing of it emptied four banks in Germany.

Back in Paris, he chanced to see Giscard d'Estaing signing a cheque. With a little practice, he could forge the President's cheques easily – and so he did.

Now he is back in Nouakchott living a life of pure luxury.

The first time that we went to the Chief's house was for a short visit on the second day we were in Walata. The main courtyard was large and liberally decorated with patterned medallions. Opposite the entrance were a number of beds rather like vast laundry hampers. Several women were lounging on these. To the right was a wall with a door in it, leading to another courtyard and what amounted to a separate house. To the left was a daïs spread with carpets and at the back of the daïs three doors into the main house.

Nema's mother lay on cushions, just inside the left-hand doorway. Occasionally she would shout to the other women in the courtyard. Another younger woman lay just inside the right-hand door. She never spoke and no-one paid her the least attention.

There were no men, apart from Nema. A few chickens pecked about in the sand on the ground.

In 1354, Ibn Battuta wrote: 'The women of Walata are of an exceptional beauty.' He was altogether surprised at the way women were treated. Moreover, 'the men show no sign of jealousy: a man can come home and find his wife in company with another man and find nothing remarkable in this.' He was even more astonished that these devout people allowed women to say their prayers side by side with men, without even covering their heads.

The women in the Chief's house were in general perhaps not of exceptional beauty, but one or two of them were very pretty. There was one whom I admired particularly. She, however, was not at all satisfied with her appearance, because she was too thin. She was not what we would call thin, but she explained that girls were expected to be fat. As a rough rule, they were encouraged to eat three times as much as men. Jeremy Swift told me that the Governor's wife in Tidjikja, when he went there, was so fat that she was quite unable to walk. Whenever she wanted to move she had to call for some slaves to carry her. The Governor thought her quite perfect. Such extremes of Mauritanian beauty, I would imagine, are becoming rarer, but a thin woman is a sad one.

While we drank our three cups of tea, the courtyard had been gradually filling up with inquisitive children, the gnome as always in the front, saluting. Nema's mother did not look too pleased. So we decided to go. One of the women asked us to call at her house on our way home. Outside Nema's house there was a huge crowd of children. It was only with difficulty that they were prevented from pursuing us into the house where we had been invited. Our hostess barred her door.

Mysteriously most of the women from Nema's house had got here before us – but our visit was short. Someone unwittingly unbarred the door and a hundred children flooded in. We hurried away, followed by all the children of the town, shouting and laughing and the gnome saluting more and more frenziedly.

After two or three days they got used to us and we could wander about quite freely.

Nema used to plan little diversions for us. He would take us, he said, to see the Chief's garden. We went down into the valley and followed the wadi up to the last well. Not far from the well was a small patch of green not more than five yards square, fenced round with thorn branches. In this pathetic garden a little mint grew and another plant which Nema said was used in a dish called something like Jiju. That was all.

About half a mile further up the wadi was a very big and beautiful acacia, one which would have been quite impressive in fertile country. Nema said it was the last of many which grew there when he was a child. This one might last another five years.

As we came back we stopped at a small graveyard, lying in the middle of the wadi among the few remaining wells. These were the graves of the French. Most of the names were illegible. I could make out three – Edouard Auguste Marie de Latard de Pierrefeu CAI, 1914, a Sergeant Infanterie de Marine Auguste Gilling, 1913, and that of the archaeologist Bonnel de Mézieres, who excavated the site of Koumbi Saleh in 1913 and died at Walata in 1942.

On another day Nema took us to Tizerte, about three miles away over the trickiest soft sand. Here there is evidence of a very large settlement presumably from the days when Walata was a large city with a population of at least thirty thousand people. All that a layman can see is a mass of broken red pottery, each shard covered with a pattern of dots. It is also possible to imagine the outlines of houses. Not far away, under a line of cliffs, is a sizeable graveyard. I suppose the ground is rocky and hard to dig in, for the graves are shallow and many dismal skulls gaze emptily from among the tombs.

In the early thirteenth century Walata was the most important commercial town in the southern Sahara. Modern historians think it likely that, when the Ghana empire was crushed by Sumanguru, the Soso king, the major Moslem families left Koumbi Saleh for Walata, which at that time was called Biru. Until it was superseded by Timbuctoo, in the late fourteenth century, Walata was a centre of trade, culture and religion. One chronicle reports: 'The caravans poured in from every country. Rich men, wise men and holy men settled there. They came from Egypt, from the Fezzan, from Ghadames, from Tuat, from Tafilalet . . .'

When all else has long since gone and now even the water is nearly finished, the holy men remain. Walata is still a Koranic centre, to which pupils come from far away. There was a young man from Sierra Leone who used to call on us in order to speak a little English. He was studying Islamic law.

Not far from us lived a holy man, Mohammed Jirdu. When I first went to see him he was sitting on one of those 'laundry-hamper' beds, instructing a young man who sat on a low stool in front of him. The young man held a small, narrow board, on which were written some verses from the Koran. Behind the old man there were many more of these boards propped up in a niche. The old man waved to me to settle down and then went on with his lesson. He had a mellifluous voice and the young man listened eagerly. It might have been a print by J F Lewis, entitled *The Lesson from the Koran*.

When the lesson was over, the holy man asked me what to do about his foot. It was wrapped in a bandage. 'I have bled it,' he said, 'but it makes no difference; it still hurts when I walk.' As he looked to be about eighty, I could only imagine that he had arthritis or rheumatism, anyhow certainly nothing that I could cure.

I promised to send him some most efficacious pills – just the thing for his problem, I said.

It was one of those pleasant occasions when one feels completely at ease with someone and the time passes agreeably. It does not matter a bit that it also passes, in practical terms, quite uselessly. Mohammed Jirdu is one of the world's optimists.

When he was young, he said, all the houses in Walata were occupied. It was after colonisation that they started to fall down. Three hundred must have fallen down, but now it would be better. The population he thought, was growing. There was no great lack of water. But, aren't the wells diminishing in number?

'Oh yes, there used to be three hundred and thirty. I suppose there are about half that now.' He thought for a bit and then added, 'Fifteen or so.' (Nobody could ever agree on the actual number. I counted six.) Mohammed Jirdu chatted happily on about the cattle raising and the agriculture – growing millet and maize. I had seen no signs of any agriculture, so I asked how it was this year.

'It is a bad year this year. We haven't had much rain at all since 1968.'

He was, I think, a little confused about everything. He seemed every so often to slip back in time. He told me that there were five family names in Walata – Sharif, Hajib, Idelba, Baty and Daralal. The Chief was always from the same family, 'Chosen equally by the authorities and the people.'

Afterwards I sent some mild, pink pills to the old man. A couple of days later he asked for some more, saying that they had worked wonders, *alhamdulillah*.

Of the five names he had mentioned one, Idelba, I had thought was the name of the tribe of all the grandees of Walata. The social hierarchy of Mauritania is immensely complex. There are castes as well as tribes. The dominant one, the *Hassans*, nominally being composed of the noble tribes of warriors who were descended from the fifteenth-century Moroccan invaders. Then come the *Tolba* or *Zouaï*, mostly Berber in origin, who are primarily holy men. The Idelba belong in this group. Then there are the *Zenaga* or *Lahme*, formerly vassals of the *Hassans*, drawn from Berber tribes defeated at the time of the invasion. Next a caste similar to the Twareg *Inaden* called *Mallemin,* who are craftsmen. Unlike the *Inaden*, they are white. Then there is an untouchable class of minstrel-jesters, the *Iggaouen*, who perform at all ceremonies. They are forbidden to marry outside their group and, perhaps in consequence of their isolation, they are known for the rudeness and impertinence of their performances. Finally, there are the *Haratin* or slaves, now nominally liberated.

One of the other names in Mohammed Jirdu's list meant something more precise to me. The Arabic teacher at the Walata primary school is called Baty ould M'bouya. He was said to belong to the oldest family in Walata.

Baty's house is not far from the school, up a steep and rocky path which runs

---

OPPOSITE, Baty ould M'bouya

between crumbling empty houses. This end of the town is very deserted, but all the houses between his house and the ridge belong to Baty's family.

The first time I called on him, we sat in the not very big courtyard from which, if one stood up, one could see the whole valley. In the evening light the sand in the wadi took on a misty colour like green corn just turning to yellow. The last camels were moving away from the well and the pigeons were sweeping round and round, their wings making a beating swoosh, the only sound in the cooling air.

Baty ould M'Bouya has a fine, lean, intelligent face, with a trim, slightly grizzled beard. He wore a light-blue robe over a black gown. At first we exchanged pleasantries and he himself brought us a thick, white drink, which he said was made with milk and ground maize and flavoured with nutmeg. He brought also a tin tray covered with little pieces of dried gazelle meat, which tasted fairly rotten.

As we talked of what I had learned of the history of the town, he became quite agitated. 'You must not believe all these people. They know nothing.' He besought me to come back in the daytime, when it was light, and we could sit in his library and he would show me his family tree and I would understand that he was a more reliable informant about the history of Walata. 'There have been seventy marabouts in my family, so you should believe me and not others.'

On my next visit we sat in a small room high up in his house, which has an even finer view over the valley. The floor is covered with good carpets and there are painted leather cushions scattered about and beds with more carpets on them. There is a pleasantly jumbled feeling about the room. On a bent iron table there is a board with fittings – a silver pot, a special stick and some kohl – a vanity table.

Baty had got out a lot of books. He sat on the floor in the middle of several piles of papers and files. The dignity of his handsome face was amusingly marred by his rickety spectacles, which were missing one arm.

He told us that his family came from Iraq in the twelfth century at the time of Haroun al Raschid. For this reason his brand mark is roughly the same as the Iraqi flag. He pointed out little patterned squares on the mirrored doors of some small cupboards which ran along one wall. 'The pattern is the Iraqi flag.' It was Baty who told me that the wall medallions were Iraqi in origin.

Unrest in Baghdad and the danger of imprisonment had led Moussa Kazim, Baty's ancestor, to flee with four companions. At this point Baty produced his family tree. It is a tattered piece of paper with writing which winds around on the paper like a snake, but with branches curling off and stopping a few names away from the main stream. Baty's voice took on a special rhythmic quality and consequential tone as he read out the names of his ancestors – Baty ould Baba ould Mohammed Abdullah ould M'Bouya ould Barbar Ahmed ould Mohammed Bouya ould Talib Abd'Rachman ... and on and on for twenty-

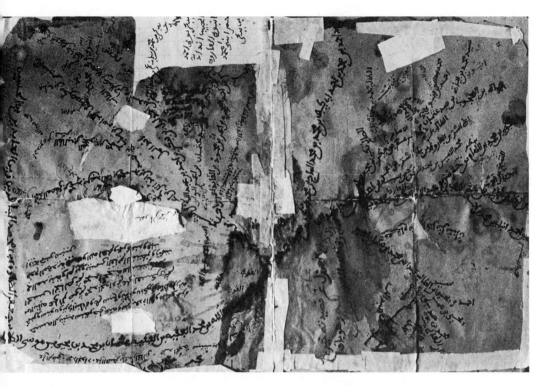

Baty's family tree

eight generations. Moussa Kazim, the one who came to Walata, was sixth from the beginning.

Baty told me that he had never been to Iraq, but he had met several relations in Medina when he went on the Haj.

As he talked it was clear that, despite all the books, a strong oral tradition continues. Baty's style of story-telling was a rhetorical one. His elegant hands formed patterns and shapes in the air – weaving baskets, fashioning cups, forming rings and fists, mountains and plains, water and stars.

Moussa and his four companions had dreamed in Baghdad of a particular place of refuge. They travelled by night, guided by a light in the sky. When the light eventually stopped over a hill they stopped. And they built a house on the hillside – the first house of Walata, for this was the place they had dreamed of.

There were already some Bambara* living in the place, he said. Moussa and his companions offered them a cowrie shell for some water. The infidel Bambara

---

*I would have thought it more likely that any inhabitants at that time would have been Soninke. The Bambarans lived much further south.

refused. The Imam with Moussa picked up three stones. He threw the first one into the well. Water gushed forth in abundance. He threw the second stone and the well flowed with blood. He threw the third stone and the well dried up.

The Bambara, when they saw the power of Islam, fled except for those who were converted. It was their turn to ask for water which was given to them and they made their way to Koumbi Saleh. Baty resumed his chanting voice to reel off the names of the Bambara – Karbalita, Kaïkita, Kamrita, Markita.

Moussa and his four companions were a teacher of Arabic, a teacher of the Koran, an Imam, a builder and a jeweller. They, said Baty, were the founders of Walata. This story was essentially the same as the one Nema had recounted, although there were some differences and contradictions. But then there were contradictions within Baty's own story. It was the story of the animals apologising to the saint that enraged Baty so much. 'It simply is not true,' he said furiously.

'The man did exist. That is true. His name was Sheik Sidi Ahmed Albakaye. He came from the west with three friends. When he died he was buried down in the valley. After a time, his three friends dreamed that the saint was lying in running water. So they dug him up and reburied him high up above the town. When they dug him up, his body was perfectly preserved. The place that he was removed from became nearly a lake. It had been a Bambaran place.'

Nema's story had been almost the same with the addition of the animal apology, but Baty's anger on that point was not to be assuaged. With much finger wagging, he warned me once again to beware of other people's stories.

I found this passion for what he believed to be the historical truth very attractive, the more so because, in all other respects, he is such a generous and peaceful man. He is convinced that by right the Chief should be chosen from his family, but he speaks well of Nema's father and bears him no grudge. 'When the French came, their plan was to divide the people of the town. So they chose Chiefs from different families. But we are not divided.'

That the people are not divided, which indeed they are not, may as much be due to the decline of Walata as to any goodwill. There is an unspoken feeling of siege about the town. The enemy is the drought and it is tightening its grip all the time. The sand drives in; another well fails. The trees wither and die; the young people leave and never come back. There is no real battle to be fought, but the shared dread binds the people together.

Sidi, in the dispensary, sits in shabby gloom behind a table. On the table are huge bottles marked Sulfaguanidine and Urotropine. He does not have many other drugs.

Sidi is not a doctor, but a nurse – 'first class' he is quick to point out. He is not old, but he is balding, thin and tired – also a trifle effeminate. He speaks beautiful French, having worked for many years in Dakar.

He explained that his task is quite hopeless. He said that he has thirty-five

Walata, a town that faces extinction as its wells dry up

The baptism at Walata

OPPOSITE, Preparing the baptismal food, Walata

LEFT, In Walata, the Chief's son proposed that Tim should marry this girl, called Tcheicha

thousand patients. The majority of these live out in the desert. He maintained that the population of Walata is ten thousand. This is quite obviously not so. I would put it at one thousand at the most – but he may have meant that ten thousand are in some way linked to Walata, while the others are pure nomads. His broader estimate is not unreasonable.

'What can I do for them? If a woman is ill a long way out in the desert it may be two days or more before I can reach her. At best I am away for four days. Meanwhile what happens here?' He has no vehicle. He has no helpers. Often, he said, the staff of the *Service Hygiene* were used as guides for foreigners.

Tuberculosis is very common, so is syphilis. The people in the desert nearly all suffer from rheumatic troubles. The most unpleasant problem of all is the appalling prevalence of Guinea worm. About two-thirds of the people suffer from this odious parasite.

It comes into the body from the water. As the wells diminish in number, those that remain diminish in quality. All of them are now hideously polluted. So the Guinea worm settles in the body, and it grows. It may grow to be several yards in length. Eventually it decides to come out of the body and it tunnels its way to the surface. Usually it comes out at the ankle or the knee. Occasionally it comes out through the eye.

In Sidi's dispensary there were many patients with Guinea worm. When the bandages were taken off the leg there would be a fair sized hole with a white thing, about the thickness of a strong bit of string, protruding. Sidi would take a small stick and wind the worm around it and keep on turning, gently pulling out inch upon inch. When the worm snapped, Sidi would bind up the leg and say, 'Perhaps we will get it all out next time.'

The worms were just another part of the siege of Walata.

Rose had met the vet by chance and he had told her of his difficulties. They were not as bad as Sidi's. He, too, had transport problems, though unlike the nurse he had two assistants. The vaccination programme was sensible, but sometimes he was short of drugs. From Rose's description he sounded interesting and I made an appointment to see him in his office, down below in the valley.

When I was on my way there, a soldier stopped me. He wanted me to go at once to the military office. There was a mild note of menace in his voice. The building was not far. I was taken straight in to an office, which was empty except for a table and a few chairs. Behind the table were two men, presumably officers. Tim and Jocelyn were with me. The officers told us to sit facing them. The more senior of the two officers (at least I took him to be the senior as he sat exactly in the middle of the table) spoke little or no French. He had enormous sticking-out ears which made me want to giggle.

OPPOSITE, The woman who paints the decorated panels in Walata, inside her own house

175

The junior started by saying that he knew I was looking for a guide called Nani. (Nani I knew to be the best guide in the area. He was working for the military, on call when they needed him.) The captain had refused permission for me to borrow Nani. This, I felt sure, was not why we had been called in. 'Then, secondly ...' There was a long pause. The one with big ears put on a magisterial face. The junior's voice took on a new note.

'Yesterday, you visited the infirmary. You asked many questions seeking out deficiencies in our services. The nurse told you he had no medicines and made many complaints. Today you have an appointment with the vet at five o'clock. You may not keep it.'

I explained that I was interested in medical affairs as I was on the committee of the International Year of Disabled People. My hope was that any information I gathered might be helpful in getting medical aid for his country. I added that he was curiously misinformed about what the nurse had told me, perhaps because I was alone with the nurse during any serious discussion.

This was translated to Big Ears, who looked unconvinced. What about the vet? I said that as I was a farmer I was interested in cattle.

The occasion was one of absurd formality. Once more I felt demeaned by my lack of courage in the face of idiot authority. This time, I tried to justify it to myself on the grounds that I was hoping to protect the nurse. I apologised for anything I might have done wrong. They leaned back, triumphant and for the most part satisfied. But they needed the last word.

'Is it not normal in every country to consult the military before speaking to a civil servant?' It seemed hardly worthwhile to say that it isn't.

Our friends in the town were most indignant about this episode. 'They are no better than apes those people in the army. They have no idea how to behave. The trouble is that we get the dregs here, the uneducated conscripts. The decent people are all with the real army fighting in the desert.'

Even Sidi and the vet did not seem much put out. I sent messages to them and they both replied that they simply did not mind about the army. They were well used to such nonsense.

On almost the last day of our visit we were invited to a baptism at Nema's house. The mysterious girl who had lain in the right-hand doorway on the day of our first visit had just had a baby. A goat had been killed on the day of the birth. Now, on the seventh day, another goat would be killed and the child would be named.

The mother is Nema's sister. She is married to our landlord's brother. It is a strict rule that the grandparents choose the child's name, if they are still alive. Failing them, the great uncle chooses. The ceremony is not elaborate.

There were about thirty women making a loud ululation when we arrived.

OPPOSITE, Preparing meat for the baptism

There was no detectable pattern to their weird noise. They just threw back their heads and, waggling their tongues like egg-beaters, howled. When they paused, two old blacksmiths chanted verses from the Koran and also the child's name – Sayid na Ali.

After a while about twenty of the ululating women and the two blacksmiths were paid off. There were very few men, only close members of the family. The sexes had separate celebrations.

Nothing very much happened. Every so often one or other of the remaining women gave an ululating cry. Inside the main house one woman beat a huge drum. People danced around. They were very pleased if any of us danced.

It was an amiable, uneventful affair. The girls were all dressed up, their hands carefully hennaed. Anyone could wander in and out. The gnome was there, of course, saluting. Nema's brother, who worked in the Ivory Coast but was back for a visit, told me that the gnome was really about fourteen, but retarded. As is often the case in simpler societies, particularly Arab societies, no-one attaches any importance to the child's misfortune. It is the will of Allah.

Sipping my tea at the party, I felt I was witnessing the end of a story which

A Walata doll's house

had gone on for several thousand years. In one corner was a woman who had brought me a doll's house. The doll's houses of Walata are not playthings for children but have a significance which no-one ever explained adequately. They are made of mud and painted. There is no roof to them, so that they look like a compartmented tray. The patterned medallions of the real house are represented by simple crosses, painted in white or indigo. The rooms are filled with miniature pots and bits of cloth. With each house there is an object quite out of proportion to everything else. I could not think what it was. When I asked, the women giggled and hid their faces. Later a man said, 'It is just a woman.' Then I could see that it was a body. The head was shapeless. The legs were the same as the head, except for a scratched line. The only faint attempt at delineation was the swelling hips and buttocks. I remembered a phrase in James Wellard's book, describing a statuette found in Queen Tin Hinan's tomb '. . . it has a featureless head, a shapeless body with the whole emphasis placed upon the hips and female pudenda.'

The Tin Hinan statuette is, in fact, a much more highly developed female equivalent of a phallic symbol. This leads me to believe that the figures which go with the doll's houses are a modern relic of something earlier than Tin Hinan – possibly a neolithic fertility symbol.

Also at the baptism was the woman who had made the patterned medallions. Her decorative work may belong to the days of the ancient empires.

Then there were the servants, or the people I took to be servants. I asked Nema how much servants are paid. '*Un "boy", tu connais le mot, gagne mille ougiyas par mois.*' (Ten pounds a month.) I said I did know the word, but what of the others? I pointed to some older workers. 'They are slaves,' said Nema.

'Yes, but surely now slaves are paid,' I said primly.

'No,' said Nema looking at me oddly, 'one does not pay slaves, that is the point of them.'

I was always making muddles of this sort. One evening when Nema had come round to see us he had brought with him a boy of about twelve. The boy sat at his feet. Nema stroked his hair and was plainly fond of him. I asked if the boy was a member of his family. Nema looked most indignant. 'No. He's a black.' I could not see any difference in colour between the two of them.

The slaves, then, were the very real and continuing consequence of the centuries of slave trading, a great deal of which had been conducted in the markets of Walata.

The decline of Walata began at the end of the fourteenth century, when the trade route from the north shifted eastward and Timbuctoo replaced Walata as the main terminus. It has been a gentle descent. An elegance which exists nowhere else in the Sahara still hangs in the air; a breath of scholarship, a last sigh of art, a whisper of philosophy. It will soon be gone. The last wells of Walata are nearly dry.

8

HOLY DOLPHINS AND AN EXPLOSION

NOUAKCHOTT MUST be the favourite in a contest for the most irrelevant capital city in the world. France had governed both Senegal and its Mauritanian territories from St Louis, in Senegal. When Mauritania achieved independence in 1960, this new state had to invent a capital. It chose a saline, marshy spot a mile or two inland from the Atlantic and one hundred and thirty miles north of the Senegal border. Here the new government built their chief city.

The result is a town of outstanding ugliness. One bank I will always remember. At ground level it has an arcade of rather feeble looking acid green pillars. Above that comes a pretentious façade of dark green marble, which looks likely to crush the pillars. Higher still are storeys covered with yellow and ochre stucco.

There are many half-finished buildings, abandoned for lack of money. One whole suburb, near the large cluster of embassies, has ground to a halt. Down by the sea is a complete hotel which cannot open and, worse, a tuberculosis hospital in the same state. Even work on the grandiose Palais de Justice seems to be very spasmodic. Nothing works very well. The electricity is often off, usually because there is not enough money to buy fuel to run the generators.

The Moors are not suited to urban life. At the outskirts of Nouakchott there are shanty-towns of tents. Even in the centre of the capital, if you peer over a wall there is often a nomad tent set up in the garden of a grand house. Mauritania is the one country where the nomad is not despised.

There is one tribe, quite separate from all others, called the Nemadi. They are simply hunters and their only real contact with the rest of the Moors is an ancient practice by which a nomad lends a Nemadi a camel. In return the Nemadi gives him animal skins and meat. The Nemadi hunt the addax and the gazelle, using spears and dogs. The authorities felt that this way of life was not suitable, much as in other countries they think nomadic living unsuitable. They decided to normalise them – that is to turn them into nomads. They gave the tribesmen flocks of sheep and goats and told them to wander about pasturing these herds. It took the Nemadi about a month to eat through this astonishing bounty. Then they went off hunting again.

Perhaps one could go further and say that the Moors are not suited to modern life. They managed to preserve their independence far longer than any other people of the Sahara. When St Exupéry was flying the mail plane from Marseilles to Dakar in the 'twenties, his great fear was of a forced landing among the Moors. They would certainly have killed him. The Reguibi, the warrior nomads of the west, were still very troublesome to the French in the 'thirties. The Préfet of Tichit told me that that village north of Walata was not colonised until 1949.

The Moors are unconcerned about the things of this century. The students at the university come and go as they feel like it. A teacher told me that, during a two-hour session, the first hour will be disturbed by people arriving late, the second by people leaving early. Similarly, when an official had it explained to him that an uncashed aid cheque could be earning thousands of ougiyas a day for his country, he replied, 'What does my country matter? What about my family? They come first.' How not cashing a cheque helped his family was not explained.

The effort to instil a sense of nationhood meets with little real success and leads to odd pretences. A girl, half French, half Moorish, called Mariem mint Derwich, told me that at the university she had become intrigued by her origins. She established that her father's family were of Berber descent. Her teachers told her to stop her researches. All Moors, whether white or black, are now taught that they are Arabs.

We camped by the sea while we were at Nouakchott. Nothing at that moment was going right. Rose had hepatitis. As the doctor at the hospital was more intent on seducing rather than curing her, she had to fly home. Jocelyn had to go to Dakar because the Saharan custom of stamping one's passport at every town one passes through had completely filled his and my brand new passports. One of the Unimogs needed a new clutch.

The only pleasure in Nouakchott was the sea and in particular showing it to Mohammed, our interpreter, for the first time in his life.

Mohammed is twenty-four. Sometimes he claims that he is a Targui. At others he denies it hotly. He has lived all his life in Timbuctoo, but has travelled to Bamako and even to Kano as a lorry driver. He has a mixture of great charm and a capacity to irritate one to a point of frenzy. He always knows better than anyone else, but is never confused by being proved wrong. He works immensely hard when it is really necessary, but has an ability to do less than anyone else I

OPPOSITE, Walata, evening

have ever known. He is fiercely chauvinistic and he would always say, 'We have that in Mali', if he saw us looking at something with interest. I could not help liking him; Rose could not bear him, mostly because of his habit of saying 'look out' or 'take care' *after* one had done something silly or painful. He thought Rose wonderful and would reveal to her quite disgusting details of a medical character, for he is a great hypochondriac.

When Mohammed first saw the sea, he could hardly say, 'We have that in Mali'. He stared and stared at it for a long time and then asked if he could drink it. I explained that it was salty. 'Can I taste it?' Of course. Even after tasting it he would not be shaken from his belief that the people of Nouakchott were the luckiest people in the world to have all that water. Yet the actual size of the ocean he refused to accept. When I told him that it was three thousand miles across to America, he didn't believe me.

It reminded me how far we were, in every sense, from the things we take for granted. Mohammed would also not believe that men had been on the moon. When I insisted, he very tentatively asked some men in the garage whether it was true. When they agreed with me, I think that he still thought that they were pulling his leg. I took him down to see the boats in the small port. He told me he had seen films 'showing boats with houses on them and spaces as big as football pitches'. He had imagined that these were science fiction.

The Twareg, and Mohammed was definitely partly Twareg, have a great fear of evil spirits. At their weddings the most toothless and ugly old hag moves about shouting and waving to distract evil *djennoun*, who want to invade young brides. Blacksmiths have the power to cast spells, and it was a parallel superstition which brought the blacksmiths to the Walata baptism. It also used to strike me as odd how misinformed Mohammed was about natural history. In common with all Twareg he believed that geckos are dangerous and was convinced that a bite from a red-headed, blue-bodied agama lizard could kill a camel. Eventually we managed to entice him into the sea up to his knees, but he never liked it. The hundreds of scuttling crabs were obviously dangerous and the dancing phosphorescence at the water's edge at night could only be *djennoun*.

The second largest town in Mauritania is Nouadhibou, on the coast four hundred miles north of Nouakchott. There is no road to it from Nouakchott, merely one of those Saharan tracks, which may be anything up to twenty miles wide and which is quite easy to lose. The alternative is to drive up the beach for the first two hundred miles to Cap Timiris.

There comes a moment, when one is travelling for a long time, that the exotic and unfamiliar come to seem almost normal. One gets spoilt and becomes blasé about circumstances which would once have been unimaginably exciting.

OPPOSITE, Walata, afternoon

Thus it did not strike us as being very extraordinary to be setting off up a beach in the desert. We had been practical and acquired a tide table, because in places dunes as high as cliffs come right down to the water's edge. To be caught in such a place as the tide came in would mean losing the trucks and everything in them.

At first it felt like a new game. The best place to drive was right down by the water. There the sand was hardest and the way more level. The trick was to be on the sand that a wave had just left. The mistake was to misjudge it; if the wheels went into a wave they would sink into the sand.

Gradually it came to us that this drive was an experience of singular beauty. We were accustomed to emptiness, but this was a new kind of emptiness with the sands of the whole Sahara stretching to the east and the Atlantic ocean to the west. But there was movement, which was new to us, the movement of the sea.

When we had travelled about thirty miles we came upon the wreck of a small coaster – the *Sancho II*, out of Tenerife. She lay rusting on the shore, full of sand and crabs. It was wondering what had happened to the crew that made me realise what a remote and rare place this was. It was on this coast in July, 1816 that the fifteen survivors of the *Meduse*, immortalised by Géricault, squabbled over their respective share of human steaks, a story which titillated the French for many weeks. Now there was no-one. Only when we camped for the night did we see some fishermen, who at first asked us to move a few hundred yards up the shore, so as not to disturb their fishing grounds, and then laughed helplessly at our attempts to catch fish with a weighted line. Nevertheless, Jocelyn caught two. They wriggled quietly back into the water, while he was busy telling us of his prowess.

If there were virtually no people, the bird life was possibly the most abundant in the world. Sometimes for a mile ahead it was impossible to see the sand, for the whole beach would be absolutely covered with gulls and terns and herons and sandpipers and plovers and scores of other birds. As we drove towards them they would rise up, wheel around and land again just behind us. Not far from the wreck, we came upon one ruffled-looking bustard. His feathers were all fussed up by the sea breeze and he looked hopelessly out of countenance. His huge, wide wings beat lugubriously as he tried half-heartedly to take off as we approached. He reminded me of the Twareg fable about the gazelle who loves the bustard. Before dawn each morning the bustard leaves her lover lest, in the day, he should see how ugly she is. Each night the gazelle tries to trap her by throwing a tent over the world and what we think are the stars are little holes in the tent.

The profusion of birds on the beach and in the sky was matched by the

OPPOSITE ABOVE, Along the coast of Mauritania, the sky is always filled with birds. BELOW, one ruffled-looking bustard

superabundance of fish in the sea. When the sea was still, a whole acre or more of water would froth with the passing of a shoal of fish. We could wade out into the middle of a shoal and be surrounded by a myriad fish shining in the dark, clear water.

I remembered how St Exupéry had looked down upon this empty coast with a mixture of alarm and of wonder at its beauty. In some ways these two days were the most enjoyable of the whole journey.

When we got near to Cap Timiris grim patches of greyish sand clutched at the wheels of the Unimogs and we had to leave the beach for fear of getting irretrievably stuck as the tide came in. As we turned inland a whole, vast shoal of fish leapt into the air, glistening like a huge sheet of sequins, as two dolphins passed below them.

The dunes here are steep and trackless, but we came eventually out onto a flat stretch of land which, running beside a long, narrow bay, forms Cap Timiris. At the end of the cape, by the open sea, is a bleak little bunch of houses and huts. A torn windsock hangs from a rusty pole. This is Nouamrhar, the only settlement of more than fifty people between Nouakchott and Nouadhibou.

Nouamrhar is a fishing village. On the day that we arrived it was too windy to fish. So, by good fortune, we fell in with one of the leaders of the community, called Mohammed Fall. He has a little shop, nothing more than a small room, and he invited us there for tea. The shop does not amount to much. There is a counter and on it a pair of scales, with two plastic plates for weighing things. Behind the counter are some rough wooden shelves with very little on them – macaroni, oil, two kinds of biscuit, tomato paste, rice, onions, sweets and a sleeping kitten. Fall's shop is the only one in the village.

As we talked and Fall prepared the tea, people came in ostensibly to buy something, but really to peer at the strangers. They brought with them clouds of flies. All writers about the Sahara make an immense fuss about flies. Geoffrey Moorhouse became quite obsessed by them, once counting thirty-seven on his arm. Rather unexpectedly, I never found them very troublesome. They would come buzzing round one's eyes in the morning impeding more sleep, but that was good as it got us moving. In the oases they were a mild nuisance, but at Walata we soon learned to keep the room dark, and the flies stayed away. Nouamrhar was the real exception to this exoneration of the fly. I had never imagined that there could be so many flies in one place. After a short while the walls of Fall's shop were dark with them. The dates on a plate on the floor between us were invisible under their blanket of flies. It did make me wonder at the total lack of interest in comfort which the Arabs and the Berbers evince. This was not the usual complement of flies to which anyone can and does become accustomed. It was a positive plague, attracted by the drying fish and the rather unusual practice which the villagers had of shitting quite openly on

186

various sandy mounds scattered through the village. It is an act they can perform very neatly, crouching down and managing somehow to keep their clothes round them like a tent, without revealing anything or, presumably, getting their clothes dirty. Given this plague of flies, it seemed to me not unreasonable to wonder why nobody thought of having a fly-screen to keep them out of the houses. Against that, the earliest tradition of these people, the Imraguen, was nomadic, so the lack of concern for comfort may be atavistic.

Mohammed Fall told us that the people of Nouamrhar were originally Berbers. He said he would show us their cemetery where, before the coming of Islam, they buried people in a sitting position. (When he ultimately did, there was nothing for the lay eye to see.) Today the tribes are mixed and the people, while Caucasian in feature, have very dark skins.

Until the onset of the great drought their lives were much easier and more varied. Every year there was enough rain for them to collect water in tanks to last through the year. Now there is virtually none. All the water for the village has to be brought either from Nouakchott or Nouadhibou. Occasionally a lorry comes from one or other town, but usually the villagers go by boat to collect water in forty gallon drums – a four hundred mile round trip. Until ten years ago they had camels and donkeys and herds of sheep. Now they have only a few goats and a sheep or two. They rely entirely on their fishing.

We had planned to camp by the beach, but Mohammed Fall asked us not to do that as it might disturb the fish. We drove down beside the bay, which the French called the Baie St Jean. After our nights by the open sea the water seemed very still. It was quite shallow. Herons waded about near the shore and a little further out, pelicans floated quietly, looking like ducks in the bath. As the light faded the bay felt rather eerie, somehow like a Scottish loch. I think it was the plopping noise of the fish jumping in the dusk, the hurrying yellow and green crabs and the harsh calls of the sea birds which produced this ghostly effect.

In the morning the wind had dropped and, when we went back to the village, the fishermen were all sitting on the sand dune just above the shore. Nothing much was happening. The men sat in small groups. Their nets hung on simple frames beside them. They chatted and Mohammed Fall introduced us to the Chief, a rather fat, unimpressive man, whose clothes were grubbier than anyone else's. The sea was still ruffled after the wind and there was quite a swell further out. Still nothing happened and we waited, somewhat perplexed by this inactivity.

Suddenly, for no reason that I could see, half of the men jumped up and stripped off their clothes down to their bathing trunks, which they wore under their *gandourahs* and *bhu-bhus*. In pairs they gathered up their fifty-feet-long nets and rushed into the sea. The sand slopes fairly steeply away from the shore, so that quite soon the men were out of their depth, swimming strongly in the dark sea.

Then I saw what was happening. Coming straight towards the shore was a huge shoal of frantic fish. Behind them, driving them towards the men, were eight or ten dolphins. Soon the fish, the men and the dolphins were all mingled together – the men encompassing the fish with their nets, the dolphins gobbling up as many fish as they could, leaping in the air, swimming back and forth to contain the fish so that they could not escape out to sea. They worked together, the dolphins and the men, in the most singular symbiosis I have ever witnessed. Without the men, the dolphins would chase the fish towards the shore and the shoal would skitter away in the shallows where the dolphins could not follow. Without the dolphins, the men would have no hope of chasing the shoal which would head out to sea beyond their reach. There is an unique beauty about the relationship, so it is not surprising that, in a simple act of heresy, the Imraguen invest the dolphins with a near divinity.

We stayed for several days watching the curious ritual being enacted four or five times a day. It appeared that there was a rota by which only a certain number of fishermen went after each shoal. For them all to go in – which would mean forty or fifty swimmers – might frighten away the dolphins. The fish caught are grey mullet. They are dried and sold for about twenty pence apiece in Nouakchott, but the main prize is the roe which is also dried and sells in Nouadhibou for about six pounds a kilo. Most of the roe is exported to Europe, where it is considered a delicacy, known in France as *poutargue* and in Italy as *bottarga*. With luck each haul will bring one hundred to two hundred fish.

The winter is the best time for mullet fishing. In the supposed rainy season and the really hot weather, the Imraguen take to boats and catch other fish. Of course, even in the good season there are times when the dolphins do not come. If this goes on for more than two or three days, the fishermen call on the marabout's help. This happened, they told me, when Jacques Cousteau came to see the dolphins in 1976. They did not come for three days. The men went to the marabout and, sure enough, there were the dolphins the next day.

When the wind stopped the fishing for a time while we were there, I asked whether we could not go to the marabout. They told me that the marabout only has power to influence living things. Of course, he could pray to Allah in the matter of the wind and Allah would do as He pleased.

They were quite certain that there was more to the arrangement than mutual convenience. Fall assured me that, if the marabout 'asked' them, the dolphins would do many things which could be of no advantage to them, but would benefit only the fishermen.

The village chief was bitterly envious of Mohammed Fall, with whom we spent most of our time. Fall, for instance, enlisted our help to put up a new windsock and the Chief thought that Fall's request to us for assistance should

OPPOSITE, A Mauritanian nomad: about four fifths of the population of Mauritania are nomadic

have been passed through him, because a new windsock was in the nature of an official matter, although Fall was in charge of the airstrip.

The Chief was constantly inviting us to his house for tea, but on the first occasion rather diminished the quality of his hospitality by happening to mention that all visitors to the village, on leaving, always presented to him anything they did not need, such as meat or rice. Mohammed Fall later apologised profusely for the Chief's behaviour. 'I am always so embarrassed by his constantly asking for things.'

I felt rather sorry for the Chief, as he plainly suffered from the most fearful sense of inadequacy. Again, the first time I went to see him, he produced his identity card which read: 'Naser ould Moktar. *Père*: Haya ould Moktar. *Teint*: Noir. *Né*: 1930. *Profession*: Chef de Fraction. *Tribou ou Fraction*: Oulad hel Lehbigou.' He needed to convince me that he really was the Chief.

The Chief, he told me, was chosen by the people. His family did not come from Cap Timiris, but from the south. An ancestor of his had married into the original Chief's family. He thought it possible that his sons would be Chief after him. It turned out later that he had no sons, only two daughters.

Under the French, Naser said, the power of the Chief had been much reduced. Now it is restored and everything of importance must pass through his hands. He did agree that there is a Préfet who endorses all his decisions. (The Préfet was away, so I could not get his version.)

With pride he told me of a military group who had camped on the beach without his permission. Their flag frightened the fish away. Naser offered to find them another place to camp. They refused to move, saying that they liked the view. 'I told them that I would break their flagpole if they did not move. They said they would shoot me if I did. So I said that was all right and I smashed the pole. The soldiers leapt into a speedboat which went faster than the wind and they rushed to Nouakchott. They went straight to the President. He asked, "Did you speak first to the Chief?" They had to say no. So they came back, bringing medicine for my people. And I settled them in a spot of my choosing.'

Naser told the story in a fine mythic style and I was rather impressed. Then he added, 'I wonder if you have brought medicine?'

The next day I sat again in his room, with its ghastly lime-green dado. Two ancient rifles hung on the wall, beside a citation for a medal of honour and two polaroid photographs of Naser. Otherwise there were only flies. Naser was once more at pains to tell me of his powers.

'If you had left your cars unguarded and something had been stolen, I would have looked at the footprints round the cars and I would have known who had been there. I would have taken the thief and cut his hand off. Even if a foreigner were to steal something I would cut his hand off.'

OPPOSITE, Mohammed Fall's wife prepares the grey mullet roes for drying

I wondered for a moment whether this were a warning, as he had no idea who we might be. But then he embarked upon a long story about his prowess as a guide and another about his marksmanship.

Life at Nouamrhar passes without much event. The feeble character of the Chief was the central topic of many of our conversations with the other villagers.

Carrying nets to the fishermen, Cap Timiris

One day a large shark appeared among the men and the dolphins. Deftly they immobilised it by wrapping one of their long nets around it. Then the men went on fishing. When they had finished, they dragged the shark ashore and killed it. Another day a boat came with half-a-dozen drums of water, brought from Nouadhibou. Then a man came home from a visit to Timbuctoo. There he had seen the Niger flowing from west to east; and all those holy men there prayed facing along the river. Obviously the sea and the Niger were *kif-kif* (same-same) so, for all these many years, the people of Nouamrhar must have been praying in the wrong direction. They should pray looking to the left down the shore. No-one could dissuade him from this position.

Nevertheless, Nouamrhar is in spirit a happy place. The young men do not disappear to towns but positively like their work. The excitement of the hunt is enough distraction. The younger boys look forward only to the day when they can join in the sport with their elders and the dolphins. They are not much interested in the school; few of them learn French or much of anything else for that matter.

As with so much of the Sahara, one wonders how much longer it can last. In some ways the people of Nouamrhar have survived the drought better than their pastoral cousins. They can manage without the few herds they had, although the material quality of their lives may have been slightly reduced. The fetching of water may be wearisome but it is not insurmountable. The main threat comes not from the desert but from the sea.

Although the shoals of fish seem impressively large, the fishermen say that the numbers are dwindling. Every so often on the horizon they see a large ship, either Russian or Japanese. And soon after there will come ashore thousands upon thousands of dead fish – small fish which would have grown to be next year's catch. The Russians and Japanese apparently use very fine nets which ensnare every fish in the sea. The ones that are too small for their purposes they throw back into the sea – dead.

In a few years, Mohammed Fall fears, this lonely outpost on a lost shore will have no possible means of existence.

Everyone was extremely helpful when the time came for us to leave Nouamrhar. It was apparently not possible to continue driving up the beach, because of rocky inlets and other hazards. The way, they said, was absolutely easy. We should set off along the bay and turn inland on a track that we could not miss.

For the last couple of days there had been an official of some sort wandering round the village. I could not make out if his role were military, political or what; but it was reassuring that he made no objection to our journey. We had been told by foreigners in Nouakchott that we ought to apply for permission if we wanted to go north of Cap Timiris. I had decided not to apply, on the grounds that people always find it easier to say no rather than yes. By driving up the beach we had avoided any serious checkpoint. Now the official also told us how easily we would find the way, so I presumed that there was no need for any concern about regulations.

We started down the bayshore. Clouds of greenish, pink-legged locusts were feeding on the salt-flat scrub. They rose in masses and whirred into the trucks and all over us. Scores of kestrels hovered overhead, swooping down again and again to feed on the locusts.

It was quite easy to find the track that was to take us inland; but in two hours, after turning east, we were lost. It is one of the most provoking things about desert tracks that they simply disappear. You are lulled into inattention by a well-worn route and do not bother with a bearing – after all, they have all said how easy it is to find the way. Then you cross a space of sand which the wind has cleaned of marks and, on the other side where you expect to find the road, there is nothing, no tyre marks, no camel tracks, just virgin sand. You cast about. You find a car track going in quite the wrong direction. It seems silly to go back to where you came from. And then, when you eventually try that, you can't find where you did come from. It isn't worrying in circumstances such as we were in that morning, merely profoundly irritating. We knew that if we headed due east we were bound to find the main inland track from Nouakchott to Nouadhibou; and that was what we had to do.

The main track, once we joined it, was in places hard enough to follow. At the most difficult part, where the dunes rose high and the way between them was impossible to guess, there were some tall markers, almost like pylons, set up every kilometre. Many of these had fallen down, once again reproaching one's inattention. It was then that I was impressed by Mohammed's skill at finding the way. Here we were in country that he had never seen before and yet, by some wonderful instinct, he seemed to sense which side of a dune to go. Even if three *balises* in a row had disappeared, Mohammed could always find the fourth, more quickly and surely than I could with a compass.

Mohammed is not a guide in any way. He calls himself a mechanic-engineer, (adding, about half-way through our journey together, the word *internationale*. '*Moi, je suis Mohammed internationale,*' he would announce). He is also urban. And yet he has the virtually unerring knowledge of where he is that one associates with highly experienced nomads. Can this characteristic be acquired or is there some genetic explanation for something which we find almost like a conjuring trick?

The way was heavy going. After the dunes came long stretches of savage rock. At last, after a day and a half, we found the railway line which brings the iron ore from the inland mines to the port of Nouadhibou. We followed it towards the town, which lies at the end of a spit of land. On our left was the sea. At this point the coast became so beautiful that we drove to the edge of some

Mohammed *internationale*

low cliffs to look at the pure white sand, the weirdly shaped rocks and the brilliant, aquamarine sea. It was a place of exquisite fascination and we thought once more how fortunate we were to see a beach of such amazing beauty with no-one to disturb its peace.

Rather reluctantly, we left the beach and cut across the sand to rejoin the track. At that moment a landmine blew us up.

This is even more provoking than losing the way. It happened in this fashion.

There was a small, obviously man-made ridge of sand. I wondered idly why someone should have made this ridge, but I was concentrating more on some camel tracks which we were following. Anthony was driving and he did not get into a low enough gear to get over the ridge. He stopped and let the truck roll back before trying again. It rolled onto the mine. I hardly remember the bang, which deafened the four of us who were in the truck for several days. I was aware first of being enveloped in a grey-black fog. Then I was floating. At first forward until my head hit the windscreen. I noticed that it was broken, but my head didn't hurt. Then I floated in a new direction – to the right. On and on I floated, at first thinking what an idiot Anthony was to have done whatever he had done, then thinking that I couldn't possibly survive this seemingly interminable flight. It made me cross. Then I landed flat on my back, about ten feet from the truck. I lay like a cast sheep for a bit. Then two things dawned on me. First, that only a mine could have done this to us. Secondly, that at any moment the petrol would blow up. So I shouted a bit.

Blast, as everyone knows, is a whimsical phenomenon. I was in fact the furthest from the actual explosion, but none of the others had been ejected. Anthony was wandering about muttering, having mysteriously concluded that the batteries had exploded. Mohammed *internationale* was to be seen dashing at enormous speed in the opposite direction. We found him later crouching like a

The vehicle that was blown up was plainly never going to move again; it was fortunate that the back wheels set off the landmine

196

rabbit in the back of the other truck. His arm had been cut. Jocelyn's only thought seemed to be for my welfare. He dragged me away from the truck and assured me that everything was all right. Indeed, the petrol did not catch fire.

Tim who had been following in the other truck immediately concluded that we must all be dead. Neglecting his duty as a photographer, he came to worry about us.

Within minutes a dozen soldiers appeared. They stood at some distance beyond the ridge and shouted useful things like, 'You shouldn't be in there,' and 'Don't move.' They eventually explained that we were in a minefield. There were many more big mines and plenty of anti-personnel mines all round us. It appeared to be something of a predicament. On the other hand, we had been wandering about quite a lot without setting anything else off. One of the braver soldiers risked joining us in order to advise us as to what to do. The truck which was blown up was plainly never going to move again. Our possessions had been flung out of the back so that it looked like a cornucopia of bedding and food. We rescued what we could in our rather dazed condition. The remaining truck had only two seats. I sat in the passenger seat and Anthony drove. We had to back out precisely along the tracks we had made coming in. The others walked in the wheel marks. It was a tense little drive, in reverse all the way, wondering whether there would be another explosion and another flight through the air.

We got out just in time to see one of the iron ore trains coming down to the coast. It was the longest train I have ever seen, perhaps a mile long, and a startling sight chugging through the empty dunes.

The repercussions, as one might say, of the incident of the landmine were both tedious and comic. The military did not know whether to be angry or sympathetic. They attempted to suggest that we had no business to be travelling in this direction. I countered this by reminding them that under the Geneva Convention it is obligatory to fence off a minefield and to mark it with danger signs every twenty-five metres. 'There is no call for a sign,' said the Brigadier, 'because everyone knows where it is.' Not quite everyone, I thought.

Their real problem was that they did not know much about the minefield. The Brigadier, explaining why we were not allowed to go back to collect more possessions, said, 'We have no plan of the field, because we did not lay the earlier mines. Of course we know where ours are.' I said I had never heard of anyone's laying a new minefield on the top of an old one to which they had no key. The Brigadier shrugged.

One official said the mines were laid by the Moroccans at the time when Mauritania and Morocco were allies and were busy seizing and dividing between them the de-colonised Spanish Sahara. Another told me that they were laid by the Polisario (the nationalist army of the Spanish Sahara, which is now called the Western Sahara). Mauritanians are never too sure which side they are on.

The Moroccans, with their idea of a greater Morocco encompassing all the Western Sahara and the whole of Mauritania and parts of Algeria and Mali, are the traditional bogey enemy. Yet I saw a group of forty-five Moroccan teachers arrive in Nouakchott to teach at the university. Ever since the military coup in 1978, and a Polisario display of force in the very capital, they have nominally been on the side of the Polisario. Mariem mint Derwich's father, for instance, is fighting with them. It is a question of trying to please everybody.

It took a few days trying to sort out our arrangements. Much of the time I spent in bed. To my bedside came army officers, police, gendarmerie – representatives of every conceivable authority. Each department asked me for a statement. When the fifth official came and sat down and asked me my name, my nationality ... I lost my temper and told him he was an idiot and that Mauritania was a hopelessly run country and would he go away and let me alone.

He arrested me. My companions assured him that I was delirious, possibly insane and quite probably on my deathbed. He would have none of it. '*Tu es arrêté. Ne bouge pas.*' I told him I had no intention of moving and succumbed to helpless giggles, which did not help. Half an hour later the Chief of Police of Nouadhibou appeared. The others tried to keep him from me, assuring him that my only hope was a long course of psychoanalysis. He paid no attention. He stood at the foot of my bed. 'Did you or did you not say that Mauritania does not exist?' he demanded with great solemnity. I nearly got the giggles again, particularly when I saw Tim's and Jocelyn's agonised faces, dreading my reply. However, I was in fact so relieved that I could give an absolutely honest answer that I gave the Chief of Police a most positive assurance that I never had said nor ever would say something so manifestly absurd. Three times he asked. Three times I gave my word. And he marched smiling from my room. Within ten minutes the original official returned. 'What is your name ...' Under Tim's stern eye, I went obediently through the catechism.

We abandoned the shattered Unimog. I flew with Tim and Jocelyn to Dakar. Anthony, Mohammed and a visiting friend drove the other Unimog to meet us. At every stop on the way, Mohammed *internationale* jumped out, exhibiting his bandaged arm and recounting tales of his bravery in the 'great explosion'.

As soon as they arrived in Dakar, Jocelyn crashed the remaining Unimog irreparably. There was nearly an ugly scene as I was still aching from the effects of the explosion, and when Jocelyn arrived with the news of the crash, he also chose that moment to remind me that I owed him £20. After two weeks of almost incredible bureaucratic confusion I managed to buy two Land Rovers.

OPPOSITE, The desert comes right down to the Atlantic on the Mauritanian coast, which was unexplored fifty years ago

TOP, Cap Timiris: a young boy beats the surface of the sea to call the dolphins

ABOVE, Men and dolphins swim side by side, each working to the other's advantage

We had abandoned any idea of trying to go north through the Western Sahara. Instead we headed east, with the whole Sahara stretching to the Nile or even the Red Sea, spread out before us. We followed the main road back towards Nema and then branched off a little northward to go to Tidjikja.

Tidjikja is the sixth or seventh largest town in Mauritania, but there was no indication of any sort as to where we should leave the main road to reach it. There are no signposts in the desert, as people seemingly never go anywhere that they do not know. In Boutlimit there was a police post. Moktar, the sergeant, offered us tea and when he heard we were English repeated over and over again, 'Margaré Tatcha, la reine Elizabeth'. (The Mauritanians appeared to be much interested in our royal family and even issued a stamp to commemorate the Prince of Wales' wedding.) When I asked Moktar where the turning for Tidjikja was, he gave one of those indeterminate waves, ending with a leftward flick.

We found the way somehow (Mohammed had gone home to Timbuctoo from Dakar) and travelled through wonderfully varied desert – at first flat hard sand with thorn bushes, then soft dunes with sands of different colours, from dark red to pure white. We were not yet used to the Land Rovers. The Unimogs had been able to get almost anywhere but they were slow. In soft sand they would grind through it laboriously. The Land Rovers, if one judged it right, would fly over the surface of quite soft sand, but might get into disconcerting swinging rhythms and feel as if they were going to overturn. I was quite relieved when we reached Moujeria, a lonely village at the bottom of a steep escarpment. Just before the village the dunes are extremely tricky to drive through. Clusters of rocks have been set down to give wheels something to grip on, but the rocks sink or are buried. There are ten bulldozers to try to keep the sand back. If the sand wins this battle, Tidjikja and several important oases will be inaccessible except by air or by camel.

At the top of the escarpment we came into one of those plateaus of burnt rock. Then the track swooped down into a beautiful valley at Nbeika, with a pretty pool of water under huge trees. It was a road of infinite variety, ending with a large natural rock gateway from which one can look down on Tidjikja – a tightly clustered town at the edge of a large wadi, with several miles of palm groves reaching out into the distance. One of the most unexpected delights of the desert is to stand above a town and listen to it. There are no mechanical noises, just an agglomeration of voices – like listening to a happy party.

Tidjikja was immensely busy, much livelier than any other town we had seen in Mauritania. The women wore bright colours, rather than the eternal indigo used by most Moorish women. The children were excited and surprised by the sight of foreigners. They crowded round pestering us and asking endless questions. They also demanded presents. 'Il faut me donner du gâteau,' one little boy insisted over and over again.

My plan was to drive on to Tichit, a distance of a hundred and forty miles. I had, as usual, been told both that the way was difficult and that it was easy. We canvassed opinion around the market place. There were two Egyptian school-teachers who said that a guide was quite unnecessary. The track ran through a valley the whole way and one could not get lost. An old man offered to come with us, but all around shook their heads by way of warning. A sensible-looking young man assured me that it was folly to go without someone who knew the way well. I decided to consult the Governor of the region.

Governor Ba received us in a large room of his residence. It had carpets covering the whole floor. There were six or seven mattresses, a radio and a cassette player, but nothing else in the room. Ba is a small, alert but world-weary looking man of about thirty-five. He told me that he had just come back from a trip round Europe. He was, he said, much travelled, having previously been to America.

He suggested that we camp in his compound as we would otherwise be plagued by the children of the town. We thanked him and he then asked if we would take the Préfet of Tichit's driver with us and a hundred and fifty litres of petrol. We agreed, although we were already vastly overloaded as we had at the time two young English girls from Dakar with us, who had come for a brief holiday.

I was puzzled that no tea was brought and was uncertain as to how long we should stay. The Governor told us how bored he was in Tidjikja, but he did not seem much interested in anything. So we left. We camped in his compound, but we did not see him again that day. He sat alone in his gloomy house.

Wandering round the town, we ran into a soldier called Ahmed who told us he came from Tichit. I understood him to say that he had fifteen days leave of which he had already used up seven in getting to Tidjikja. The bus-truck in which he was travelling had broken down. He could not transfer to another because his ticket had been clipped. There was no transport going to Tichit. He had heard we were going there. Could we take him?

There was no possibility of taking him as well as the chauffeur and the petrol. Then the chauffeur, Baba, came and asked for a forty-pound fee for guiding us. This so incensed me that in the morning I went to the Governor and asked whether it was essential for the chauffeur to go, provided we took the petrol.

Ba looked coldly at me and said that he would not impose his will on me. Of course, the spirit of Mauritania was that if the state needed something, one gave it gladly. If one had said one would do something, one did it. I replied that I understood perfectly the spirit of Mauritania as he saw it. The spirit of Great Britain was perhaps a little different – compassionate, for example, towards a soldier who had not seen his family for nine months. But I was in Mauritania, so I would take the chauffeur, who dared to ask to be paid for a lift, and leave the soldier. Ba was quite unmoved by such pomposity.

Then it turned out that they had no containers for petrol. They had hoped to use mine. I had no intention of undertaking what I expected to be a four- or five-hundred-mile journey without the maximum amount of petrol that I could carry.

'If you can't take the petrol, you will be able to take your precious soldier,' Ba said acidly.

Ba, I concluded, was a thoroughly second-rate little man, presumably the beneficiary of some corruption. He was the only person in the entire Sahara who did not offer us any token of hospitality. He strutted about in a western business suit, which was wonderfully inappropriate and, I should have thought, rather offensive to the local population. More to the point he knew little about his job and his region was ill-run. The hospital, the only medical facility for hundreds of miles, was not open. For most of the day he did nothing but sit listening to his western tapes of bad popular music.

The odious Baba turned up with at least a hundred pounds of luggage, which he assured me was for the Préfet of Tichit.

The journey was beautiful. For some way we travelled down the wadi. At one point it narrowed to a gorge with cliffs on either side. Where it widened out again was a lush place where a shadoof, the oldest kind of water-lifting gear, was used to irrigate the rich crop of vegetables. Then the way climbed to a rocky plain and later plunged down a steep incline into almost pure sand which stretched for nearly a hundred miles to Tichit, broken only by patches of grassy tussocks and a little scrub. The whole journey from the main road to Tichit was the epitome of what people imagine the Sahara to be like.

At the steep incline, we met a lorry which was having great difficulty getting up the hill. While everyone pushed and shouted, I talked to one of the passengers on the lorry. He lived at Tichit.

'I will be back in five days,' he said. 'You must wait and I will show you a place where there is gold. As much gold as you could want. And you can take it. But in this place there are also devils. So many devils. But if you are good, really, really good, you can beat the devils and take the gold. But if you are even a little bit bad, the devils will win.' He did not have time to tell me what that would entail, as they had managed to get the lorry to the top of the hill.

Tichit sits on the edge of a long range of hills which runs all the way to Walata, some two hundred miles to the south-east. Four or five thousand years ago these hills formed the shore-line of an enormous lake, which is now a depression known as the Aouker. Along the edge of this lake there were highly populated prehistoric settlements. It is thought that as many as three hundred thousand people may have lived in the caves and stone-built villages along the cliffs of the Dhar Tichit. They were a prosperous people, owning large herds of cattle. They kept grain in huge earthenware pots, just as the people near the Niger do today. All along this range one can pick up from the sand mortars and pestles, axe heads and exquisite arrow heads. As one would expect, there are rock carvings of warthogs, leopard and other wild animals.

The modern town of Tichit, which was founded in about the twelfth century, commands a fine view over the huge dunes of the Aouker. Like the prehistoric villages, it is built entirely of stone without mortar. According to legend the town has been rebuilt seven times, but what actually has happened is that when a house falls down, which is quite frequently, they built another on the rubble. The tower of the mosque, about fifteen feet square and sixty feet high was rebuilt, with amazing skill, only three years ago. There was a house being built while we were there. It was of average size, which is to say that it was going to have four or five rooms. There were twenty-five stonemasons working on it. They said it would take a month to build and would need fifteen thousand stones.

There are three quarries from which they get the stone. One has red stone, one almost white and the other a blue-grey, like slate. Some of the houses are built with red and blue-grey in broad stripes. Many of the rooms have triangular, rectangular and arched niches, apparently of the same patterns as those in the excavated houses in Koumbi Saleh. Théodore Monod describes the architecture as being manifestly Berber in style, uncontaminated by hispano-moorish influences. Certainly, there is absolutely no reason why anyone should ever go to Tichit and so it has preserved its customs in virtual isolation. The French did not even come here until 1949 and the prefecture was not built until the early 1950s less than ten years before independence.

The people of Tichit are predominantly black, belonging to a group called Masna, who speak Aouker, a southern dialect unknown elsewhere. The population is said to be seven thousand, but as at Walata I found this impossible to believe. The population of the region is put at 37,000.

We arrived at the prefecture which stands on high ground overlooking the village. The Préfet, Ibrahim Boumédienne, came out to greet us. He is a very tall, thin man with a small beard. He has a kindly face that melts into a mildly embarrassed grin. He invited us to stay in his house for as long as we liked. He was the very opposite of Governor Ba.

We unloaded the luggage including the heavy boxes which Baba had brought. He had behaved extremely tiresomely on the journey, so we played out a childish charade by way of relieving our feelings. Baba protested when we took his boxes off. Couldn't we take them in the car down the hill to his house? No, no, we said. Didn't he remember he had brought them for the Préfet? We must give them to the Préfet. Baba had to hump them home himself.

The prefecture is a large building. Most of the rooms open onto a wide enclosed passageway which runs round two sides of the building. The Préfet gave us two rooms. There were six of us with the two girls from Dakar.

The Préfet proved to be the most charming, if rather distant host. He never ate

Ibrahim Boumédienne, Préfet of Tichit

with us, but he would send us delicacies such as camel hump and liver. His roguish Senegalese cook, Sidi, took advantage of this situation. He would tell us there was nothing for dinner, so we would buy rice or whatever. Then the Préfet would send us something. The next day Sidi would give us some awful millet. Where is the rice? 'Lost,' said Sidi. You cannot lose rice, we said. *'Eh bien, c'était un cadeau.'*

When we had eaten, the Préfet would come to talk to us. He was an educated man and had been to the university in Nice for three years in the early 1970s. He, like Governor Ba, felt lonely and cut off in Tichit, but his attitude was quite the reverse of the Governor's. He had a lot of time on his hands, because although he had been in his post for nearly two months he had been quite unable to leave Tichit itself to make a tour of his region. In the first place, he had no petrol for his Land Rover. The alternative, which for some inaccessible areas was essential, was to borrow twelve camels from the military, but this so far he had been unable to do.

He had decided to write a *'dossier'*, as he called it, on Tichit. The difficulty here was that the man in charge of the library refused to let him borrow any of the books. He could look at them in the library, but not take them to the prefecture. This would, I gathered, have been somehow beneath his dignity. 'Of course, I could order him to let me have them, but that would be far too drastic.' He was rather engagingly sensible of his power, but quite modest. When I asked him on arrival whether there was anyone to whom we should report, he had replied, '*Non. Içi c'est moi qui est l'état.*' It was said with his enigmatic smile, and I could not be sure whether the words had any historical echo for him or not.

He seemed to give up a shade easily on his '*dossier*', but while we were there the ninety-year-old librarian was away camping in the desert. I also suspect that the Préfet was not truly academic by nature. He described things which were eight hundred years old as prehistoric and thought the nineteenth century mosque immensely ancient. His background was purely nomadic. His family had suffered severely during the drought. His father lost one hundred and fifty cows and two hundred and fifty camels in the worst year.

The Préfet had a great national pride, but without any great hope for the future of the country. The resources of Mauritania are too few. Apart from the iron ore, the major products are salt, gum arabic and camels. The salt comes mainly from the area between Nouakchott and the Senegal border at Rosso. The gum arabic, which is used locally as a panacea, is extracted from the acacias in the south. Camels are bred everywhere. The number of camels born every year is in the region of one million. In Tichit alone ten are killed every day. A moderate camel is worth about two hundred and fifty pounds. A rich nomad may own several hundred. The Préfet told me a story about a man who took water by train from Nouadhibou to his herd of nine hundred camels near Choum. With the possible exception of the iron ore, there is a dwindling market for all these products.

If the prospect for Mauritania is gloomy, it is even less promising for Tichit. While its extinction is not so imminent as that of Walata, it does seem inevitable. The palm groves yield reasonable dates. Not long ago, a company was formed to try to market the dates commercially. It failed. The packaging and transport problems proved to be too great. Beneath the palms, the people grow tomatoes, lettuce and mint. In some years, they can grow carrots but, at the time of our visit, there had been absolutely no rain for over a year so it was not possible. In the past there were grain fields, but now hardly any remain and the yields from them are negligible. There are some local salt deposits, but the salt is of very inferior quality and is used only for animals.

Despite all that, the Préfet did not seem unduly downcast, nor in any particular hurry to rectify his country's problems. He spent the whole of one afternoon, quite contentedly, watching Baba tinker ineffectively with his Land Rover.

We offered to take the Préfet on an expedition to see some rock carvings beyond Akrejit, about twenty-five miles along the Dhar Tichit. Ahmed, the soldier, had given us a chicken by way of thanking us for bringing him home. He mentioned that his father was a guide. His father was tall and thin and appeared very old. He wore a long, heavy overcoat. Despite that he could walk as spryly as any of our party and could climb the cliffs more rapidly. Ahmed's father spoke no French and rather halting Hassanic Arabic. Nevertheless he and the Préfet between them managed to exchange more misinformation about the not very interesting carvings than I could have thought possible.

At Akrejit itself, a small settlement with a nineteenth-century fort, the Préfet went off to do some business with the local leader. Tim and I had tea with a sad man called Mahmoud, who had lost his few beasts that year because of the shortage of grazing. Now he had decided that he must find a job perhaps in Tidjikja or, worse still, in Nouakchott. What job could such a man find, who had done nothing all his life except tend his meagre flocks?

He was by no means unintelligent. I noticed an empty can of soya bean oil in his house. On it were the words: 'Furnished by the people of America. Part of the World Food Project'. I asked him if he knew that it was a present from the Americans to him? 'A present to the government of Mauritania,' he said, 'but not a present to me. I have to buy it.' (We often saw aid of this sort being misused. In Agadez there were sacks of sorghum, with the same legend, being offered openly for sale.)

As we were leaving the next day, we offered to take Mahmoud to Tidjikja. Apart from anything else, I was not absolutely sure that we would be able to find our way back easily, as the wind would have wiped out all our tracks.

On our way back to Tichit we passed a caravan of about two hundred camels. The Préfet said there were still occasionally trains of a thousand, heading towards Senegal. Only that morning he had signed *laisser passés* for four hundred and fifty in three different groups. They were beautiful. When camels are bunched together, their long, long legs look like young trees in a spinney, swaying and crossing in the wind. Their heads like huge snakes have a purposeful air. They seem to know where they are going, in a way that horses and cattle never do. Their sedate, silent movement over the surface of the sand has a touching, timeless quality.

For as long as man can survive in the desert, the camel will survive with him.

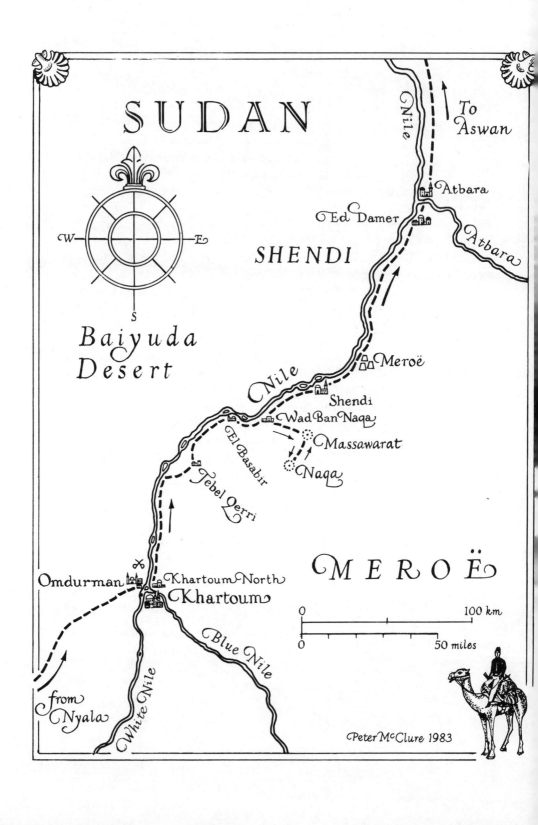

SUDAN

SHENDI

Baiyuda
Desert

Nile

MEROË

To
Aswan

Atbara

Ed Damer

Atbara

Meroë

Shendi

Wad Ban Naqa

Massawarat

El Basabir

Naqa

Jebel Qerri

Omdurman   Khartoum North
Khartoum

Blue Nile

from
Nyala

White Nile

0   100 km

0   50 miles

Peter McClure 1983

9

DERVISHES AND PYRAMIDS

W E THEN embarked on a long, long diversion. I suppose there are few people who have driven from Dakar to Cairo via Kano, Calabar, Bangui and Khartoum. Perhaps there is some obscure merit in the doing of it, but that sort of thing has no appeal for me. In any case, it was not what I had set out to do.

My original plan had been to go through Chad up to the Tibesti mountains, where the cave paintings are finer even than those in the Tassili; then to take a broad sweep round Libya and make my way to western Sudan; go to Khartoum and travel down the Nile; and finally to launch out into the western desert of Egypt. This, I soon realised, was impossible. The Libyans were both irritating and unreasonable. In London they told me to get visas in Tunis. In Tunis they asked why we had not got them in London. There was no question of driving around on one's own. No unmarried woman under thirty-five would be admitted and a married woman would have to travel with her husband. Anyone could come to Libya, they said, provided he had an invitation from an official source. So it went. In short, the country is closed to anyone who might just want to go out of interest.

This was a bitter disappointment. Leptis Magna, the whole Fezzan, Murzuk, Ghadames, Ghat. So much Saharan history has taken place in Libya and we could not see it. Once again, the only way a traveller can go there is in the way that René Caillié travelled, by camel, disguised as an Arab. Libya had been accessible for barely a hundred years.

Chad, of course, had a war. We got visas easily enough, but the Tibesti, which contains some of the few virtually unexplored regions of the world, was the centre of the fighting. The road through Abeche towards the Sudan was said to be mined. I judged that one mine was enough for one year. Furthermore, there was said to be absolutely no petrol for any purpose. Chad, then, is another closed country. The German explorer, Nachtigal, was almost the only visitor to Chad in the nineteenth century. The French did not really occupy the country until 1929. Chad had been accessible for barely fifty years.

Sadly, we abandoned any hope of going through either Libya or Chad. Rather than return to Niamey the same way that we had come, we swept southward in order to see Djenné and Mopti and to pass through the Dogon country. En route we encountered the Paris to Dakar rally.

Cars of all kinds rush through villages which otherwise see perhaps only two or three vehicles a week. People of many nations completely ignore the ones they are passing through. They scatter orange-coloured cardboard luncheon boxes as they race past a cluster of huts. Amazed children, their bellies swollen with hunger, gaze listlessly at this incredible display of affluence. 'I am in a hurry,' the drivers say in half a dozen different languages, addressing people who have no notion what a hurry is. They grab food from a market stall and throw half-eaten tomatoes away.

Is it priggish to think this offensive? Or do the people enjoy it – a spectacle, something they have never seen before? Is it fun perhaps? I am glad when it is over.

We stop at Bourko, a beautiful village in the mountains not far from Mopti.

Quentin was arrested but Tim got this photograph

There is a stream with a ford. A baobab stands at the stream's edge. This is what the Aïr must have been like, not all that long ago. But it will go. The desert will encroach. Between here and the Niger at Gao, the old guide book promises us elephants, lions, ostriches. They are not there.

It is four months since we were at Gao. On the ferry over the Niger I have my passport taken away by a policeman, because I tell him to leave Tim alone as he is getting a photograph which will disappear if he pauses to show his photographic permission. Bagna Touré is so pleased to see us again that he soon has my passport back.

At the Niger border, poor Boureima Guindo still has his *maladie sexuelle*, but we shake hands in a sad farewell to the western Sahara.

To reach the Sudan, we had to cross Nigeria, Cameroon and the Central African Republic. What might have been agreeable would have been to have driven across the northern parts of these countries, which are comparatively little visited and which, at least, have some connection with the Sahara. This idea was frustrated by bureaucracy. While each of the countries we had to pass through had a consulate in the country next to it, none of them had a consulate further afield. To get from one country to the next, we had to go to the consulate in the next-door country. All the consulates were in the south of all three countries.

No journey through strange countries is without its pleasures, its surprises and, above all, its comedy. Rose rejoined us at Kano. Her aeroplane arrived at four in the morning. We laid out our sleeping bags in the car park to wait for her. The mosquitoes were ferocious, so we put up nets. The car park guard came over and asked if we intended to sleep there. Rather sheepishly we said yes, expecting to be told to move. 'Sleep well,' he said, 'I will watch over you very carefully.'

Kano was awful, I thought. Nothing but hideous, hooting traffic jams. I thought of Buchanan, sixty years ago, setting off on his long trek. This was the terminus of the caravan routes in his day. Now only a few walls of the old city remain. Otherwise you might be in some ghastly industrial town in any poor country.

South of Jos, a customs man waved us down. We had long since given up being puzzled at finding customs posts in the very middle of countries. He wanted to see our passports and carnets for the cars. This had already presented problems. In Senegal, where I had bought the Land Rovers, no-one had heard of carnets – a convenient system which enables one to take a car through a country without any customs formalities. A carnet is a kind of bond, guaranteeing that one will re-export the car.

I explained that we had no carnets, but that at the Nigerian border, the kind customs chief had given us a temporary importation certificate. 'That is not legal. You will go back under escort to Illela.' But that is eight hundred miles.

Could we perhaps go to Jos, fifty miles back, and discuss the matter with the chief there? 'No.'

He looked implacably at me and I thought it time for a little boasting. 'I am a member of an international organisation authorised by the United Nations. They will be distressed to hear how I have been received in Nigeria.'

He thought for a while, as we sat sweating in the sun. 'I believe you. I believe you are a member of an international organisation. I say that you may go on. The others and the cars will go back to Illela.'

We pondered this arrangement for a while. We all pictured my wheeling myself alone over the next four hundred miles to Calabar. Somehow we managed not to laugh. We decided to say nothing more, but just to wait. He wandered off, telling his minions to watch us. Twenty minutes passed. Then he came back. 'You may all go.' We smiled, shook hands vigorously all round and left. We had learnt a lot in a year.

The first night that we reached real jungle, we were much exercised as to where to camp. As we went through a small town called Obudu, a Land Rover raced after us. When we stopped, two Frenchmen jumped out and asked us to stay with them. They were road builders. Their road was finished, most of their companions had gone and they wanted company. So we stayed in the luxury of their camp. The following day they took us up the road they had built. It climbed at first through the steamy vegetation of the jungle, but soon through steep, wooded valleys where rushing streams tumbled down rocky gorges and wild, red, flame trees glowed on the hillsides. Beside the road, at one point, there was a huge forest fire. Round the edge of the flames, swooping through the smoke, hawks circled, waiting to pounce on small creatures escaping from the blaze. After less than an hour we came out onto rolling grassland, like English downs. Here there was a cattle ranch and a garden where strawberries grew. It was cool and gloriously nostalgic. It must be one of the more amazing contrasts one can achieve in so short a time.

We got our Cameroon visas in Calabar. The border is not far and it is a satisfactory border. After crossing a bridge the road narrows and, for some reason, the jungle is suddenly full of brilliantly coloured butterflies. The people, all at once, are immensely helpful. As one drives through a village, the children rush forward all shouting with a rhythmic cry. Eventually one distinguishes it as, 'Welcome, welcome, welcome'.

This part of Cameroon was, before independence, British – although it was originally a German colony. It had been thought that it would naturally, on independence, join up with English-speaking Nigeria. A referendum, rather lackadaisically undertaken, showed an absolute determination to join with the French Cameroons. The result has been wonderfully successful. The children, particularly in the formerly British section, learn both English and French and are proud of it.

It always happened that we arrived at the places with consulates at the weekend and therefore had to waste days waiting for the offices to open. To avoid this in Yaoundi, the Cameroon capital, we stayed by the sea at Victoria, under Mount Cameroon.

Victoria is extraordinarily German in appearance. Wandering along the coast, back towards Nigeria, we came upon the ruins of German houses, grand places with large, pretentious porticos. The jungle twisted round the pillars, soon no doubt to pull them down. They might have been ruined Mexican temples. Hidden in the courtyard of one was the remains of a pre-war Buick, concealed by its German owner perhaps hoping to find it again when Hitler triumphed.

At Idenau, by the mouth of a river, there is a palm oil factory, a superb Heath Robinson affair. One ancient steam engine, driving a complicated system of innumerable belts, works dozens of machines for shelling, crushing, cooking, stirring and straining the palm nuts. Anthony spent hours peering at all this weird machinery. Meanwhile, a mile further on, we found a small, empty swimming pool. It had been for a group of German settlers. At the far end of the pool, rather roughly scored into the concrete edge, is a swastika and a date – 2 September 1939. It was somehow ironic to think that on the day after they finished their pool, the war which was to lose them their possessions began.

We came into the Central African Republic near Bouar. It was a typical introduction to that wretched country. Whoever was driving stopped the car just after the stop sign, but well short of the frontier barrier. As we went into the frontier post, the man at the desk said, 'For a start that will be eight pounds for driving past a stop sign.' 'Eight pounds for each vehicle that is,' said the man behind him.

That's all right, we said. Make out a receipt. 'Only the commandant can issue receipts. He is not here.' We will wait. 'He will not be back till three this afternoon.' It was ten in the morning. Never mind, we said. We can wait. We are tired and hungry. We will make a nice picnic and have a welcome rest.

Ten minutes later they came out and said we could go on. They had incidentally blithely accepted our Cameroon temporary importation certificate instead of a carnet. We really *had* learnt a lot in a year.

Our journey from Bangui northward to the Sudan was in many ways the worst part of the whole year. After the first few hundred miles, the road became little more than a stream bed. There were a few pleasant hours in the morning, when the ghastly damp of the night had dried out. The sun slanted through the jungle trees and the butterflies danced in the beams of light. In the afternoon there were biting flies which invaded the cars in their hundreds. They had needle sharp proboscides which inflicted a yelping pain, even through thick clothes. There was no evening spring in the jungle. Even before the flies gave up, the mosquitoes started. The nights were sodden.

The narrow road was so deeply rutted that we had to drive with one wheel in a rut and the other in the centre of the track. On several occasions, the Land Rovers tipped so far over that we had to walk beside them pushing on the side to prevent the car from scraping along the wall of the sunken road. It was frightening and exhausting.

Villages were few, though the people were friendly, offering to sell us skinned monkeys to eat. I rather liked the village custom, which I had first noticed in Cameroon, of burying people by the hut in which they lived. Just outside the door of a mud hut there might be an elaborate tombstone, with a goat lying on it. Death is very much accepted as a part of the natural cycle. The other custom of great charm was the decoration of the mud walls of houses. Often there were pictures of lions, or of people. Less frequently there were large aeroplanes, painted in primitive style. It was a long time before I discovered that these were put on by people who had been on a pilgrimage to Mecca.

In the north of the Central African Republic, petrol was running short. There were, as always, varying reports about the fuel situation in the Sudan. One person said there was none. Another, who had just come from there, said there was plenty. We had nearly enough to get us to Nyala, one hundred and eighty miles beyond the border. I bought a few gallons at five pounds a gallon. The merchant who sold me the petrol had travelled all over the central part of Africa. He had even been to Nouakchott. 'Only an eighter,' he said. It turned out that he judged towns by the number of storeys in their tallest buildings. 'Nairobi is a forty-twoer, the best town in Africa.' At the same time he encouraged us with his non-architectural opinion that, 'The Sudanese are the nicest people in Africa.'

That night we slept just beyond Birao, about an hour's drive short of the border. At last we were out of the jungle and back in Sahel country, with masses of acacias, Abyssinian rollers, sandy patches and beautifully dry air. We slept without mosquito nets again and lay looking at the tiny holes in the gazelle's tent.

Soon after we lay down for the night, I heard some slight sounds – a gentle creaking, then a soft breathing and some whispered words. Fifty yards from where we lay, a small train of twelve camels was passing in the moonlight. The ropes round their burdens creaked and the animals snorted softly. Three or four men were guiding them through the night. They were probably smugglers. Silently they padded on and I went to sleep feeling that at last I was home again.

We left the Central African Republic in the morning. The way ran past a large stretch of water. Herons and cranes waded in the lake and near the edge great, ground hornbills lumbered along. We drove up to the Sudanese customs post with a fine flourish and got stuck in the sand. We were out of practice after nearly three months away from the desert.

At once our merchant friend was proved right. The Sudanese officials, after so many disagreeable bureaucrats, were polite and helpful. It was a second home-coming.

The contrast between Birao and Umm Dafog is the difference between black Africa and the Sahara. Despite the painted aeroplanes, we had been passing through primarily Christian country. A small village might have two or even three rival mission churches. Now we were in a purely Islamic atmosphere. It was more alive, busier, more humorous, certainly more to my taste.

Was there any petrol? 'No, *malish*. There is bound to be petrol at Rahad el Berdi, *inshallah*.'

We were not very worried. We could reach Nyala, a reasonably big town, provided we did not get lost. We got lost almost at once. We went about twenty miles out of our way, then we went through a long stretch of heavy sand. After that, we had no hope of reaching Nyala on the petrol we had left. We camped in a beautiful place where a family of parrots, the first we had seen, chattered in some tall palms. In the morning we came to a large village, the name of which I have forgotten. The district official received us with great courtesy. When we asked for petrol he said there was none, but his monthly allowance of twenty gallons had just arrived. He would give us four gallons. When I protested (rather feebly) he said it was his duty. He would have liked to give us more, but we would be able to fill up at Rahad el Berdi, *inshallah*. He would not even let me pay for the four gallons.

There chanced to be an English agricultural adviser from Nyala visiting the village. He said he was going back to Nyala that evening and that he would look out for us on the way, in case we ran low on petrol. We had a merry lunch in a sort of tea shop. The young villagers came to try out their English. I felt strangely lightheaded.

At Rahad el Berdi they said they had had no petrol for several months, *malish*. We would get plenty in Nyala, *inshallah*. About twenty miles short of Nyala we stopped and camped. We reckoned that we had just enough petrol to get one car to Nyala. John Bennett, the agricultural adviser, found us and took Jocelyn into Nyala, with the idea of bringing him and some petrol back in the morning.

That night I got malaria. It had been marvellous that, with the exception of Rose's hepatitis, we had none of us had any illness. The desert is an extraordinarily healthy place. Of course, from indifferent water one may pick up some mild stomach upset, but the desert seems as inimical to germs as it is to everything else. The people of the desert, if they have enough to eat, suffer few diseases, although they have fearful eye complaints. In the oases, there is sometimes bilharzia and a certain amount of malaria in the south. Wounds heal with amazing rapidity in the dry atmosphere.

So I blamed the jungle for my malaria, though in some ways it was quite enjoyable. The world was transformed. I floated through strange mountain scenery. I was never alone. When Tim and the others left me, there was always some imagined person to whom I could talk. For a week John Bennett and his wife put up with my lying raving in their house. Meanwhile the others tried to buy petrol. There were a few gallons to be found in the *souk* (market) at twenty pounds a gallon. As we had eight hundred miles to go to Khartoum with two cars over heavy sand, it seemed a little expensive.

Once again, the local official tried to help. He could not sell us enough to get to Khartoum, but offered some which might have got us to El Obeid. In the end, we decided it was easier to accept the offer of two lorry drivers to transport the cars on their new Scania lorries, which belonged to the Water Department.

I flew ahead with Tim, while the others travelled with the cars. The two lorry drivers more than justified the opinion of the Sudanese put forward by the Birao merchant. It took a week for the lorries to go from Nyala to Khartoum. They would not allow Rose and the others to pay for even a cup of tea throughout the whole journey. They always saw that she, Anthony and Jocelyn got the best pieces of whatever they had for lunch at the wayside stalls and the best places to sleep in the huts where they spent the nights. When we all went to say goodbye to them the day after they arrived, the lorry drivers were amazed to be given presents. They were also put out because they were meant to leave that morning for Port Sudan. They were still there when we left. The Water Department could not get any diesel for the lorries.

There is a romance about Khartoum which I have always found irresistible. The events which made it famous are comparatively recent and are so easily evoked, without much straining of the imagination. I had an elderly cousin who was brought up in Cairo. He used to say he saw or, if he didn't, could have seen General Gordon on his way to Khartoum. Not long ago, then; I can never pass Gordon's palace, now the Presidential palace, overlooking the Blue Nile, without imagining that strange hero's last hours and without thinking that we have still not reached the centenary of his death.

Across the river from the palace lies the *Melik*, one of Kitchener's gunboats, still used as the headquarters of the Yacht Club. Then at Omdurman, not more than three miles away, beyond the confluence of the two Niles, there is the Mahdi's tomb which Kitchener desecrated and the Khalifa's house, now filled with relics of the battle of Omdurman.

About twenty years ago, I sat in the shade of a fig tree in a garden in Omdurman. My host was a Sudanese Field-Marshal, then nearly eighty years old. He had not fought at the battle of Omdurman, as he was only twelve at the time, but he well remembered the day, the slaughter and the searing tragedy of the day.

The Field-Marshal had made a great study of the battle. He had made beautifully detailed maps showing, first, Kitchener's progress up the Nile, then a general plan of the area of the battle, then plans of the exact positions of the Khalifa's forces, then the various actual engagements which made up the day.

He had these maps hung on a frame and, as we sat in the garden and he narrated the events of the battle, a young boy turned up the maps in order, like an advertising presentation. Every so often, the Field-Marshal would get up and, with a silver-tipped cane, point out some special detail of importance.

He told the story beautifully, with considerable drama and pathos, but curiously little rancour. As a Sudanese, his sympathies lay largely with the Khalifa, though he disliked the autocratic nature of the man and acknowledged his cruelty. As a soldier, he admired the generalship and the administrative abilities of Kitchener, though he was distressed by the savagery of the British. So as the story unfolded, he would switch sides from one to the other, in his enthusiasm for whichever leader he was speaking of.

The Field-Marshal conjured up for me the spirit of the Sudanese people in the 1880s. After a period of intelligent Governorship by Gordon from 1877 to 1879, he was succeeded by the corrupt Egyptian, Raouf Pasha, who reverted to supporting the slave traders, to permitting bribery, to the brutalities of torture, flogging and ruthless tax-collection. So it was that, early in 1881, stories began to circulate of a holy man from Abba Island, one hundred and fifty miles south of Khartoum on the White Nile near Kosti. Mohammed Ahmed ibn el Sayid Abdullah was a demagogic, religious fanatic with oratorical powers which could whip his followers to fever pitch. Soon he was preaching holy war against the corrupt Egyptians* and their infidel associates.

The Mahdi, as he was known, claimed to be a reincarnation of the Prophet. Such was his rapid rise to power that, by 1883, he had captured the important desert town of El Obeid. The British, under Gladstone's premiership, took one of their periodic stands of pretended unconcern or affected disinterest. After an Egyptian uprising which had threatened the Suez Canal, they had been forced to occupy Egypt, defeating the rebels at the battle of Tel el Kebir. They felt disinclined to involve more troops.

The Egyptians themselves raised an army with the idea of wiping out the Mahdi. They employed Colonel William Hicks of the Bombay Army to lead the expedition of eight thousand men. This army followed the Nile to El Dueim, south of Khartoum, and then turned west across the desert to El Obeid. On 5 November 1883, the Mahdi with fifty thousand men swept down on the now ragged group of men, unused to desert travel, let alone desert fighting. The ridiculous chain mail and metal helmets. which some of them wore, did nothing to help them. All but two hundred perished.

As a result of this defeat, Gordon was sent back to Khartoum with instructions to evacuate the garrison stationed there and, in essence, leave the Sudan to the Mahdi. It was this last part that he could not bring himself to do. He had imagined that he had to deal with another rebel of the kind with whom he had

---

* They called the Egyptians 'Turks' – a term still in quite common use today.

been so successful during his first stay in Khartoum. The Mahdi was a very different matter – a savage repressive fundamentalist, who instituted the death penalty for anyone who drank any alcohol or smoked any tobacco; at the same time a man who could command blind allegiance.

There is no need to rehearse the story of the siege of Khartoum and the death of Gordon on 26 January 1885; and the arrival of Sir Charles Wilson, heading the advance party of the relief force, two days too late.

British vengeance had to wait for fourteen years; but, given the legend which grew up about Gordon, it was inevitable that there would have to be wiped out what Queen Victoria said she so keenly felt – 'the *stain* left upon England. ...'

No vengeance was necessary upon the Mahdi himself. The victory over Gordon somehow undermined his spiritual fortitude. He retired almost at once to a life of debauchery in his house in Omdurman. Indoors, he abandoned the patched *jibbeh* symbolic of poverty and renunciation, which had been the uniform of himself and his followers. Instead he put on fine linen shirts and conveniently loose pants. Girls of all ages and colours pandered to his quite secular whims, as he lay on golden brocade cushions, being fanned with ostrich feathers. Only with great difficulty could his immediate advisers persuade him to get up, dress his now fat body in his patched *jibbeh* and go out to the mosque to lead the faithful in prayer.

This way of life was perhaps not pleasing to Allah. In five months the Mahdi died. He was just forty-one.

The Khalifa Abdullah, who succeeded him, was a man of quite a different character. He had no popular magic, but possibly a certain contemptuous charm. He was very much a nomad, but quite exceptionally cruel and ruthless. He managed to consolidate the power which he inherited from the Mahdi, partly by using the religious prestige of the dead leader and partly by the straightforward methods of any despot. Nevertheless the Khalifa was surrounded by enemies. The fame of the Mahdi had spread to the Middle East. There were hopes that fundamentalists in Egypt might rise as they had in Sudan. An expedition by one of the Khalifa's emirs into Egypt met with a severe defeat. The British were a thorn on his Red Sea flank, where they still held Suakin. To the south, the Abyssinian Copts harrassed his armies.

Then disease, locusts and famine struck. It was estimated that two thirds of the Sudanese population died or were killed during the fourteen years between Gordon's death and the battle of Omdurman. Of course, the Khalifa's brutalities contributed handsomely to this amazing statistic. He ordered, for instance, the amputation of the left foot and right hand of every member of a tribe which had refused to fight for him.

The decline in the power of the Khalifa (though there was no reason to suppose that he would not have survived many years) coincided with the British fear that the French might try to occupy the Sudan. It would be the natural course in the achievement of the double objective of creating a French band stretching from the west coast to the east coast of Africa and frustrating the British efforts to create a similar band from the north to the south of the continent. By 1896 the time had come for the British, under the guise of avenging the death of Gordon, to reoccupy the Sudan. Sure control of the Nile was vital to British interests. Two years before, Kitchener had become the commander (Sirdar) of the Egyptian forces at the age of thirty-four. The year before, the tentatively imperial Liberals, under Gladstone, had been replaced by the confidently imperial Conservatives, under Salisbury. This time it would be no hasty affair. No chances would be taken.

For me, on this Saharan journey, history repeated itself in a looking-glass manner. My Field-Marshal friend had long since died and, unfortunately, I had even lost the notes I made of his narrative of the battle. By chance, I fell in with Colonel Dermot Blundell of the Grenadier Guards. He was living in Omdurman for some military training purpose. Being an energetic man, he has made a particular study of the battle of Omdurman. He offered to take me out to the battlefield and explain, in situ, how the day had gone.

We drove out to the Kerreri Hills, for it was about four miles from Omdurman that the battle took place. From the top of a steep hill, called Jebel Sirkab, we looked out over the whole landscape. The Colonel, dressed in civilian clothes and wearing a straw hat with a Brigade of Guards hatband, began to sketch out the story of the events leading up to the battle.

He described the elaborate preparations which Kitchener made for the expedition into the Sudan. He had first set about building the railway south from

Colonel Dermot Blundell describes the battlefield of Omdurman

Egypt. This project was in the hands of a Canadian subaltern and the average progress was two-and-a-half miles of line completed every day. The railway was envisaged as part of a grander scheme, whereby it would run from Cairo to the Cape, through land which was all controlled by Britain. Next, Kitchener requisitioned from Thomas Cook's the steamers which they used for taking tourists up the Nile to Luxor and Aswan.

It was not until April in 1898 that Kitchener's forces met the first contingent of the Khalifa's army. The young man leading the Sudanese was the Emir Mahmoud. He attempted to outflank Kitchener. When that failed, he dug trenches and built a zeriba or stockade of thornbushes behind which his soldiers waited for Kitchener. Some of them were chained so that they could not run away. A thorn zeriba is quite an obstacle if it is high enough – particularly, as the Colonel pointed out, for Scottish troops wearing kilts. But the battle of Atbara was a short-lived affair. Covered by artillery such as the Sudanese had never dreamed of, the British troops ('the Majors and the Captains first,' said the Colonel) stormed the zeriba. Nine thousand Sudanese died, six hundred British.

The Colonel did not mention something I remember the Field-Marshal's mentioning. Kitchener rode in triumph back to the town of Berber on a white horse. There the prisoners were marched past him. In front was the handsome Mahmoud. His feet were shackled. His hands were tied behind him. Round his neck was a collar. If he paused or tripped, his captors jerked on his collar, dragging him forward. The soldiers and the people threw muck at him.

'What, meanwhile, was the Khalifa doing?' the Colonel asked rhetorically. At that moment, the desert wind blew his straw hat off. The question rang on in my head and, from twenty years before, a picture of the old Field-Marshal came back to me, asking an identical question in the same tone of voice. They were, in a way, exactly alike, these two soldiers from the opposing sides. Both loved the story of the battle, the thrill of a feat of arms. Both struggled desperately to be fair to the other side, each, unconsciously perhaps, censoring the worst excesses of his own people.

Anyhow, what the Khalifa was doing was pondering whether he should attempt to halt Kitchener at Sabaloqua. He had prepared fortifications there, the remains of which can still be seen today. It was a good position, for Sabaloqua is a cataract which forms an ideal bottleneck for a defensive position – a gorge with hills on either side. It would have put Kitchener at a considerable disadvantage. Why did he not make a stand there? Partly, perhaps, because he did not know the country. Moreover it could have been easy to cut his supply lines. 'Sadly,' that is from his point of view, 'he decided against it,' said the Colonel with great impartiality.

The Khalifa might have had a better chance if he had managed to lure Kitchener out into the desert, away from his gunboats. He did not like that idea, although his experience of desert fighting was much superior to Kitchener's, because it meant leaving Omdurman open for the infidel to walk in. He could also have fought in Omdurman itself which had earthwork fortifications along the Nile. They are still there in part. But to fight there would endanger the women and children. Omdurman at that time had a population of 400,000. 'A seething, insanitary but almost holy city, while Khartoum was a ghost town,' said the Colonel. In the event these fortifications were destroyed by Kitchener's gunboats with their six-pounders, using a new gunpowder called lyddite.

The Khalifa had another reason for choosing the battlefield that he did. It was said that the Mahdi had prophesied that the infidel would be destroyed on the hills of Kerreri. There is a suggestion that he never said this, but that it was put about that he had by British Intelligence under the guidance of Major F R Wingate.

The Colonel now explained to us the course of the battle. The Jebel Sirkab, on which we stood, was a little less than two miles due west of the place where Kitchener made his zeriba on the west bank of the Nile. Looking down, we could imagine his twenty-four thousand troops, eight thousand of them British, drawn up on the banks of the river. They had been marching since dawn. By eleven o'clock, when they hoped to camp, the temperature was already 125° in the shade and 170° in the sun.

The gunboats, commanded by three future Admirals of the Fleet – Beatty, Keppel and Hood – covered the troops. They had already attacked the Khalifa's gun emplacements and knocked a large hole in the eighty-foot dome of the Mahdi's tomb. There was certainly more scrub in the desert eighty-five years ago. The troops were able to cut enough bushes to make a satisfactory zeriba three quarters of a mile long and half a mile deep. Inside this protection they waited. Two rows of soldiers six feet apart at the front then another two rows thirty yards behind them. They had twenty-four Maxim machine guns and fifteen forty pounders. The men were armed with magazine-fed, Lee-Metford rifles which were extremely accurate over a long distance (they were still in use in the Second World War).

When darkness fell the soldiers all lay fully clothed, ready in case of a night attack. Kitchener did not really expect one, 'although I suspect everyone else did', said the Colonel. He ordered reveille for 3.40 a.m., which would give time to prepare for a dawn attack.

Meanwhile, what of the Khalifa? He had, on the morning of 1 September, when Kitchener's troops were gathering thorn bushes for the zeriba, addressed his sixty thousand warriors, in the big square before the mosque. Then he left for the desert. Every man was asked if he were joining the battle. Anyone who replied no was stabbed. There was some mild skirmishing between scouting patrols on both sides, reconnoitring in attempts to estimate each other's strength.

Much of the night the Khalifa spent trying to decide between a night attack and a postponement to the following day. The majority of his Emirs argued in favour of attacking by night. Ibrahim el Khalil was especially anxious to engage the enemy at night. The Khalifa's son, Sheik el Din was opposed to it. As he commanded the Khalifa's bodyguard and consequently had rifles, his arguments were likely to prevail. And so they did.

It was a grave mistake. Half the Dervishes★ were armed only with swords or spears, though it is true that the spears had savage fish hook barbs on them. The remaining half had captured rifles (the Hicks disaster alone had yielded fifteen thousand rifles), many of them sawn off. Their marksmanship was further hampered by their absolute refusal to lie down to shoot. Obviously, with this limited weaponry, it would have been very advantageous to have fought in the dark, hand to hand fighting in any case being more in their line.

Instead the first attacks came at five forty-five in the morning. Four miles of moving Dervishes. A guardsman who had lain grumbling in the zeriba declared that it was the best sight he had ever seen in his life. And the slaughter began. Forty shells a minute poured from the gunboats. Each shell killed twelve men. Four thousand Dervishes led by Ibrahim el Khalil, ten thousand under Osman Asrak charging across three thousand yards of open ground. The closest any Dervish got to the zeriba was four hundred yards. By half past seven, seven thousand Dervishes lay dead, strewn across the sand in their patched white *jibbeh*. Another two thousand were wounded. At this moment the British casualties were six.

It seems to me that a night attack must have succeeded at any rate to some extent. Kitchener's searchlight could only illuminate the desert for three hundred yards beyond the zeriba. If the Khalifa's men got so close from three thousand yards away, surely so many thousand men could have overrun the zeriba with only three hundred yards to cross. The Colonel assured me that historical researchers have played war games assuming a night attack. Still Kitchener wins. It may be so, but it would have been a very different victory.

Even as it was, all was not done. The Khalifa had allowed for the possibility of the failure of his first frontal attack. He wanted to draw the British out and attack them on their right flank. He still had many troops and many fine fighters, including Osman Digna, who at Tamai had performed the almost unheard of feat of breaking a British square.

Meanwhile, Kitchener made his only real mistake of the day. Thinking to cut off any chance of retreat towards Omdurman itself, he moved out the Twenty-First Lancers, including the young Winston Churchill, to perform one of the last real cavalry charges in British military history. They charged a group

---

★ Alan Moorehead points out that the word 'Dervish', used to describe the Mahdi's followers, is not accurate. It was British soldiers' slang imported from the Middle East and India. Among the Arabs the Mahdi's warriors were known as Ansar. Nevertheless the term is still widely used – e.g. by the Colonel.

of one hundred and fifty Dervishes. Suddenly there rose from a depression behind the hundred and fifty a further two thousand. The Lancers did not, indeed could not, pause. They rode on, cleaving their way through the howling Dervishes. It took ninety seconds before they emerged on the far side. Twenty-four Lancers died. Then they turned, 'drew their carbines and finished the affair,' as the Colonel put it. The Lancers had breakfast in the depression, but the Dervishes withdrew leaving some sixty dead, but many wounded.

Alas, for the Khalifa, his Emirs made more than one mistake. General Macdonald was indeed drawn out, but the Khalifa's surprise misfired. The group led by Abdullah Abu Siwa had gone too far in pursuit of a small British detachment which had escaped to the north. Then the Khalifa's half-brother Emir Yacoub, who was hiding with sixteen thousand men behind the Jebel Sirkab, hesitated. His 'fatal hesitancy', as the Colonel called it, gave Sir Hector fifteen minutes to reform. Only a handful came within two hundred yards. Then came Abdullah Abu Siwa with four hundred Baggara horsemen in the lead. They charged, but they were late. Macdonald had turned. They all died.

The battle was over by eleven thirty when Churchill wrote, 'Sir H Kitchener shut up his glasses, remarking that he thought the enemy had been given "a good dusting".'

The 'dusting' meant that twelve thousand Dervishes were dead, ten thousand wounded. The British dead numbered forty-eight. Their total of dead and wounded was barely more than four hundred.

It is hard to find excuses for Kitchener's behaviour after the battle. The Colonel made none, admitting quite frankly that, as the British went towards Omdurman, they killed the wounded on the sand. Many of them were crawling towards the Nile in the hope of finding water.

I remember the Field Marshal's struggle to keep his indignation at bay when recounting the story of the end of the battle. He drew my attention to Winston Churchill's strange and uncharacteristic view of surrender. Many of the Dervishes offered to surrender but according to Churchill there is no obligation in war to accept a man's surrender, provided you make it plain to him that he should fight on. Quite how this was done is not clear, but the offers of surrender were refused.

The explanation given at the time for the killing of the wounded was that the Dervishes had a trick of pretending to be dead and that when you passed an apparently dead body, it would jump up and stab you. It seems hardly likely that they would lie doggo for twenty-four hours. But the British were still killing the wounded the next day.

The Field-Marshal, I recall, explained that in an ordinary battle the number of wounded usually exceeds the number of dead by about three times. At Omdurman the number of dead exceeded the wounded. It is comforting that soldiers on both sides have since become much more civilised.

Kitchener, of course, may have been an exceptional case. There was something exceedingly vicious in his treatment of the Mahdists. He made his headquarters in the mosque and he desecrated the Mahdi's tomb, digging up his body and throwing his skeleton into the Nile. He kept the skull, having some idea of turning it into an inkstand. This aroused general horror and prompted Queen Victoria, in a mood of royal trade unionism, to express herself much shocked, pointing out that the Madhi had been, after all, 'a person of a certain importance'.

Immediately after the battle Kitchener went south to Fashoda where he exhibited the other side of his character. It was at Fashoda that Capitaine Marchand had set up a French outpost and it was him that the Marquis de Morès had hoped to join up with, when he set out to offer support to the Mahdi. Now that the Mahdists were finished, it was time to put an end to any pretentions the French might have in the Sudan. With considerable tact Kitchener established a British post beside the French one. The French Government, unwilling to get involved in any serious conflict with the British, ordered Marchand to withdraw. The dreams of men like de Morès were finally over. The western Sahara would for the next sixty years be French and the eastern Sahara British, with, for a brief time, an Italian buffer in Tripolitania.

While the maps of the Sudan are the best in the whole Sahara, the tracks are somehow more difficult to find. As soon as one deviates from a main route, it is imperative to work with a compass bearing. Otherwise one gets lost. As we had only just enough petrol to reach Egypt, we could make few diversions. At the same time, I very much wanted to see the ruins left by the people of Meroë – an early civilisation of people whom Herodotus called 'Ethiopians', meaning 'burnt faces'.

Herodotus tells us that the Persian king Cambyses sent spies to find the Table of the Sun in the land of the Ethiopians. This table was famous as it was in the middle of a meadow and it was huge and spread with large quantities of meat, which were replenished every night by the magistrates. It is hard to guess at the origin of such an improbable tale, but Meroë itself was very real and important.

The Meroïtic civilisation lasted from the sixth century BC until 350 AD. Remarkably little is known about it. Various classical writers provide little sidelights. Diodorus Siculus describes their ritual murder of their kings by the priests, which continued until King Ergamenes, a contemporary of Ptolemy II in Egypt, staged an early military coup, persuading the army to kill the priests instead of him. Strabo, writing in 7 BC, said they ate millet, from which they also made a drink. (A millet drink called *marisa* is still made in Shendi, the nearest town to the pyramids of Meroë.) Pliny wrote of Meroë, saying it was ruled by a Queen Candace. Juvenal said the women of Meroë had breasts bigger than fat babies.

Recent researches indicate that the people were brown-skinned with sharp features, rather Mediterranean in looks with some negroid traces – much the same as the people of Nubia today. They had tribal markings on their faces, enlivened with blue tattooing. They bred cattle and raised crops. It seems that they mostly fought with bows and arrows and spears. No relics of swords have been found, although there is one representation of a sword in the Sun Temple at Meroë. (There is some speculation that it may have been the antecedent of the Twareg sword.) Despite this, they worked a lot with iron and even used the 'lost-wax' process. (Again, devotees of Meroë postulate the notion that the process came to West Africa from Meroë.)

These rather simple sounding, desert people must have been inspired with unusual energy and talents, for they sprang from almost nowhere and their power and fame spread over the whole known world.

Egypt had ruled over what is now the northern Sudan for well over a thousand years before the first known, independent, Nubian state appeared in the ninth century BC. This state, known as Kush, had its capital at Napata and was the direct forerunner of Meroë.

Their system was monarchical and their kings divine. The queens often ruled and were possibly all known as Candace, rather than just the one Pliny wrote of. It seems likely that the royal descent was matrilineal. It is interesting that when James Bruce, the Scottish explorer who first spotted the ruins of Meroë, went to Shendi in 1722 he met the Sittina or queen of the region. She wore a purple stole and a large gold crown, from which her plaited hair fell to below her waist. Bruce fancied that she was the reincarnation of Queen Candace and he kissed her hand. She jumped in royal surprise, saying that no-one had ever done such a thing to her before.

The Kushites became so powerful that, under Piankhy (751–716 BC) they conquered Egypt and ruled as the XXV (Ethiopian) Dynasty until 654 BC, when the Assyrians advanced and Tanwetamani, the last Kushite king of Egypt, retired to Napata. It was not long after this, possibly in 591 BC, that the capital of Kush moved to Meroë. For two centuries or so, some of the ancient rites such as acclamation had to be performed still at Napata, and the kings, up to Nastasen (?335–315), were buried at Nuri. After that, Meroë was supreme.

The first places I wanted to see were Naqa and Massawarat es Sofra. These are two, primarily religious, Meroïtic centres, discovered in 1821 by Linant de Bellefonds and drawn a year later by Frédéric Caillaud, the son of a French jeweller who had joined a punitive expedition mounted by Mohammed Ali, the Egyptian ruler, and commanded by his son Ismail.

We managed to find a man who lived at Naqa who was grateful for a lift. He guided us over a maze of tracks well to the east of the route we had been following. Amid rolling dunes, lying in hilly country, we came to a well where camels were pulling up water in leather buckets, from a depth of at least a hundred feet. Near the well there are two quite small ruined temples. The first one, known as the Kiosk, had a curious effect upon all of us because its arches are Roman in style. It was the first time for so long that we had seen anything of beauty which stemmed from our own culture. It made us, momentarily, quite homesick.

The other temple, the Lion temple, is Egyptian in style, with some Indian influence. The Meroïtes started building in the Egyptian manner, but quite soon after the fall of the Kushite dynasty they introduced their own variations. The carving on the Egyptian temple is vigorous; the beautiful snake columns having lion heads and a startling picture of a man being eaten by a lion. In the Kiosk there are representations of good, fat ladies, plump enough to please Juvenal. Round about are mounds of unexcavated buildings, but it is thought that Naqa was populated mostly by people in temple service.

There was no-one to guide us to Massawarat es Sofra, so I took a bearing with my rather primitive compass (my good one had been stolen) and followed the track indicated by one of the cameleers, flicking a little finger a fraction to the right. The track, of course disappeared after about half an hour. 'Do you know where we are?' the others asked. Of course. We went on for an hour or so. There was a range of hills to our right, with a hint of a gap in them. There were no tyre marks. It was a bit to the right of my bearing, but his little finger had flicked. We travelled on over virgin sand. To go too far to the right meant heading straight into the lost wastes of the Nubian desert.

The way became steep and the sand deeper. There were no marks. 'Are you sure this is the right way?' they repeated. Absolutely. We certainly had not got enough petrol to risk getting seriously lost. My compass looked so small, like a toy one. Was it accurate? The map showed a clear track. The others became alarmed. 'You're lost, aren't you?' they said furiously. Certainly not. We will rejoin the main track just beyond those two hills. They looked deeply sceptical, but not half so sceptical as I felt. Then, just past the two hills, there was the track. We had achieved a wholly undeserved short cut. Sudanese tracks were always like that, but I was not always so lucky.

Massawarat es Sofra lies at the edge of a wadi in country which looks as if it came out of a cowboy film. It was a beautiful place in which to camp, but it was somewhat disappointing in other ways. There is one very much restored temple in the most straightforward Egyptian style and, at a little distance, a large jumbled area of tumbled figures and pillars, with a few reconstructed rooms.

The next day we drove to Shendi, where the market has been famous for centuries. When John Lewis Burckhardt, a Swiss scholar, went there in 1814, he estimated that five thousand slaves a year were sold at Shendi. Alan Moorehead, in *The Blue Nile*, writes:

'A thousand miles away from any part of the world that one could call civilised,

224

you could buy such things as spices and sandalwood from India, antimony to blacken the eyelids, medicines, German swords and razors, saddles and leather from Kordofan, writing paper and beads from Genoa and Venice, cloth, pottery and basketware of every kind, soap from Egypt, cotton, salt and Ethiopian gold. There was a lively sale in monkeys that were trained to do tricks, and Shendy's wooden dishes, battered and blackened by being held over a fire, were famous. The market was also renowned for its sale of Dongola horses, and for camels and other beasts to carry these goods across the desert.'

Even today the market is lively and surprisingly large – the inheritor of thousands of years of desert and Nile trading, started by the people of Meroë. Chinese pans have replaced the German swords, but I was able to buy a drug from Switzerland to ease a torn muscle and there was plenty of cloth, pottery and basketware. No monkeys, that I could see, but surely camels.

That evening we came to Meroë itself. Among barren hills, overlooking the Nile, there stands a cluster of sharp-pointed pyramids the top ones forming a dramatic skyline. These are the tombs of the kings and queens of Meroë after 315 BC. These pyramids are quite different from any Egyptian pyramids, being much steeper and also much smaller. The effect is unpretentious and yet impressive. Here, unlike at Massawarat, it seemed possible to imagine the strong, energetic desert people who built the pyramids and the masses of unexcavated buildings hidden under the surrounding desert sands.

Several of the pyramids have now been restored, so that instead of being the dark red terracotta colour of the sandstone they are built from, they are covered with smooth grey plaster. This, of course, is what they would have looked like when they were new, except that much of them would have been painted. The restoration is the work of a German architect who has become an archaeologist. Dr Friedrich Hinkel is no doubt regarded as a controversial figure, because he is a practical man rather than an academic. He is also perfectly charming, rather good-looking with bloodhound bags under his eyes, and positively bristling with enthusiasm.

He started working in the Sudan in 1960 at Massawarat. Soon he was employed on the dismantling of the Nubian temples which were destined to be flooded by the building of the Aswan dam. Hinkel's ingenuity was proved when it came to moving the colossal statues from Argo Island. Lacking all heavy equipment and having no trailers, he fell back on ancient methods. He took barges to the island when the Nile was full. Then he waited until the river dropped and loaded the statues down into the barges. Then he waited again for a year until the river was high once more and he could tow his barges to Khartoum.

For the last few years Dr Hinkel has been working at Meroë. It is because he

OPPOSITE, Dr Friedrich Hinkel

227

is a practical man that he has made many fascinating discoveries. The early archaeologists burrowed into the pyramids from the top and from the sides in a fruitless search for the tombs. They did not realise that the burial chambers are, in fact, underneath the pyramids. They also did not realise that all the stone was plastered over. The stone is roughened to take the plaster, because you cannot paint directly onto sandstone. Even where there are reliefs these were whitewashed to a thickness of half a millimetre and then painted.

What interested Dr Hinkel most was the method of construction. It is assumed that the large Egyptian pyramids were built by making large ramps of sand which were raised as the pyramid grew higher. This was not possible at Meroë as the pyramids are too close together for this to work. Dr Hinkel was intrigued by two things. First the pyramids are all truncated, stopping nine-tenths of the way to the top. Then another piece is put on and the whole finally capped with a round stone to keep the rain out. This suggested to Dr Hinkel that the builders used some kind of lifting gear that would not allow them to finish the apex. The other interesting thing was that there is a long cedar pole running directly up the middle of the pyramid. This pole, he thought, could have a religious significance connected with tree worship. Or, more probably, it could be to do with the method of construction.

Dr Hinkel gets quite worked up as he explains the extreme difficulties of building a pyramid. The main problem is keeping the angle the same on all four sides. It was possible that the pole was a help in measuring outwards from the centre. Then he had another idea. Perhaps the pole supported a shadoof, the oldest form of lifting gear, which is known to have been in existence in the third millenium BC. The shadoof needs a central pole, but its use would also mean that the apex would be impossible to construct in the same way and also that the pyramid would have to be very steep. Both these points are true of the Meroë pyramids.

Then Dr Hinkel had a piece of extraordinarily good fortune. In March 1979, when he had only three days before packing up before the summer heat, he found a faint drawing on the wall of the antechamber to the pyramid known as number eight. It is, he says with excitement, the earliest, indeed the only, record of the building of a pyramid. It is quite simply the architect's sketch, showing, as a modern architect's drawing would do for a symmetrical building, only half the pyramid.

The sketch is one metre seventy high and its scale is one to ten. The pyramid is truncated, and the cap is exactly one tenth of the pyramid's height. All these facts fitted Dr Hinkel's theory and enabled him to identify the pyramid as being pyramid number two built about 50 BC. Perhaps most interesting of all is that the pyramid was built according to what we call the Golden Section, that is to say that they worked on a proportion of eight to five, which is 1.6. The Golden Section is 1.618.

From where we camped, the sun set behind the main group of pyramids and, as I looked at their silhouettes, I felt somehow happy that these pyramids are so deserted, unlike the great pyramids of Gizeh with their daily hordes of tourists. The Meroïtes preserve their mystery – a people who understood so much, whose taste was in many ways more appealing to me than that of the grand pharaohs. No-one has yet penetrated their language. We know so little about them, except that they were swept away by Noba tribesmen from the west in 350 AD, about twenty years after the last pyramid was built.

The pyramids of Meroë are not quite so deserted as they were a few years ago, when Alan Moorehead wrote that the ruins, 'stand silently in the tremendous heat, and except for occasional parties of archaeologists hardly anyone visits them from one year's end to another.' The road which runs beside the Nile and past Meroë is, for the most part, little frequented. Most people heading north or coming south from Egypt take the train. Lately, however, there has been a change. Since the route to India from Europe has been closed by the events in Iran and Afghanistan, the 'overlanders' have taken to going to Africa rather than the East.

On about four routes in the Sahara, one meets these travellers, usually in organised groups in large trucks, but often just two people in a Volkswagen. It is hard to know what they go for, unless it be just the going. The route we were now on is especially popular because it is the most easily managed if the object is to go from the north of Africa to the Cape.

Some two hundred miles north of Meroë we left the Nile at Abu Hamed and followed the railway where it takes a short cut across the Nubian desert. It is a stark, hot land, with no wells. From Abu Hamed to Wadi Halfa it is six days by camel. The making of the railway must have been a formidable undertaking.

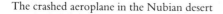

The crashed aeroplane in the Nubian desert

Every so often there are stations in the middle of nowhere. Beside one of them was a crashed aeroplane, which the nomads appeared to use as a lavatory. The stationmaster of this particular station offered us some *araghi* and tea and some lambs-tongue lettuce which he grew in a shady spot. He allowed us to ride up the line a little on one of those hand-propelled trucks which appear in American comedy films. Memories of films proved misleading as it was immensely hard work to get up to ten miles an hour, unlike the films. The stationmaster said no train was due for two days.

Soon after that, we met a truckload of overlanders. They planned to camp that night at Meroë. Would it be a good place to stop, they asked, and would there be any 'toilet facilities'?

Wadi Halfa is the end of the road; and the railway. Here you have to embark on an ancient-looking steamer to travel down Lake Nasser to Aswan. This is not the original Wadi Halfa (where Sir Evelyn Baring secretly buried the Mahdi's skull which Kitchener had sent to him). That lies several miles to the north under the waters of the lake. The new Wadi Halfa, or at any rate the part near where the boats moor, is an appallingly scruffy shanty town built on barren sand, surrounded by some bare hills.

Nothing happens there, except for the train terminus and the completely haphazard arrival and departure of the ferry boats. There are a few seedy cafés, an extraordinary number of cloth shops and tailors, and, tucked away at one end, a couple of shacks where some exhausted-looking whores offer sweaty solace to waiting travellers. Next door to these shacks, a man sells bottles of foul-tasting *araghi*, perhaps to give his neighbours' customers Dutch courage. It is said that he laces this date spirit with battery acid to give it a bit of zip. I bought a bottle and found it so nasty that later I gave it to a garrulous mechanic on the boat. He drank it all and was still with us the next day, albeit a bit subdued.

We had to wait four days for a boat. We camped at night outside the town near the lake shore. There were fewer scorpions there than at the place where most people camped. In the day, we amused ourselves by having shirts and trousers made by various tailors. The cotton was excellent, but the stitching was ungainly. Otherwise we sat in one of the cafés and there met the leader of a group of overlanders. He is called Martin Crabb. He and his wife, Rita, had already been waiting for a week for a boat and were destined to wait another two weeks for the only barge which could take their large Bedford truck. Martin had sent his customers ahead on a passenger ferry, so that they could wander down the Nile in Egypt, while waiting for him to catch them up.

Martin has been taking groups of overlanders through Africa for several years. Sitting in the café, drinking quantities of *karkadeh*, he explained to me something about the people who go on these tours, which can last nearly five months. It had always seemed to me that the overlanders were well-named, that they skimmed along over the surface, barely noticing anything about the countries they went through; travelling, as it were, in a capsule of their own environment. They talked to one only of the ease or difficulty of the road, of the ease or difficulty of buying things and above all the price of everything. There was even one American girl in Bangui who said to Tim that she was longing to get back to the real things of life – movies and hamburgers.

Martin believes that that is more the spirit in which they set out, perhaps with a vague interest in seeing something different, but that it does not last. A small minority come to escape from some problem. An even smaller minority read diligently all that they can find on the countries they will go through. Martin's company always provide plenty of books. He says that he has never yet had a passenger who on arriving in a town has asked him where the library is. It is usually, 'Where's the cake shop?'

Gradually their attitude changes. It is this change that makes the job, which is otherwise an almost endless series of frustrations, interesting to Martin. The overlanders are, at first, genuinely surprised at finding that the everyday things which they are used to are simply not there. They are shocked by the poverty. It seems to make no difference that they have seen it all on television; the actuality is as startling as if they had never seen a documentary film. Then the climate is too much for them. They have heard about heat, but never been able to imagine it.

After a few weeks of fairly rugged experience, they stop making bad taste jokes about the 'natives', they learn that it is possible to live without a stereo, they become properly interested in the lives of other peoples. Martin believes that their whole perspective changes. It is a most encouraging theory, although I fear that he is somewhat idealistic.

Apart from that, he made me think that such a group would provide a fascinating study for a sociologist. The overlanders come from a wide range of social backgrounds. On one trip he had a brain surgeon and a coal miner. For the first two weeks, there is a honeymoon period during which everyone is exquisitely polite to each other. Then, as Martin put it, they harden up a bit and start to vie for position in the group. What is confusing to them is that people who are used to respect, for example, lawyers and professional men, suddenly find that they are far less regarded than, say, a mechanic who has a practical skill to offer. The humorist is esteemed above almost all others. Love affairs are very cautiously entered upon. People recognise that, if they make a wrong choice early in the trip, it will be extremely awkward over so long a time. Only very rarely does anyone become ostracised by the group. Bickering is usually rapidly stamped on and any victimisation apparently engenders a protective spirit in the rest of the group. Altogether, Martin managed to soften my impression of overlanders, though I could wish that when they find no 'toilet facilities' at Meroë, they would not use the dark corners of the ruins.

Mediterranean Sea

Matruh
Alexandria
Port Said
El Alamein
Cairo
Siwa Oasis
Siwa
Qattara Depression
El Faiyum

Bahariya Oasis
El Minya

Farafra Oasis
Asyut

EGYPT
Nile

W — E
S

Dakhla Oasis
El Kharga
Great Oasis of
El Kharga

Red Sea

Aswan

Lake Nasser

300 km

Abu Simbel
Ferry
0
200 miles
Wadi Halfa

LIBYA

SUDAN
Nubian

Peter McClure 1983
Desert

10

'CHILDREN OF THE DARK'

TO WANDER about the battlefields of El Alamein forty years after the events is to marvel afresh at the folly and courage of men. It is so hard to imagine those great armies facing one another in this bleak, drab place. The desert here has nothing romantic about it – a flat dreary scrubland, characterless and not even alarming. It is true that there is the sea, brilliantly turquoise, washing a beach of pure white sand; but you cannot see it from where they fought. Just behind the beach, the sand piles up to form a barrier between the sea and the desert. And that sand looks scrubby and dirty.

The soldiers, we are told, came to love the desert. Now as they approach old age they reminisce about the sunsets, about the nomads stealing the Colonel's trousers, about Tony who wore galoshes in his tank but never shut the top down because he said it was too hot. It is difficult to imagine anyone loving this blank, uninspiring land and even more difficult to imagine how they can erase the memories of the corpses and the stench and the flies.

Today there is a small village at Alamein with two petrol stations, an inn of a sort and a museum. The museum does not help much. The obsolete tanks, all painted cream, and the funny old field guns look like toys. There are some one-man shelters which remind one of daleks. Nothing seems real. The battlefield at Omdurman was so much more comprehensible. This seems inexplicable in so many different ways.

How could one explain to anyone that here it was that good prevailed over evil; that with these toys on foreign soil the people of a now lost empire slogged it out with other foreigners to preserve the world from an insane fantasy? Why here in Africa? Why the people who now cling together in a European community of nations? It seems so idiotic, when at the time it seemed so noble.

The helmets and the rifles have all been picked up, the tanks have been carried away, the mines have all been exploded, often at the cost of a Bedouin life or that of his camel. Nothing remains, except for the memorials – memorials so revealing of the character of the nations which put them up that the tragedy of them nearly tips over into absurdity.

The memorials are spread over some ten miles of the desert. Coming on the road from Alexandria, the first is the Greek one – a small awkward copy of a classical temple. Then a South African one, dissociated from the rest of the former British Empire, a simple block of stone.

Next comes the memorial of the Empire. From the road you see little: just the roof of a comparatively modest building, compared, that is, with the ones that come later. It is built on the side of the sandbank, looking away from the sea out over the melancholy desert. The building is a cloister with a garden and a field of crosses below it. The concept is both understated and old-fashioned and in many ways charming. No-one else has attempted to lay out lawns in the desert and to grow flowers and to plant trees among the graves. In fact, these are the only graves of this kind.

On the cloister walls are engraved the names of those whose bodies were never found. The lists are chillingly long. They are also a stirring reminder of the vastness of the Empire. Mingled with the English, Scottish, Welsh and Irish regiments there are scores of others – the Seventh Rajput Regiment, the Cyprus Volunteer Force, the Druze Regiment, the Second Battalion Hyderabad Infantry, the Sudan Artillery ... As one might expect with the Empire, the officers' names are listed first, in order of seniority, the men follow after. It is fair to add, however, that in the graves beneath the crosses officers and men lie indifferently, side-by-side.

The overall impression is touching and innocent of bombast or vainglory. 'Their name liveth for evermore', says an inscription on a sarcophagus, and one wishes it were true.

Travelling westward towards Libya, the next monument is a large milestone announcing the distance to Alexandria. It is ironic in that it commemorates those who were never to reach Alexandria, the Italians who died in the first battle of Alamein, when the Axis advance was halted. The inscription reads: *Manco la Fortuna non il Valore* 1.7.1942. The poor Italians, ever dreading accusations of cowardice, attribute defeat to ill-fortune.

Soon after the milestone are two more stones, not more than three hundred yards apart. The first marks the forward minefield of the Allies, the second the forward minefield of the Axis forces on 23 October 1942. There is an eerie sense of confrontation in the closeness of these two stones.

Beyond them on the ridge of the dune stands a huge, octagonal edifice of rough sandstone, with the distant appearance of a gasometer or, more charitably perhaps on closer inspection, a fortress with neither windows nor any relieving feature whatsoever. There is but one door approached by a little flight of steps. This is the German memorial. Inside, the centre of the octagon is open to the sky. Round the open space are eight recesses, in each of which there are three sarcophagi bearing the names of German towns. In the middle of the open space stands an obelisk. At the base of this there is an inscription:

Here rest 4200 German soldiers of the Second World War.
Let their death be a strengthening and enlightenment for us.

Quite how is not clear, but in this solid, heavy monument, the Germans seem to feel that the war was as pointless as it now seems to us all. Their inscription to thirty-one unidentified soldiers of unknown nationality says roughly:

'Death took everything here – name, age and race. It took everything worldly and rendered it meaningless. Only one thing remained as a light in the dark legend of this boundless war in this disenchanted world. You stood here in war whether enemy friend or brother.'

Whose war was it, I wondered rather peevishly, that disenchanted the world? It is depressing this memorial, as heavy and blind as the war that inspired it.

A few more miles and there is the Italian memorial. Another octagon, but what a difference. Ignoring the fact that it is the biggest memorial of the lot, the delicacy of this pale, tapering building is a source of pleasure. In just the way that they got their milestone wrong, they got their main memorial exactly right.

At the roadside is a chapel and beside it a small mosque. The Italians are the only ones to recognise that this European war was conducted on Egyptian soil. The chapel is dedicated to, '4800 Italian soldiers, sailors and airmen. The desert and the sea did not give back 38000 who are missing'. There is also a plaque here to, 'the soldiers of peace – technicians and Italian workers who lost their lives in the construction of the Aswan dam at Esna and Esfina 1898–1951'.

Behind the chapel, a road climbs straight and steeply to the main building. On either side of the tapering octagon is a wing with steps mounting to a terrace. Ahead is a door. Inside all is light. The octagon is hollow, rising to a skylight. On the far side of it, a huge wooden cross, perhaps twenty-five feet high, appears to hang over an altar beyond which the building opens out to a wide window looking over the sea. It is the only memorial to make use of the sea.

Round the walls of the octagon and of the two wings are individual plaques of perfect white marble, beautifully lettered with the name of each of the dead. The plaques are arranged in strict alphabetical order, regardless of rank. There is an atmosphere of cool peace in which any sound echoes perfectly in the hollow of the tall spire – an effect reminiscent of the Baptistery at Pisa. This is a monument built by the most unwarlike and the most unmilitary people. That it is, perhaps, a little cold in feeling may give one to think that good taste and war can never have anything in common.

The Italian War Memorial

The oasis of Siwà was for me one of the prime objectives of the whole journey. As early as the sixth century BC and probably much before that, Siwa had a famous oracle, the oracle of the good Amun, which was consulted by people from all over the civilised world. Alexander the Great went himself to ask questions of the oracle in 331 BC. In addition, I knew that the customs of the Siwans were said to be very unusual. That old prude, Byron de Prorok visited the oasis in 1926. He camped, he said, on a hill covered in skulls. In the evening he heard sounds of revelry and went down to see what was happening. The sight that met his eyes was such as could not be recorded in any decent book.

'The scene now becomes too degenerate to describe. The cults of the dead gods are alive again; Tanit, Baal and Moloch hold sway once more! Through the ages they have been kept alive by the hidden fires of passion, forever ready to burst forth in the bodies of these uncivilised children of the desert. . . . Beyond question, Siwans are the most degenerate people in all the world.' Finally, Siwa had had a certain importance in the second world war. The oasis seemed to encompass every aspect of Saharan history.

The one drawback was that Siwa lies very close to the Libyan border and thus in a sensitive military area. In Cairo I found out that it was not easy to get permission to go there. The British Ambassador was ineffectual. A charming Belgian diplomat tried for permission on my behalf, but was told that manoeuvres were going on at Siwa and that no-one could go. I met a minister, who could not help. At the press centre they told me that in the past year twenty journalists had applied for permission to go. None had been allowed. They would apply for me, but it was pointless. I was told that the Swedish Ambassador had been trying to go for two years with no success. After many days I gave up.

That evening I had a drink with a merchant friend and, merely by way of conversation, mentioned my disappointment at not being able to see Siwa. 'But why ever not?' he said. I explained. 'I will arrange it,' he said. And he did. Three days later I was driving along the coast road to Mersa Matruh, where Cleopatra had her summer palace and where she made love with Anthony. I would have preferred to try to cross the desert from Bahariya, Farafra, or even El Kharga. It was from the last of these oases that the Persian king Cambyses in 524 BC sent an army of fifty thousand men, according to Herodotus, 'with orders to attack the Ammonians, reduce them to slavery and burn the oracle of Zeus'. (The name Siwa dates from only about six hundred years ago. Classical writers called it simply the Oasis of Jupiter-Ammon, hence Ammonians.)

This army disappeared entirely. It never reached Siwa. No survivors returned to Kharga or anywhere else. Herodotus does say: 'There is, however, a story told by the Ammonians themselves . . . that when the men left Oasis (i.e. Kharga) and in their march across the desert had reached a point about midway between it and the Ammonian border, a southerly wind of extreme violence drove the sand over them in heaps as they were taking their mid-day meal, so that they disappeared forever.' One day, perhaps, the sand will blow away and expose the army of Cambyses, with its weapons and its armour preserved in the dryness of the desert. It is a treasure hunter's dream.

We would not have been encouraged to go that way, but we followed instead the route that Alexander the Great took, almost directly south from Mersa Matruh, which in his day was known as Paraetonium. The desert through which the route runs is uninteresting and bare. Callisthenes, the historian who went with Alexander, maintained that after a few days they ran out of water and were saved by a providential rainfall. They were also, according to Callisthenes, guided by two crows which croaked at them if they went in the wrong direction. Curiously enough, a swift travelled with us for miles, swooping beside the moving car. We stopped and put water out for it, but it wouldn't or couldn't drink. For Alexander it must have been a gruelling march of seven or eight days. It took us about eight hours.

Siwa lies in a depression nearly sixty feet below sea-level. One comes upon it quite suddenly. The track, after running across a plateau, plunges over an escarpment. As one drops down about six hundred feet, one sees an enormous number of palm groves stretching ahead for several miles. The depression is about fifty miles long and varies between five and eighteen miles wide. Large areas of this expanse are barren desert with large salt lakes, but the fertility of the groves is a delight after the drabness of the desert.

The Governor* greeted us with exceptional courtesy and arranged for us to be put up in an apartment in the government resthouse. He apologised for having to charge us each fifty pence a night. The resthouse, a row of half-a-dozen two-roomed apartments, is about half a mile from the actual town of Siwa.

The Siwans of classical times did not live here but a few miles to the east, at a place which is now called Aghurmi. We wandered there through lush groves of palms. There are about a quarter of a million palms in the oasis, but unlike most Saharan oases there is a wide variety of other crops. Olives predominate, but there are lemons, figs, pomegranates, peaches, mulberries and carob with their sweet locust-bean pods. There are barley and wheat, but no rice because this is forbidden in an attempt to wipe out malaria (mosquitoes thrive in paddy fields). More surprisingly the Siwans love flowers. They grow roses and a lot of peppermint. As one goes through the groves every so often one comes upon one of the two hundred and eighty springs. They are large like huge wells, surrounded by low stone walls. The water looks a dark, gunmetal colour and bubbles stream up round the sides where brilliant green moss grows. Young naked boys play by the springs, diving off the walls sending sluggish ripples across the thick surface of the water. It seems a happy place. The oldest of these springs was known in classical times as the Fountain of the Sun, and its waters were reputed to be cool by day and warm by night.

Aghurmi stands on a rocky hill. There is a ragged village below the hill, but the sides of the hill itself are covered with tumbling masonry. At the top are the ruins of the temple of Amun to which Alexander came. It is possible to make out something of the site of the oracle, although over the centuries it has been used partly as a mosque and partly just as a place to live. There is an open space

---

* I had a vexatious recurrence of malaria in Siwa. I have a clear recollection of making copious notes; a recollection not borne out by the skimpy evidence of my notebooks. The Governor's name and various other details, alas, escape me.

The oasis at Tichit

Ahmed Ali Saleh's daughter dressed in traditional Siwan jewellery

LEFT, The old town at the oasis of Siwa

which was a courtyard where the procession of the god was held. The image of the god at the time of Alexander took the form of an *omphalos*, or navel, which was decorated with emeralds.

Beyond the courtyard is the temple itself with four chambers and the sanctuary of the oracle. The sanctuary is ten or eleven feet wide and twenty feet long. To one side of it runs a narrow corridor which leads nowhere and seems to serve no purpose, unless it were a place where a priest could hide and give sonorous verbal answers to questions put to the oracle. This would have been unusual for an Egyptian oracle. The more common method was for priests with attendant singing virgins to carry the symbol of the god in a barque and, when questions were posed, the god would answer only yes or no – making the bearers of the barque move forward for 'yes' and backward for 'no'. The only other movement was a violent trembling which indicated that the god was enraged by the question. It seems to me unlikely that this limiting binary system of reply would have been quite adequate for the answers which we know were given by the oracle at Siwa, although the priest could supposedly elaborate. Sometimes the oracle could claim to be terse. Pindar was a great devotee of Amun and sent a poem to the priests, engraved on a triangular stele. It was still there when Paunsanias visited Siwa about six hundred years later, in 160 AD. When he was old, Pindar sent messages to the priests of the oracle asking for the greatest good fortune a man could enjoy. Shortly after, he died. This was judged to be their reply.

Such was the reliability of the oracle of Amun that Eubotas, who won the running race in the ninety-third Olympiad (408 BC), took with him to the games a statue of himself. He had been told by Amun's oracle that he would win – so a statue of the victor was on view immediately after the race.

When Alexander arrived at the temple he was greeted by the priest as the son of Zeus-Amun. There is some confusion about the actual words the priest used. They may have been meant merely as the title which would ʌave been accorded to any Egyptian king or they may, by a mistake in Greek, have implied more than the priest intended. However, when Alexander's Macedonian followers asked whether they might give their leader divine honours, the oracle replied that this would please Amun.

What questions Alexander himself asked is not known, as he went alone into the sanctuary. All he would say when he came out was that what the oracle had said pleased him. From that time onward, Alexander was a devout believer in Amun and the myth that the god was his father rather than Philip gained credence, not discouraged by Alexander. The oracle was not always so obliging to him. When his friend Hephaistion died, he sent to ask the oracle whether his lover could be worshipped as a god or demi-god. The answer came that he

---

OPPOSITE, The pyramids at Meroë

239

could only be considered as a hero. It is said that Alexander wanted to be buried at Siwa. The funeral procession started from Babylon but Ptolemy insisted on Alexander's being buried at Alexandria.

The oracle lasted many more centuries. Strabo in 23 BC maintained it had almost disappeared, but Paunsanias said it was still active nearly two hundred years later. Certainly it seems probable that the worship of Amun continued until some time in the sixth century AD.

The present town of Siwa was built in 1203 AD. Since the decline of the oracle and the arrival of the Arab invaders, the fortunes of the oasis had suffered grievously. There were only forty men left and seven families. They decided to move from Aghurmi and to build a fortress town on a nearby hill, to protect themselves against raids. The town at first had only one entrance through the high wall surrounding it. No-one was allowed to build outside the walls, so that as the population increased the houses grew taller, some being as high as seven or eight storeys. The houses were built of *karshif*, a salty mud which sets almost as hard as cement. It has, however, the awkward habit of dissolving in the rain.

Since 1826, the rule about building has been relaxed, so that most houses are now built outside the walls and the very occasional rains have largely destroyed the old wall and old buildings so that the ancient citadel now looks like a melted, surrealist milk chocolate town. One can still walk through this crumbling, medieval fortified town and find a few inhabited houses, some of them curved, with rounded walls and some still as high as five storeys. On some parts of the hill the houses are built in the rock, being little more than caves. The streets are astonishingly narrow. Two donkeys could never have passed one another. But one comes across pleasant corners where streets meet, roofed over and with seats carved out of the mud walls so that people could sit and talk in the cool.

The life of the town today goes on mostly in open places at the foot of the hill. We used to sit in one or other of the dusty cafés and talk with any Siwans who were not too suspicious of strangers. Communication was difficult because the language they speak is a Berber dialect, having similarities to the language of the Mozabites and the Twareg. We were lucky to meet Ahmed Ali Saleh, one of the schoolmasters. He had trouble with his car and hoped that Anthony might repair it. He also had a friend who ran a soft drinks business. His new deep-freeze could not be persuaded to cool anything. Anthony again was expected to explain this. In the event that was simple. Being so delighted at possessing what must have been the only deep-freeze in Siwa, the owner had filled it so full of bottles that the wretched machine would not shut.

Ahmed Ali Saleh was a tall, soft featured man with pale eyes and rather thick lips. His family was one of the aristocratic ones of Siwa and they had been considerable landowners. The new laws of ceilings for land ownership have

---

OPPOSITE, A young boy disappears into the Fountain of the Sun

meant that large properties have had to be divided up. Such laws always have loopholes, particularly if families are large enough. This is certainly the case with Ahmed who, when I asked him how many children he had, said, 'Seven. Ah is it seven or eight? Oh yes, eight. Six girls and two sons.'

He is still prosperous. One of his daughters is married. For her trousseau he had to buy her eighty dresses, costing twenty pounds each and fifty shawls at ten pounds apiece. On top of that he would have to buy her a house. In all, the marriage cost him over five thousand pounds.

Ahmed dressed his daughters Esma and Hadida for us in the elaborate silver jewellery – bracelets, rings, necklaces, earrings, some of which are so heavy that they have to be hung over the ears. Sometimes the whole collection of jewellery can weigh as much as ten pounds.

The Siwans, on the whole, are rather reluctant to talk about their customs and their history, perhaps realising that various aspects of both are rather out of the way and a foreigners' interest is possibly both patronising and prurient. Ahmed preferred to refer me to someone else when I talked to him about the ritual battles which were a curious feature of Siwan life for many centuries.

Soon after the building of Siwa in the thirteenth century the seven families fell into two rival groups, one lot known as the Easterners and the others the Westerners. The Easterners or *Sharqiyin* were also known, according to Dr Ahmed Fakhry as *al-Takhsib*, which means, 'pleasant, open hearted and non-aggressive', while the Westerners or *Gharbiyin* were known as *al-Lafayah*, which means, as Fakhry delicately put it, 'almost the opposite of the nickname of the other group'.

The affairs of the town were run by a council drawn from the members of both factions. Whenever a disagreement between the two sides became serious, they would settle the matter by staging a fight. The fights took place on the flat ground outside the walls. A day would be appointed and the two sides arranged themselves in two rows facing each other. Every able bodied man was expected to take part. Each family had its established position in the row. The Adadisah of the Easterners, for instance, always faced the Awlad Musa of the Westerners. The people who had moved back to Aghurmi, the al-Bawinah, always fought with the Westerners. The women watched the battle, shouting like cheer-leaders and throwing stones at anyone who tried to run away. The fight might go on all day. When it grew dark, they all went home and started again the next morning. Victory came when one side or the other fled from the battlefield.

The coming of firearms put a slightly different complexion on affairs. So that the slaughter might not be too great, it was agreed that the two sides would range up facing each other in their usual positions. At a given signal each man would fire just one shot. They would gather up the dead and wounded. Then

OPPOSITE, Ahmed Ali Saleh, a Siwan schoolmaster

they would square up to each other again and fire another shot. So it went on until one side or the other gave up. In this way not more than ten people were usually killed. Nevertheless, the population today is only five thousand and was then probably only three thousand, so a loss of ten men must have been serious.

Ahmed and the friend he took me to see, Sheik Abdullah Mosalem, assured me that Dr Fakhry had got muddled up and that it was the Easterners who had the unpleasant reputation and nickname. There seems to be some supporting evidence for this in the events of 1712. The Easterners wanted to widen a street, something which could not be done without the agreement of the council. The Westerners vetoed the plan. There was a huge battle, known as the battle of al-Ramlah. The Easterners won. They then imposed four conditions on the Westerners. One, that the Easterners should have first pick of any merchandise brought from outside. Two, that Westerners could only sell things through Easterners. Three, that if a Westerner met an Easterner in a narrow place, he must give way to the Easterner. Four, that if a Western garden worker broke off while singing a song and an Eastern garden worker took up the song and finished it, then on no account might the Western garden worker start singing again. The Westerners accepted these rules which were not changed for fifteen years when another battle reversed this situation. Mysteriously, between battles, both sides lived together in a small place and inter-marriage was not uncommon between rival families.

The other even stranger arrangement of the Siwans, which led de Prorok to call them 'children of the dark', was the role of the garden workers, or Zaggalah. Zaggalah strictly means club bearers and part of the purpose of this group was to act as guardians of the town and the gardens. The Zaggalah were recruited from the poor relations of the landowning families, being excluded rather in the manner of the younger sons of the British aristocracy. They tended the palms and the crops and in return were fed, clothed and given forty bushels of the best dates and twenty bushels of barley each year.

They were aged between twenty and forty. They were forbidden to spend the night within the walls of the town. Furthermore, they were not allowed to marry until they reached the age of forty. The effect on a group of young men denied all contact with women may easily be imagined. They made a cult of homosexuality and it seemed to catch on even within the town. Marriages between men and youths became perfectly accepted and formal marriage contracts were drawn up. According to one source the bride price paid for a boy was more than the fixed amount given to a girl's parents. The banquets and celebrations were equally lavish.

With some innocence and great delicacy Dr Fakhry writes that the Zaggalah's 'gayest parties are those held in the evenings, when they get very drunk and begin to dance in a circle. Each one puts a girdle around his waist and another above his knees and moves round and round, jerking his body, leaning forward and putting his hands on the shoulder of the man in front of him. The musicians sit in the middle, or at one side, and the dancers are supposed to sing together, but in their excitement one hears shouts and shrieks as if they were wounded animals. It does not take long before the onlookers observe that some of the dancers come very close to those in front of them and the dance turns into erotic movements.'

In 1928 when King Fouad visited Siwa he was deeply shocked to learn about the male marriages and he forbade the custom. Thereafter, the Siwans gave up written contracts for these unions. But when King Farouk went to Siwa in 1945, he asked whether it was true that the Siwans still practised 'a certain vice'. The sheiks hung their heads and did not answer. The king gave them no presents. Against that, the sheiks did not think much of Farouk because he came in dressed

The groves of Siwa, where an abundance of fruit and flowers is grown

245

in shorts and an open-necked shirt, while they were all dressed in the robes of honour and carried the swords which King Fouad had given them. They told Fakhry that Farouk 'neither looked like a king nor behaved like one'. As Fakhry added wryly, one cannot be sure whether it was the lack of presence or the lack of presents that disappointed them most.

Ahmed, the schoolmaster, told me that the lively parties of the Zaggalah still go on, but that they mostly take place in April after the date harvest. We were there late in May, when it was getting too hot for parties of that sort, or so I would imagine. The pressures on the Zaggalah are less nowadays. Fifteen years ago the law forbidding them to marry was relaxed and they are now allowed to marry at twenty.

The isolation of Siwa has meant the preservation of customs which exist nowhere else in the Arab or Berber worlds. Sheik Abdullah Mosalem, as we sat on his beautiful carpets drinking tea, told me the story of the original *ghul*. 'Long, long ago there was a girl from an important family, who suffered from a severe skin ailment. It was so unpleasant that she went to live by herself in the desert. She grew lonely and sad. After a while she befriended a beast and eventually she coupled with the beast. She had a child. The child was hairy and red-eyed and it used to attack people and eat them. If it happens now that a woman is widowed twice she is said to eat husbands and is called *ghulah*.'

Fakhry maintains that any widow is called *ghulah* (feminine of *ghul*). As soon as her husband dies she is taken to one of the springs, washed, and dressed in a white mourning gown. Then she is shut up for four months and ten days in absolute seclusion. One old woman may bring her food and she is allowed to talk to immediate relations only through a closed door. At the end of the time, she is taken blindfold (in case she should look into anyone's eyes) to the spring and is finally washed of her evil, which is just as well, particularly as she is not allowed to change her white gown during the whole time of her incarceration. A year after her husband's death she can marry again. Where this amazingly harsh custom came from it is impossible to tell. No other desert people practise it.

The Siwans do appear to have a remarkable resistance to outside influences, coupled with an acute sense of business. There is, of necessity, a large garrison of soldiers stationed at Siwa, but it is noticeable that, while the Siwans are perfectly polite to them and very pleased to sell them anything, they hardly mix at all in a social way. Naturally, there is no question of the soldiers' talking to Siwan women, if only because one hardly ever sees a woman in the streets and, if one does, she is so shrouded in her voluminous clothes that it is impossible to tell anything about her. So in the cafés the soldiers sit in separate groups, while the Siwans carry on as if there were no-one there.

The Siwans are purely pragmatic when faced with any external threat. If they recognise that they cannot defeat an invader they welcome him. In the first world war they fought for the Senoussi against the British, but when the British forces captured Siwa in 1917, the people greeted them with cheers and pledges of loyalty.

In the second world war much the same spirit prevailed. British, Australian and New Zealand units were stationed there. The Italians bombed the town regularly, fortunately often with bombs which failed to explode. For safety, many of the Siwans took refuge in the tombs on the Jebel al-Mawta, the hill where de Prorok camped. In digging out shelters among the graves on this 'hill of the dead', they uncovered many unknown tombs, some of them beautifully decorated and dating from the sixth century BC. The Siwans sold to the soldiers any area of fresco which took their fancy. It is strange to think that in Brisbane, Dunedin or Huddersfield, there may be fragments of the tomb of Si-Amun, a half-Greek merchant or landowner of the third century BC.

Then the Italians occupied Siwa and were enthusiastically received, as was Rommel who came to see the troops there and gave the sheiks seven and a half pounds of tea and ten thousand lire, which the Italians were good enough to buy back when their turn to be kicked out arrived.

Ever since the visit of King Fouad there has been talk of a tarmac road to Siwa. Now, for military reasons, it looks as if it really may be finished – it reaches out some fifty miles from Mersa Matruh. It is unlikely that even Siwan reserve would survive such easy access for more than a few years.

Watching the passers by, Siwa old town

When we reached the tarmac after bumping back over the barren desert between Siwa and the coast, I felt a sudden sense of loss. The journey was over. It was exciting to be going back to Europe, to families, to friends. Moreover, it was time to go. We were all tired; several of us had acquired disagreeable worms. Anthony had lost four stone. Indeed, by the time we reached Siwa there were only Tim, Anthony and myself left. Jocelyn had flown back from Khartoum, looking awful; Rose had gone home from Cairo after one last magisterial triumph over the customs men of Egypt. Nevertheless, I felt sad.

The sense of loss was composed of many emotions. To travel for so many months with the same people is to create a bond which has no parallel in everyday life. It was interesting that we hardly ever had an open, violent disagreement. A few frosty days was about the worst of it. We avoided dispute by the simple expedient of grumbling endlessly about one another's faults when driving in the Land Rovers. As we changed places every few hours we could all be certain of being able to rid ourselves of any impatience with anybody else in the course of a day. There was the great advantage of there being no question of being overheard. The desert can play strange tricks with sound. One day at Wadi Halfa, Rose, Anthony and Tim were standing on a high hill at some considerable distance from me. They were all complaining about my behaviour. 'Do be careful, he might hear,' said Rose. 'Don't be ridiculous,' said Anthony, 'he couldn't possibly hear us up here.' But I could.

We were, by the end of the journey, so attuned to each other that we almost resented outsiders. In one sense we were bored with each other because we had exhausted our conversation; in another we were so involved with each other that even now what the others are doing is of paramount importance to us all.

Much of my regret was the loss of freedom and the return of responsibility. It is true that we were all responsible for each other. Stupidity could end in absolute disaster. To make a muddle about the water or the petrol or to cause a fire could have meant that we would all die, but that kind of responsibility is perfectly easy to accept. The quality of freedom that we were losing was the kind which does not have to worry about time, one in which houses, things, conventions make no demands, a state where money may not change hands for days at a time – a kind of limbo.

Then the desert itself. No matter how much we longed for cool water, for interesting food, for the comforts of civilisation, the charm of these things, when we reached them, had always quickly faded. In towns or cities our spirits were always low. We all of us brightened up as soon as we were in the empty spaces again.

As we passed through Alamein once more, I remembered wondering how anyone could have loved this scrubby desert, as the soldiers of the Eighth Army were said to have done. Leaving it, I realised how much it could mean. None of our lives would ever be quite the same again.

EPILOGUE: A DISTANT MIRAGE

N O LONG journey ever turns out in the way one expects. Perhaps it is the charm of travel: if one knew just what would happen in advance, it would rob the enterprise of most of its point. When I set out on this expedition, I had a very clear idea of what it would be like. I knew, for instance, that I would like to find out all about the Foreign Legion. I was certain that I would ignore all the oil-fields. There were various figures of Saharan history I wanted to investigate. General Lapperine, for example, whose *Méhariste* scouts were the real conquerors of the desert for the French. I was setting out to see the last of the nomads, whose way of life I felt sure would have disappeared in another ten years. Once before I had seen the nomads of Saudi Arabia, just before they were settled on the land. In the Sahara I thought I might already be too late.

Hardly any of this worked out in the way that I had expected. The Foreign Legion, I came to realise, was a particularly brutal, largely German group of vicious mercenaries who had very little to do with the Sahara proper. It was involved in the ruthless and shameful suppression of all nationalist or merely independent movements in the more populated areas of Northern Algeria and Tunisia. There was nothing to attract me to write about it.

There is a great deal that is attractive about General Lapperine, who, as a young Major, built up a swift-moving, light-travelling group of camel riders, the famous *Méharistes*, which transformed the French colonial army from a lumbering, useless old-fashioned force into the conquerors who at last defeated the Twareg. James Wellard points out that such was their skill and mobility that in the summer of 1905, 'one of his officers, Captain Dinaux, crossed the Sahara *four times in the hottest season of the year* without losing a single man or animal'. In some ways he is no longer relevant, in the way that de Foucauld is still relevant, for the holy man's followers are ubiquitous, or that Aurélie Picard is relevant in that the Tidjani are even more so. More importantly to me, I saw nothing connected with Lapperine. Had we managed to get from In Gall to the place where Lapperine's aeroplane crashed in 1920 and where he died thirteen days later, I might have felt differently. Mechanical problems prevented us.

I was determined to write about nothing which I had not seen, with the exception of Buchanan and the Taralum. It was for this reason that our failing to get into Libya and Chad was such a disappointment. Had there been petrol in Sudan, I would have liked to have written about the talented and eccentric District Commissioners in the Darfur, one of whom was Wilfred Thesiger's mentor.

Against the disappointments must be set an equal number of exciting surprises – that Aurélie Picard's house should still be standing, the beauty of Walata, the fishermen of Nouamrhar and so many hundred days on which the magic of the desert was an almost tangible delight.

My original expectation that the way of life of the desert had nearly disappeared was probably the most absurd of all my misconceptions. The Sahara has been changing for thousands of years and it is changing now. I would be surprised if Walata can survive another fifty years. The tarred roads across the desert will make a crossing of the Sahara even easier than it is today. The oil wells have already lured people out of the oases and shown them a completely different life. But the Sahara is not Saudi Arabia. Its oil has brought some wealth. It has provided schools and electricity in Algeria, and even more unexpected things in Libya. Nonetheless, most of the countries of the Sahara – Mauritania, Mali, Niger, Chad, the Sudan – are the poorest countries in the world, and in them fundamental change will be long in coming.

There is a sub-division of the Fulani, Jeremy Swift told me, who are being studied by some aid organisation or sociological survey team. Their language differs from the rest of the Fulani who are being studied. Therefore, for computer purposes, key things in their lives are given numbers. Camels, of course, are one. Tea is seventeen. The tribe have caught onto this numerical language. 'I have lost my one,' they will say. Or a man wanting to make tea without having to give it to everyone will ask his friend, 'shall we seventeen?' and off they go to brew up behind a bush. Such contacts with modernity, however ridiculous, do nothing materially to alter their lives. They must still wander, searching for ever-diminishing pastures on which to feed their long-horned cattle.

What other way of life can the people of Iherir adopt? Unless they abandon their valley, there is nothing else they can do but grow dates and a few crops and pasture the camels.

The desert may become even more inaccessible for political reasons. I think

OPPOSITE, This old man and his colleague (p. 242) cured people of rheumatism and arthritis by burying them in sand

of an old man in Siwa who used to make a living treating foreigners for rheumatism. He buried them up to their necks in the sand of particular dunes and let them stew for long periods. The sands, he maintained, had special properties which acted nearly as a panacea. 'When,' he asked me, 'will people be allowed to come here again?' He showed me his visitors book which revealed that he had had no clients for many years.

Such inaccessibility will, if anything, preserve the way of life of the peoples of the oases. With little material progress, with the implacable spreading of the sands, with the increase in political dissension, the isolation of many stretches of the Sahara will be even greater than it is today. Already in some places we are back in the days of René Caillié.

BIBLIOGRAPHY

BATTUTA, IBN   *Travels in Asia and Africa* Translated by H.A.R. Gibb, London, 1929

BAZIN, RÉNE   *Charles de Foucauld* Translated by Peter Keelan, Burns, Oates & Co., 1923

BLANCH, LESLEY   *Wilder Shores of Love* John Murray, 1954
Pavilions of my Heart Weidenfeld & Nicolson, 1974

BODLEY, R.V.C.   *Wind in the Sahara* Robert Hale, 1947
Sounds of the Sahara Robert Hale, 1968

BOVILL, E.W.   *The Golden Trade of the Moors* Oxford University Press, 1968

BUCHANAN, ANGUS   *Sahara* John Murray, 1926

CAMPBELL, DUGALD   *Camels through Libya* Seeley Services & Co., 1935

CLOUDSLEY-THOMPSON, JOHN   *The Desert* Orbis, 1977

DRESDEN, DONALD   *The Marquis de Morès: Emperor of the Bad Lands* Oklahoma University Press, 1970

FAKHRY, AHMED   *The Oases of Egypt: Volume I, The Siwa Oasis* American University in Cairo Press, 1973

FRISON-ROCHE, ROGER   *Djebel Amour* Flammarian (Paris), 1978

GAUTIER, E.F.   *Sahara: The Great Desert* Columbia University Press, 1935

HASSANEIN, A.M.   *The Lost Oases* Thornton Butterworth, 1925

KEITH, AGNES NEWTON   *Children of Allah* Michael Joseph, 1965

LANE-FOX, ROBERT   *Alexander the Great* Allen Lane, 1973

LEO AFRICANUS   *History and Description of Africa* Translated by J. Pory and edited by R. Brown, (London), 1896

LEVTZION, NEHEMIA   *Ancient Ghana and Mali* Methuen, 1973

LIEBLING, A.J.   *Liebling Abroad* PEI Books, 1981

MONOD, T.   *Méharées. Explorations au Vrai Sahara* (Paris), 1937

MOORHEAD, ALAN   *The White Nile* Hamish Hamilton, 1960
     The Blue Nile Hamish Hamilton, 1962
MOOREHOUSE,   *The Fearful Void* Hodder & Stoughton, 1974
  GEOFFREY
NORWICH, JOHN JULIUS   *Sahara* Longmans, 1968
OSSENDOWSKI,   *The Breath of the Desert* Allen & Unwin, 1927
  FERDINAND
PROROK, BYRON DE   *Mysterious Sahara* John Murray, 1930
ST-EXUPÉRY,   *Wind, Sand and Stars* Translated by Lewis Galantière,
  ANTOINE DE   Penguin, 1966
SHINNIE, P.L.   *Meroë* Thames & Hudson, 1967
SWIFT, JEREMY   *The Sahara* Time-Life, 1975
TRENCH, RICHARD   *Forbidden Sands* John Murray, 1978
TURNBULL, PATRICK   *Sahara Unveiled* Hurst & Blackett, 1940
VUILLOT, P.   *L'Exploration du Sahara* Libraire Coloniale (Paris), 1895
WELLARD, JAMES   *The Great Sahara* John Murray, 1964

INDEX

257

Nile, river, 6, 143, 214, 218, 227, 229
nomads: begging, 21, 23; and bureaucracy, 78, 93-4, 146-8, 181-2; camels, 65, 69, 94, 181; comfort, 14, 186-7; disappearance, 249; education, 22, 146, 183; herds, 127; improvidence, 21; navigation, 8, 194; *see also* Twareg
Nouadhibou (Mauritania), 183-6, 187, 189, 193, 194
Nouakchott (Mauritania), 164, 166, 167, 181-3, 187, 189, 198, 204, 212
Nouamrhar (Mauritania), 186-93, 250
Nyala (Sudan), 212, 213, 214

oil industry, 65-9, 250
Olivia, *see* Wentworth-Rump, Olivia
Omdurman, battle of, 214, 216, 217-22, 233
ostriches, 122
Oued Taroda (Algeria), 93
Ouibed (Algeria), 39-40, 42
Ouled Sayrh tribe, 40
overlanders, 229-31

papers, *see* bureaucracy
passes, desert, 14, 21, 24
Paulmier, Father, 106
peanut industry, 127
Peter, *see* Macdonald, Peter
petrol, 200, 201, 203, 207, 212, 213-14
photography, 71, 74-5, 78, 118-19, 131
Picard, Aurélie, 52-63, 249-50
Pliny, 112, 222, 223
Polisario, 152, 153, 197-8
Pouplard, Father, 108
poverty, 159, 208, 250
'Prioux' stones, 92-3
Prorok, Count Byron de, 111-13, 236, 242, 247
pyramids, 227-9

Rachman, Abdul, 162
railways, 217-18, 229-30
Reguibi tribe, 182
regulations, *see* bureaucracy; passes
relationships, 74-6, 248
religion, 108, 156, 193
remoteness, 91, 126, 248, 253
Reygasse, Maurice, 111
Richard, Father, 108
Richaud, Resident-General, 28-30
rivers, 127-9
rock carvings: Akrejit, 204-5; Djanet, 78-83
romance, 6, 26-7, 92, 115, 183-4, 233
Roman influence, 15-16, 112
Rose, *see* Cecil, Rose

Sahara: extent, 5, 127, 129; influence of, 52; lure of, 5-6, 76; overlanders, 229-31; rock paintings, 78-83; unrest, 102-4, 123, 141
Sahel region, 127, 133, 138, 141, 156, 160, 212
St Exupéry, Antoine de, 10-11, 24, 132, 182, 186

Saleh, Ahmed Ali, 241-2, 246
salt trade, 118, 122-3, 124-5, 144, 152, 156, 204
sand, variety of, 7, 37, 92
sandstorms, 88
sea and desert, 182, 183, 184-98
Sedrata (Algeria), 47, 49
Senegal, 181, 209
Senoussi sect, 77, 91, 93, 105, 123, 247
Serouenout (Algeria), 91-2
Sharqiyin, 242
Shendi (Sudan), 224-6
shitting, public, 186-7
shops, 117, 186
Sidi, Walata nurse, 174-5
sincerity, Arab, 26
Siwa (Egypt), 236-48, 253; customs of, 242-6
skinks, 42
slaves, Mauritanian, 179
slave trade, 93, 117, 143, 224
SMERT, 133, 134
smuggling, 126, 212
Sodom apples, 9, 70, 111
Sonatrach, oil, 65
Songhay empire, 133, 134-7, 142
Songo (Mali), 83
Sonni Ali, 133
Soso, kingdom of, 138
Souf, the, 39, 40
Spanish Sahara, 197-8
Stendhal (H. Beyle), 6
Stone circles, 92-3
story-telling, 137, 166-7, 173
Sudan, the, chapter 9; 250; drinks, 117; hospitality, 214; journey to, 207, 209, 211; petrol, 212; war in, 215, 216-17, 222
Suez Canal, 215
Sumanguru, King of Soso, 138, 169
Sundjata, 138
superstition, 179, 183, 189, 201
Swift, Jeremy, 122, 153, 155, 168, 250

Tabello (Aïr), 122, 123
Tagdemt (Algeria), 47
Taghit, battle of (1903), 99
Tahert (Algeria), 47
Tahir, Mohamed, 119, 120
Tahouat (Niger), 127
Tamachek language, 73, 100, 102

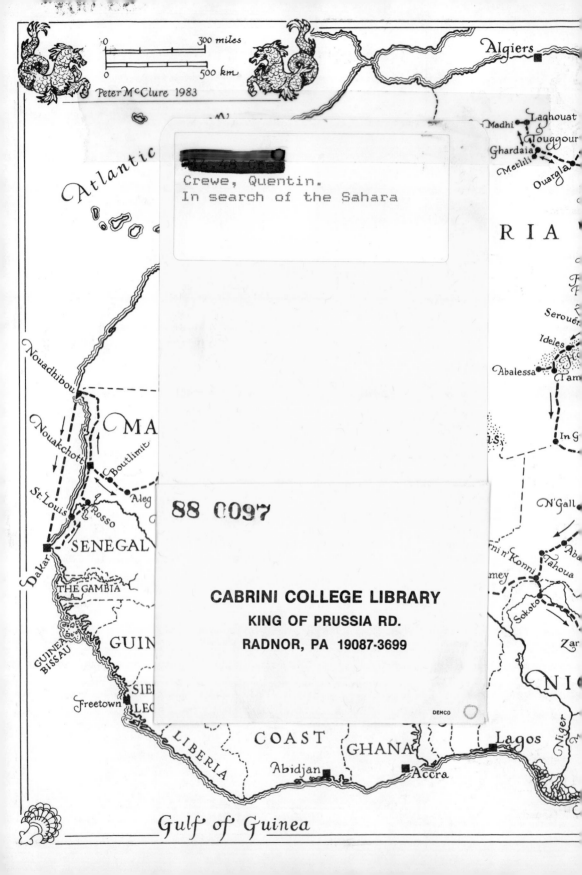

Peter McClure 1983

0   300 miles
0   500 km

Algiers

Madhi   Laghouat
         Touggour
Ghardaia
Merhli   Ouargla

Atlantic

RIA

Serouér
Ideles
Abalessa   Tam

Nouadhibou

MA

Nouakchott
Boutlim
St. Louis   Rosso
Aleg

N'Gall

SENEGAL

Dakar

THE GAMBIA

GUINEA
BISSAU

GUIN

SIE
Freetown   LE

LIBERIA

COAST   GHANA   Lagos
Abidjan   Accra

Niger

Zar

NI

In G

ni n'Konni   Abe
Tahoua
mey
Sokoto

Gulf of Guinea

DEMCO